Keep this book. You will need it and use it throughout your career.

About the American Hotel & Lodging Association (AH&LA)

Founded in 1910, AH&LA is the trade association representing the lodging industry in the United States. AH&LA is a federation of state lodging associations throughout the United States with 11,000 lodging properties worldwide as members. The association offers its members assistance with governmental affairs representation, communications, marketing, hospitality operations, training and education, technology issues, and more. For information, call 202-289-3100.

LODGING, the management magazine of AH&LA, is a "living textbook" for hospitality students that provides timely features, industry news, and vital lodging information.

About the American Hotel & Lodging Educational Institute (EI)

An affiliate of AH&LA, the Educational Institute is the world's largest source of quality training and educational materials for the lodging industry. EI develops textbooks and courses that are used in more than 1,200 colleges and universities worldwide, and also offers courses to individuals through its Distance Learning program. Hotels worldwide rely on EI for training resources that focus on every aspect of lodging operations. Industry-tested videos, CD-ROMs, seminars, and skills guides prepare employees at every skill level. EI also offers professional certification for the industry's top performers. For information about EI's products and services, call 800-349-0299 or 407-999-8100.

About the American Hotel & Lodging Educational Foundation (AH&LEF)

An affiliate of AH&LA, the American Hotel & Lodging Educational Foundation provides financial support that enhances the stability, prosperity, and growth of the lodging industry through educational and research programs. AH&LEF has awarded millions of dollars in scholarship funds for students pursuing higher education in hospitality management. AH&LEF has also funded research projects on topics important to the industry, including occupational safety and health, turnover and diversity, and best practices in the U.S. lodging industry. For more information, go to www.ahlef.org.

00841TXT01ENGE
PP-3477

HOSPITALITY 2015

The Future of Hospitality and Travel

Educational Institute Books

HOSPITALITY 2015

The Future of Hospitality and Travel

Marvin Cetron, Ph.D.
Fred DeMicco, Ph.D.
Owen Davies

American Hotel & Lodging Educational Institute

Disclaimer

This publication is designed to provide accurate and authoritative information in regard to the subject matter covered. It is sold with the understanding that the publisher is not engaged in rendering legal, accounting, or other professional service. If legal advice or other expert assistance is required, the services of a competent professional person should be sought.

—*From the Declaration of Principles jointly adopted by the American Bar Association and a Committee of Publishers and Associations*

The authors, Marvin Cetron, Fred DeMicco, and Owen Davies, are solely responsible for the contents of this publication. All views expressed herein are solely those of the authors and do not necessarily reflect the views of the American Hotel & Lodging Educational Institute (the Institute) or the American Hotel & Lodging Association (AH&LA).

Nothing contained in this publication shall constitute a standard, an endorsement, or a recommendation of the Institute or AH&LA. The Educational Institute and AH&LA disclaim any liability with respect to the use of any information, procedure, or product, or reliance thereon by any member of the hospitality industry.

Contents

Foreword

In mid-2009, the world is in one of the worst recessions it has seen since the Great Depression of the 1930s. Inevitably, this downturn has hit many parts of the hospitality industry as hard as anything in recent memory. In bad times, both consumers and businesses cut elective spending as fast and deeply as they can. Travel is one of the first expenses to go.

We see the results throughout the global tourism industry. At hotels, restaurants, cruise lines, and tourist destinations, prices are off sharply. Yet for many, income is off even more. According to the UN World Tourism Organization, international tourism in the first four months of 2009 was down 8 percent from the same period a year earlier. In Europe, it was off by 10 percent, in the Middle East by 18 percent. The WTO expects 2009 to come in as much as 6 percent below 2008, but that assumes the decline will slow in the second half of the year. If not, annual results could be considerably worse.

Throughout the tourism and hospitality industry, hosts have been scrambling to attract customers despite the sour economy. With Disney's theme-park profits down by 50 percent in the second quarter of 2009, the company has been offering discounts on tickets and hotel rates for the first time in its history. (To compensate, prices for parking, snacks, and drinks have been rising, while restaurant portions have shrunk.) A new dollar menu has made McDonald's the only chain in the restaurant industry whose profits have grown during the recession. Cruise lines have been filling ships by offering shorter trips, cutting port stops, and dropping prices. In late 2008, four-day Caribbean cruises were going for less than $100 per person! Even for companies whose customers are still coming in, shrinking profits have brought growing pain.

Survival during this grim time would have been easier, or at least more certain, if industry executives could have anticipated the downturn and planned for bad times. In fact, a few executives did manage to foresee what was coming. Yet, they were no more numerous than the economists who predicted a recession owing to their uncommon insight, rather than natural pessimism. There weren't many. Anticipating changes, such as the shift from fat times to lean, is a learned skill. And if this recession teaches us anything, it shows that every executive, middle manager, and student in the tourism and hospitality industry needs to learn how to anticipate change.

That is where this book comes in. The subject of this volume is change and how to foresee it. When today's senior executives were beginning their careers, we were just starting to understand that something new was abroad in the world, a process of transformation that our parents had not recognized and our grandparents had not faced. After World War II, most people had expected things to go "back to normal." Twenty-five years later, many of us were still adapting to the idea that it was not to be.

The process of constant change began earlier—arguably much earlier—but it became a way of life in the 1950s, when American executives fanned out across the world, spreading the Gospel of capitalism; their students built Germany, Japan, and other countries into mighty international competitors. People whose grandparents had been born, lived, and died on the family farm began following their jobs from Nebraska to Texas to New York and even London, Paris, or Tokyo. Tiny restaurants specializing in hamburgers and fried chicken spawned vast chains that transformed the world's eating habits. Hotels proliferated to meet the growing demand for accommodations. First airlines and then telecommunications knitted the world together into one global economy. Hospitality companies were born, grew, shrank, merged, and grew some more.

Somewhere along the way, we came to understand that change is now a permanent part of our lives, and one that is moving faster every day. No one can manage a business or plan a career without being able to anticipate where technology, demographics, and other transforming forces will lead us. Unfortunately, making successful forecasts has been a difficult skill to learn, not only because forecasting itself is challenging, but because few specific resources have been available to help with the task.

It is here that *Hospitality 2015* shines. Marvin Cetron is a pioneer of forecasting, with a remarkable record of successful predictions in business, technology, politics, and lifestyles; he has been working with travel and hospitality executives to project the course of our industry for some thirty years. Fred DeMicco is one of the leading educators specializing in the hospitality industry, and he too has demonstrated a consistent ability to anticipate our needs. If anyone can teach practical forecasting for travel and hospitality and show us what lies ahead, these authors are the obvious choices.

In fact, they have managed this task remarkably well. In the pages ahead, the authors explain the basics of forecasting as it is done by one of the art's most capable practitioners. Then they examine specific areas of travel and hospitality—airlines, hotels, restaurants, and others—and apply their techniques to spell out where current trends are leading our industry. By the time you are done with these basic lessons and practical examples, you should have a much better sense of what lies ahead and be ready to begin making sound forecasts of your own.

However, change is not the only critical issue in hospitality. It is not even the most important, as the authors themselves clearly recognize. More than any other, the hospitality industry exists to provide service to its customers. Quality of service is the issue that dominates the working day of tourism and hospitality personnel, from housekeepers to the CEO. It is the issue that should most concern you.

There was a time when hospitality providers could compete effectively on the basis of location and price. Today, multiple hotels are available almost anywhere people want to stay, and the Internet enables consumers to find the lowest price for everything they buy or do. Much the same trend is seen in other branches of the travel and hospitality industry.

This competitive pressure has begun to remove the traditional selling points from the customer's decision-making. For repeat guests, the most important issue is how satisfied they were on their last visit. For new patrons, one of the most important is the reputation we have built among previous consumers. In short, "location, location, location" has been replaced by "service, service, service." This is the one area left in which we can distinguish ourselves from everyone else who wants the customer's business.

The payoff for exemplary service is greater than it has ever been, and the penalty for disappointing your customers is worse, because potential guests can easily learn exactly how good your service has been. When they make reservations through Internet sites such as Expedia, Priceline, or OpenTable, they can look at reviews of your hotel, resort, or restaurant from every customer who has been moved to provide one. Some websites specialize in nothing but reviews, while others provide discussion forums for vacationers, business travelers, or diners. Word of mouth now comes, not from hundreds of people talking with a few close friends, but from hundreds of thousands broadcasting to the entire world. And those messages can be read virtually forever. On the Internet, a bad review from a single irritated guest can damage your reputation for years to come. But a guest's unexpected pleasures also can pay dividends long into the future.

When we look ahead in the hospitality industry, we are trying to foresee more than economic conditions, new technologies, or the political environment. More than anything else, we need to anticipate what services our guests will value in the future. Then we must figure out how best to meet those evolving needs. This is a constant challenge.

The future is about high-quality, highly personalized service. Exactly what that means depends on your business. For a hotel or resort, it can be developing the friendliest, most informative data systems, so that guests can make reservations effortlessly over the Internet and be confident that your staff will "remember" their preferences from previous visits. For a quick-service restaurant, it can be providing an extra drive-through lane to speed traffic and installing better loudspeakers, so that customers and staff can understand each other. For full-service restaurants, it might be improving the menu, listing calories and carb counts not only for the entrees but for salad dressings and other options. New possibilities will arise daily, as your customers' needs change and technology brings new ways to meet them.

The chapters ahead can help you to anticipate future needs. Yet in the end, your company's success depends most on your own attention to detail.

Marv Cetron tells of staying at a top-of-the-line hotel, part of a chain that is well known for its devotion to quality and customer service. One of the chain's customer-pleasing efforts was a money-back guarantee that room service would deliver breakfast in ten minutes. While waiting for his breakfast one morning, Marv happened to open the door to the hall—and there was the waiter, looking at his watch and carefully counting down so that he could deliver the rapidly cooling meal exactly on schedule, just as the company had promised!

No matter how hard you try, there is always some way to make your service just a little bit better. Identifying that opportunity can be a challenge, but your customers will appreciate the results. So will your bottom line.

So read on. One of the best ways to identify opportunity—or threats such as an oncoming recession—is to keep a practiced eye on the future. You will learn how in the pages ahead.

Robert A. Gilbert
President and CEO
Hospitality Sales and
Marketing Association International

Dr. Marvin Cetron, president of Forecasting International, is one of the preeminent forecaster-futurists in the world. For some fifty years, he has pioneered corporate and government forecasting, developing many of the techniques that other forecasters now use daily. He remains one of the most active and respected practitioners in this field.

During this long and productive career, Dr. Cetron has consulted for 450 of the *Fortune* 500 firms, including Best Western and Capital One; more than 100 government agencies, among them the Central Intelligence Agency, the Transportation Security Administration, and the National Security Agency; and 150 professional and academic associations, including World Travel Market, the National Restaurant Association, the International Association of Exhibition Management, and the Hospitality Sales and Marketing Association International. He served as an advisor to the White House for every administration, Democratic and Republican, from the time of John Kennedy through the Clinton years.

Dr. Cetron's 1994 study, *Terror 2000: The Future Face of Terror*, circulated privately at the Pentagon, predicted virtually the entire course of terrorism in the years since. Specific forecasts included the rise of large-scale terrorist attacks by Muslim extremists, coordinated attacks on widely distant targets, a devastating assault on the World Trade Center, and the deliberate crash of an airplane into the Pentagon.

He is a member of the Board of Advisors of both Pennsylvania State University and the University of Delaware.

In July 2009, a Google search on the names "Marvin Cetron" and "Marvin J. Cetron" returned more than 183,000 references to Dr. Cetron and his work.

Dr. Frederick J. DeMicco is ARAMARK Chair and Professor at the University of Delaware Department of Hotel, Restaurant and Institutional Management at the University of Delaware and Conti Professor of Hotel and Restaurant Management at Pennsylvania State University. He is one of the world's leading educators in the field of hospitality management. He teaches courses in international management, food service management and leadership, with research in the areas of cost control, total quality management, gerontology, and managed services. In the past, he has been Associate Director in the School of Hotel, Restaurant and Recreation Management at Penn State University, where he was Professor-in-Charge of the HRIM undergraduate program.

Dr. DeMicco is on the Editorial Board of the *Hospitality Research Journal*, as well as author and co-author of more than seventy-five publications in the area of hospitality. With Dr. Cetron, he wrote *Hospitality 2010: The Future of Hospitality and Travel*. His textbook, *Contemporary Management Theory: Controlling and Analyzing Costs in Foodservice Operations* (fourth edition), co-authored with James Keiser and Robert N. Grimes, is used at approximately one hundred CHRIE-affiliated universities.

Dr. DeMicco completed his Ph.D. in Hotel, Restaurant and Institutional Management at Virginia Polytechnic Institute and State University. He is ranked twelfth among the 119 most cited international hospitality faculty.

Owen Davies is a veteran forecaster and writer in the fields of medicine, science, technology, and the future. Trained as a biochemist, he became a writer and magazine editor instead. Since 1971, he has written or edited nineteen books, uncounted magazine articles, and many business reports and other specialized works. In the early 1970s, he was a cub reporter for *Medical World News*, then considered the *Newsweek* of the medical community. Between 1979 and 1981, he was senior editor at *OMNI*. He has been a freelance writer for the last twenty-five years. His magazine works have included articles in *Forbes, Newsweek International, Self, Health, The Futurist, Institutional Investor, Managing Automation,* and other leading general-interest and trade publications.

Since 1986, Mr. Davies has served as a consultant to Forecasting International, in Falls Church, Virginia. He has participated in more than one hundred studies for the Special Libraries Association, Saab-Scania, Glaxo, and the Pentagon, and many other prominent companies, government agencies, and trade and professional organizations.

1

Practical Prophecy for Beginners

DO YOU WORRY when attending meetings off the beaten path? Imagine being taken hostage by terrorists while vacationing in the Middle East or visiting a business partner in South America? Limit your options to jobs or investments in the United States because you never know what's going to happen in foreign lands, even when they appear to be stable?

Who could blame you? Whether you are a business executive scoping out foreign competition or a college student thinking about spending a semester abroad, national stability is one of the most important factors to consider when making plans that involve other countries. It also can be one of the most difficult to measure. After all, stability is not a single factor, but a complicated vector sum of economic conditions, demographic trends, political forces, religion, technology, personalities, and more—an endless list of factors. If revolutions, coups, wars, and weapons tests regularly take the CIA by surprise, how can you be expected to know what's brewing in faraway places?

That reasoning applies just as well to a host of other problems you will inevitably face in a career in the hospitality industry. How will demographic changes affect the food preferences of diners at mid-priced restaurants? How will technology continue to change hotel management? What can you expect from the economy over the next one, five, or ten years? You will encounter these and many similar issues in the years ahead. And you will be expected to respond to them correctly.

We can help. In fact, that is the whole purpose of this book.

Forecasting Tools and Techniques

Over some five decades of work, Forecasting International (FI)—the firm founded by one of the authors and long employing another—has spent much of its time evaluating the stability of nations for clients ranging from the Department of Defense to *Fortune* 500 companies to foreign governments. In the process, we have managed to anticipate developments that took many onlookers by surprise, from the fundamentalist revolution in Iran to the collapse of oil prices after the spike of 2008.

The credit goes to a series of tools and techniques that make it possible to evaluate the vital signs of the future, much as a doctor takes your temperature and blood pressure to assess your health. They can ease your worries—or steer you away from potential trouble.

Consulting the Oracle: The Delphi Poll

One common forecasting technique is the Delphi poll. In a Delphi poll, a panel of experts fills out a questionnaire designed to elicit the members' views about the issues being studied. The answers from this first survey are then circulated among participants, and the poll is repeated. In the second round of questioning, participants reconsider their original views in light of the opinions of their peers. This usually results in a narrower range of replies and a more "solid" consensus, as any extreme views are mitigated by further thought and perhaps a bit of peer pressure. The Delphi technique has been used in several thousand studies and is generally held to produce the most reliable analyses and forecasts available.

FI has used Delphi studies with much success in a wide variety of fields. However, we often modify the basic method by including a number of participants who are professional forecasters rather than subject specialists. This change frequently produces useful results that a more narrowly focused study might overlook. The forecasters tend to consider data from other fields that the specialists would not, and their insights trigger new ideas from the specialists in the second round of questioning.

For example, we consulted both forecasters and subject specialists for a study of future terrorism performed for the Department of Defense in 1994. Nearly seven years before the September 11 attacks, we were able to predict virtually the entire course of terrorism as it has developed since then. Specific predictions included the rise of international terrorism based in the Muslim extremist movement; a second, much more successful attack on the World Trade Center; a terrorist incident in the Midwest by an American-born extremist connected to the militia movement; and even the deliberate crash of an airplane into the Pentagon. (The State Department made us remove that last item from the report for fear of giving someone an idea they might not have on their own.) In reviewing this study, we concluded that it would not have been nearly so wide-ranging and accurate had it been limited to terrorism specialists. In fact, most of the predictions above originated with forecasters and were strongly supported by their peers, but were rejected by the majority of specialists. The experience with the Department of Defense study led us to adopt this more inclusive kind of study panel whenever we use the Delphi technique.

Fictional Futures: The Scenario

Another useful tool is the scenario. *Merriam-Webster Online Dictionary*'s first definition of the word scenario is "an outline or synopsis of a play." As descriptions borrowed from other fields go, this one is not bad. Scenarios are portraits of alternative futures that might conceivably develop from today's world. They are not forecasts in that we do not expect tomorrow's reality to resemble them, except in limited and unpredictable ways. A good scenario can make us see the evolution of a future we would scarcely recognize if we were magically transported into the middle of it.

That is very much their purpose. Scenarios often are used in developing forecasts in order to help identify issues that need further research. They also can broaden our imaginations, allowing us to envision a wider range of possible futures. Sometimes we use them to broaden the imaginations of our clients, enabling them to consider forecasts that they otherwise might find too unlikely to be taken seriously.

Scenarios begin with drivers—a defined set of forces that we choose to examine. Will new technologies dominate future society? Will the capitalist economic model continue to spread throughout the world? Will a sudden change of heart sweep across the globe so that environmentalism guides our decisions? Scenarios can spin out any combination of postulates, each one leading to a different, yet convincing, future. The only limitation is that scenarios must be internally consistent. A scenario of economic decline, for example, is unlikely to include full employment or a wealthy middle class; joblessness and privation are the order of that day.

One of the most commonly used scenarios, and one that has had a powerful influence on the work of Forecasting International, is the 2050 Global Normative Scenario, evolved by the United Nations Millennium Project in 1999. It represents a consensus vision of the future compiled from the ideas of more than 1,000 participants in a continuing attempt to anticipate what is to come. In the Millennium Project's scenario, the world of 2050 has changed in many ways. Predictably, it is driven and dominated by science and technology. The Internet, biotechnology, artificial intelligence, nanomachines, and space colonies all have contributed to this prosperous new world. Technology, global communications, human development, and enlightened economic policies have worked together to make the world a better place than seemed possible at the end of the twentieth century.

Another tool uses three scenarios: one optimistic, one pessimistic, and one that deliberately parts company with most of the trends we see around us today. These scenarios grew from the work of the Global Scenario Group of the Stockholm Environment Institute. Over the last few years, the Brookings Institution, the Santa Fe Initiative, and FI all have employed this approach in a wide variety of contexts. The three scenarios are commonly known as Market World, Fortress World, and Transformed World.

Market World projects a glowing capitalist vision of economic reform and technological innovation. In this scenario, developing regions are quickly integrated into the global economy. Countries privatize government-run industries, cut through tangled regulations, trim public spending, and let the market have its way. In the real world, this formula has turned many underdeveloped Asian lands into industrial powers.

Fortress World represents the dark side of capitalism. Economies grow rapidly, but the boom leaves whole regions of the world untouched. The poor become poorer. The environment suffers. Terrorism grows. By 2050, all we can see ahead is growing desperation and violence as what little remains of the social contract continues to disintegrate. The global economic meltdown in the second half of 2008 can be interpreted as a small taste of this world.

Transformed World steps outside the either/or of capitalist vision and nightmare. In this scenario, a pragmatic idealism replaces consumer society's will to get and spend with an altruistic desire to provide for basic human needs and the shared vision of a better life for all. Environmentalism prospers. Urban crime, drug use, and poverty decline as education, employment, and the city environment improve.

By 2050, democracy has become almost universal. With many shared values and general tolerance for what differences remain, the world has all but achieved a single global civilization. It has become a stable and happy place at last.

These three scenarios are largely generic, and that is the basis of much of their value. In the process of adapting them for each study, we often learn things that would not turn up in a more straightforward examination of the future. Dozens of forecasts have been performed for the hospitality industry. So far as we know, none of them anticipated the sudden collapse of travel that followed the September 11 terrorist attacks, or the effect of the SARS (Severe Acute Respiratory Syndrome) epidemic on travel in Asia in 2003. These are insights that could have been derived only by asking "What if?" And that is the realm of the scenario.

If This Goes On... (Trend Analysis)

One of the most valuable forecasting techniques is trend analysis. It comes in two forms: trend extrapolation and trend correlation. The basic idea of trend extrapolation is that the changes we see happening around us are likely to continue, and the future will grow out of them. Any reasonable forecast has to assume that technology will continue to deliver new miracles, that countries where birth rates are out of control are likely to have much larger populations in the years ahead, and so on. We need good reasons to deviate from those straight-line projections, and those reasons can be among the most useful insights derived from a study.

Trend correlation is even simpler in principle. Some trends follow others. Thus, when you know where one trend is headed, you can be reasonably sure about the other. For example, a rise in the number of construction permits issued in a community reliably foretells an increase in the number of buildings built. A rise in birth rates presages a long-term increase in the demand for housing, schools, and eventually hotels, restaurants, and other aspects of the hospitality industry.

About fifteen years ago, we developed a unique tool to help with trend analysis. After some thirty years in forecasting, we reviewed what we knew about the future and condensed our knowledge into a list of trends that we could see changing the world; this list is available in Appendix A. We have updated the list frequently over the years. The number of entries varies from time to time as trends mature and die and new forces arise to shift the course of events. At the moment, FI is tracking fifty-five major trends in world politics, technology, national and international economies, and other important aspects of global society. These are the broad forces that will help to shape the future, and they give us a necessary context in which to consider any specific subject.

Since developing our list of trends, we have used it to predict the future of companies, industries, and entire countries. In each study, we look at the specific circumstances of the subject—say, the hospitality industry—and try to figure out how these circumstances will interact with the broader trends. How will the economy affect them? What about demographics, technology, and changing societal values?

Trend extrapolation has its limitations. Unlike scenarios, this is not a technique for "thinking about the unthinkable," as the pioneering forecaster Herman Kahn wrote in a book about nuclear war. Over time, surprises occur that cumulatively change the course of events. Barring a surprise on the scale of September 11, forecasts are likely to be very accurate over the next year or two, slightly less accurate over five years, significantly off course after ten years, and seriously wrong twenty years ahead. Nevertheless, extrapolating trends can be useful even for long-range forecasts, because the process itself helps us to identify the areas in which surprises are most likely and will have the greatest impact. In this way, it provides a basic framework for understanding the future.

Trend analysis is the most valuable tool we have for charting the most likely path of future events. The chapters ahead all grew primarily out of this process.

National Stability

In an age of terrorism, and for an industry that is exposed to risks all over the world, one of the most important issues is the stability of foreign lands. Do we dare to put a new hotel, resort, or restaurant in a given country? Should we consider moving out of existing operations there? Can airlines and cruise ships safely stop at its air and sea ports? We have seen all too often that a country that appears stable today can erupt into violence almost without warning.

And yet, invariably, there are subtle warnings, if only we recognize them. Identifying the warning signs and figuring out what they mean are jobs for forecasters.

Indicators

For this purpose, we supplement our trends with a series of indicators that we collect for each country under study (see Appendix B). These include a wide range of economic, demographic, technological, and military data. Nearly all of them are readily available. After half a century of working with classified information under government contracts, we have found that at least 95 percent—and probably closer to 98 percent—of what you need to know comes from unclassified sources.

Whenever possible, we like to find the same information from two or more independent authorities, just for confirmation. We use the Bureau of Labor Statistics and the U.S. Census Bureau for economic and demographic data, Jane's for military data, the Worldwatch Institute for environmental data, and *The Economist* and *The Christian Science Monitor* for a wide variety of information. Other useful sources include websites operated by the United Nations, the World Bank, and the International Monetary Fund. We read *The Futurist* as well for invaluable background.

The indicators in Appendix B have proved to be extraordinarily useful and versatile. Not all indicators are important for every nation. Each must be weighted according to the conditions in the country at hand, and thus far that has been largely a task for experience and human judgment.

FI tracks more than forty indicators that can be valuable in assessing the stability of a nation. For a definitive analysis, we wish to include as many of them as possible. For a quicker but still very good investigation, the list can be pared significantly. The exhibits throughout this chapter give basic data for a number of countries.

As they stand, these exhibits have some important limitations. For a practical study, we would have to fill in some gaps. Most exhibits include only the most

=========================== **Military Indicators** ===========================

Exhibit 1
Global Military Spending FY 2008

Rank	Country	U.S. dollars (billions)
1	United States	711.0
2	China	121.9
3	Russian Federation	70.0
4	United Kingdom	55.4
5	France	54.0
6	Japan	41.1
7	Germany	37.8
8	Italy	30.6
9	Saudi Arabia	29.5
10	South Korea	24.6

Exhibit 2
Status of World Nuclear Forces, 2009

Rank	Country	Total Warheads (est.)
1	Russian Federation	8,800
2	United States	5,535
3	France	< 350
4	China	160–400
5	Israel	200+
6	United Kingdom	200
7	India	65–140
8	Pakistan	~60
9	North Korea	~10

Exhibit 3
Weapons Exports, 1999–2006

Rank	Country	U.S. dollars (billions)
1	United States	72.8
2	Russian Federation	59.7
3	United Kingdom	21.7
4	France	13.6
5	China	11.8
6	Israel	7.1
7	Germany	5.5
8	Ukraine	3.3
9	Italy	3.2
10	Spain	2.5

Exhibit 1 Source: Christopher Hellman and Travis Sharp, "The FY Pentagon Spending Request—Global Military Spending." The Center for Arms Control and Non-Proliferation 22 February 2008 (www.armscontrolcenter.org/policy/securityspending/articles/fy09_dod_request_global/).

Exhibit 2 Source: "Status of World Nuclear Forces 2009," Federation of American Scientists. Accessed May 11, 2009, at www.fas.org/programs/ssp/nukes/nuclearweapons/nukestatus.html.

Exhibit 3 Source: *CRS Report for Congress: Conventional Arms Transfers to Developing Nations, 2000–2007*, 23 October 2008.

prominent countries in that category. The United States is listed in the exhibits for nuclear warheads (Exhibit 2) and gross domestic product (GDP) (Exhibit 4), for example, but its oil reserves are omitted (Exhibit 7). In other cases, such as freshwater supplies (Exhibit 8) and the number of trouble-prone young men (Exhibit 22), data are provided for selected countries that either are of general interest or

======= **Economic Indicators** =======

Exhibit 4   GDP, 2007

Rank	Country	U.S. dollars (billions) (purchasing power parity)	U.S. dollars (billions) (official exchange rates)
1	United States	13,780	13,840
2	China	7,099	3,251
3	Japan	4,272	4,384
4	India	2,966	1,099
5	Germany	2,807	3,322
6	United Kingdom	2,130	2,773
7	Russian Federation	2,097	1.29
8	France	2,075	2,560
9	Brazil	1,849	1,314
10	Italy	1,800	2,105

Source: *CIA World Factbook* (www.cia.gov/library/publications/the-world-factbook/index.html).

Exhibit 5   Competitiveness

2008–09 Rank	Country	2007–08 Rank
1	United States	1
2	Switzerland	2
3	Denmark	3
4	Sweden	4
5	Singapore	7
6	Finland	6
7	Germany	5
8	Netherlands	10
9	Japan	8
10	Canada	13

Exhibit 6   Exports, 2008

Rank	Country	U.S. dollars (billions)
1	Germany	1,530
2	China	1,465
3	United States	1,377
4	Netherlands	910
5	Japan	777
6	France	761
7	Italy	566
8	Russia	476
9	United Kingdom	469
10	Canada	462

Exhibit 5 Source: World Economic Forum, *The Global Competitiveness Report 2008–2009* (www.weforum.org/pdf/gcr/2008/rankings.pdf).

Exhibit 6 Source: *CIA World Factbook* (www.cia.gov/library/publications/the-world-factbook/index.html).

have a significant connection with that issue. For a real-world study, the missing data would have to be sought out. Fortunately, nearly all these figures can be found readily on the Internet.

In many of these exhibits, the countries are simply rank-ordered. For practical work, we would need to weight each indicator to reflect its significance to the country. For example, the United States does not appear on the list of nations with the largest oil reserves (Exhibit 7), yet that very lack of supply is extremely important to the nation's economy and foreign policy. Iceland, in contrast, has more

===== **Resource Indicators** =====

Exhibit 7
Oil Reserves, 2007

Rank	Country	Billions of barrels
1	Saudi Arabia	265.7
2	Canada	178.6
3	Iraq	118.7
4	Iran	137.2
5	Kuwait	101.6
6	United Arab Emirates	87.9
7	Venezuela	89.1
8	Russia	71.8
9	Libya	40.5
10	Nigeria	36.5

Exhibit 8
Freshwater Supplies, Selected Countries

Country	Annual renewable water resources (cubic miles/year)	Cubic meters per capita
Afghanistan	65.0 (1997 est.)	8,878
Australia	398.0 (1995 est.)	77,528
China	2,829.6 (1999 est.)	8,712
India	1,907.8 (1999 est.)	6,502
Iran	137.5 (1997 est.)	7,711
Iraq	96.4 (1997 est.)	13,088
Israel	1.7 (2001 est.)	975
Pakistan	233.8 (2003 est.)	5,585
Russia	4,498.0 (1997 est.)	133,799
Saudi Arabia	2.4 (1997 est.)	379
United States	3,069.0 (1985 est.)	871,150

Exhibit 7 Source: Average of three estimates presented at www.eia.doe.gov/emeu/international/reserves.html. Accessed June 2, 2009.

Exhibit 8 Source: "Total Renewable Freshwater Supply, by Country," Pacific Institute. Accessed June 2, 2009, at www.worldwater.org/data20082009/Table1.pdf. 2005 population data from United Nations Population Division, "World Population Prospects: The 2008 Revision Population Database." Accessed June 2, 2009, at http://esa.un.org/unpp/index.asp?panel=2.

fresh water per person than any other country on the planet, yet it is omitted from Exhibit 8 because this asset has not given it prominence on the global stage.

Weighting these factors correctly sometimes requires practice, but simple logic will carry us though most studies. It helps not to view the data as a mass of discrete facts, but as elements in a complex network of mutual influences.

Most important, the data presented here are single points. They present a snapshot of each country, when a video would tell us much more. For any study carried out at FI, we would look not at GDP or military spending, but at trends in those data. The whole point of forecasting is not to find out where the subject stands, but where it is going.

Case Study: United Kingdom

For a better idea of how this works, let us take a country and see what we can find out about it. We will look at the United Kingdom, which is globally significant and is represented in many of the exhibits. On the way, we will supplement the exhibits with data that are readily available online and with some of our own background information.

For a start, the United Kingdom had a GDP of $2.773 trillion in 2007, the latest year for which information was available (Exhibit 4). This made it the sixth

---

Purchasing Power Parity

You will run into "purchasing power parity," or PPP, whenever you examine national economies. It applies a "fudge factor" to income or wealth data in order to tell us more about local standards of living than raw numbers could.

One famous version of PPP is the Big Mac index, developed by *The Economist*. In July 2008, a Big Mac cost $3.57 in the United States and 670 forint in Hungary. The official exchange rate was 144.3 forint per U.S. dollar. Yet when you compare the price of the Big Mac in each country, the effective exchange rate—the implied PPP—was 187.7 forint per dollar. Those smaller PPP forints suggest that money may not go as far in Hungary, and life may not be quite as comfortable as the official exchange rate implies.

Since raw numbers don't always tell the whole story, the *CIA World Factbook* gives two measures of GDP for each country. (GDP per capita, however, appears only as PPP.) According to the CIA's figures, Hungary's GDP in 2007 was $138.4 billion at the official exchange rate, but $191.7 billion according to a more formal version of purchasing power parity. This higher PPP number suggests that Hungarians may be more comfortable than the official exchange rate would lead us to expect.

There is a conflict here, of course. The Big Mac index tells us that Hungarians are poorer than they appear, while the CIA says they are wealthier. One of these versions of PPP is misleading, or things have changed in Hungary between 2007, when the CIA's number was current, and July 2008. If we were studying Hungary rather than the United Kingdom, we would need to explore this issue carefully. Serious forecasters spend quite a bit of time sorting out this type of discrepancy.

---

largest economy in the world. A quick look at the online edition of the *CIA World Factbook* shows that this translates to a comfortable $35,000 per capita, measured by purchasing power parity. This places the United Kingdom at roughly the same level as Germany, a bit ahead of France and behind Japan, and significantly behind the United States.

The United Kingdom is a major exporting country, ranking ninth in the world according to dollar value of exported products (Exhibit 6) and twelfth in the World Economic Forum's index of business competitiveness (see Exhibit 5 for the top ten). Another economic factor that seems interesting is that the United Kingdom still has not adopted the euro, the currency of nearly all its partners in the European Union (EU). This means that its companies may face some risks from currency exchange even when they trade within the EU. It also suggests that some people visiting the Continent from abroad may decide to stay there, rather than going through the hassle of converting their money to pounds Sterling in order to see England, while those who visit Britain may not travel further. This is not likely to be more than a small handicap for the British hospitality industry, but it could be worth looking into in a more thorough study.

In resources, the United Kingdom does not have enough oil or fresh water to rank among the top ten in Exhibits 7 and 8, and it is not among the ten largest exporters of farm products, according to data from the Food and Agriculture Organization of the United Nations. However, it does rank as the eleventh largest agricultural exporter. This is an interesting accomplishment for a few small

═══════════════════ **Technology Indicators** ═══════════════════

Exhibit 9
Nobel Prizes in Science, 1901–2008

Rank	Country	Total*
1	United States	233
2	Germany	84
3	United Kingdom	79
4	France	31
5	Switzerland	20
6	Netherlands	15
7	Russia/USSR	14
7	Austria	14
7	Sweden	14
10	Japan	13
10	Italy	12

Exhibit 10
Patents Granted, 2000–2005

Rank	Country	Patents per million population
1	Republic of Korea	1,113
2	Japan	857
3	United States	244
4	Finland	214
5	Sweden	166
6	Germany	158
7	France	155
8	Russian Federation	135
9	Slovenia	113
10	Netherlands	110

Exhibit 11
Internet Users, 30 June 2008

Rank	Country	Percent
1	Greenland	92
2	Netherlands	90
3	Norway	88
4	Iceland	85
5	Canada	84
6	New Zealand	81
7	Australia	79
8	Sweden	78
9	Japan	74
10	United States	74

Exhibit 12
Personal Computers, 2006

Rank	Country	Per 1,000 people
1	Israel	1,221
2	Canada	876
3	Switzerland	865
4	Netherlands	854
5	Sweden	836
6	United Kingdom	758
7	United States	762
8	Denmark	696
9	Singapore	682
10	Japan	676

* Totals include foreign-born scientists working in the country of record.

Exhibit 9 Source: http://nobelprize.org.

Exhibit 10 Source: United Nations Development Program, *Human Development Report 2007/2008* (http://hdr.undp.org/en/media/HDR_20072008_EN_Complete.pdf).

Exhibit 11 Source: Internet World Stats (www.internetworldstats.com).

Exhibit 12 Source: World Bank, *World Development Indicators, 2008* (http://books. google.com/books?id=O67oDJW01pwC&printsec=frontcover&dq=%22World+ Development+Indicators:+2008%22#PPA310,M1).

islands, and for some studies we might want to delve into that further. In addition, we remember that the United Kingdom once pumped quite a bit of oil from the North Sea, and another check with the *CIA World Factbook* reveals that there are large reserves of coal and natural gas as well as oil. News reports also indicate that

Diplomacy Indicators

Exhibit 13
Top Donors of Foreign Aid, 2007

Rank	Country	U.S. dollars (billions)
1	United States	21.75
2	Germany	12.27
3	France	9.94
4	United Kingdom	9.92
5	Japan	7.69
6	Netherlands	6.22
7	Spain	5.74
8	Sweden	4.33
9	Italy	3.93
10	Canada	3.92

Exhibit 14
U.N. Security Council, 2009

Country	Membership ends
China	Permanent
France	Permanent
Russia	Permanent
United Kingdom	Permanent
United States	Permanent
Austria	2010
Burkina Faso	2009
Croatia	2009
Costa Rica	2009
Japan	2010
Libya	2009
Mexico	2010
Turkey	2010
Uganda	2010
Vietnam	2009

Exhibit 15
Environmental Treaties of Selected Countries, 2008*

Rank	Country	Number
1	France	293
2	Germany	272
3	United Kingdom	244
4	Sweden	214
5	Russian Federation	163
6	United States	162
7	Canada	141
8	Japan	119
9	Brazil	113
10	China	93
11	India	93
12	Israel	81

*Country may be either a signatory or a party to the treaty.

Exhibit 13 Source: Assessment of Foreign Aid Spending by Donor Countries in 2007 (www.results.org/website/article.asp?id=3558).

Exhibit 14 Source: UN Security Council (www.un.org/sc/members.asp).

Exhibit 15 Source: Socioeconomic Data and Applications Center: Environmental Treaties and Resource Indicators, Columbia University (http://sedac.ciesin.columbia.edu/entri/CountryISO.jsp).

========================= **Social Indicators** =========================

Exhibit 16   **Exhibit 17**
Quality of Life*   **Educational Participation, Selected Countries, 2006**

Rank	Country		Country	Primary school	Post-secondary
				% of relevant age group**	
1	Iceland				
2	Norway		Brazil	140	24
3	Australia		Russian Federation	129	70
4	Canada		Iran	118	27
5	Ireland		India	115	11
6	Sweden		China	111	22
7	Switzerland		United Kingdom	107	59
8	Japan		Australia	104	73
9	Netherlands		Japan	100	55
10	France		United States	98	82
12	United States		Niger	51	1

  * UN Human Development Index

** Percentages may exceed 100 owing to enrollment of students outside the official age range, enrollment in multiple institutions, and other factors.

Exhibit 16 Source: UN DP Human Development Reports (http://hdr.undp.org/en/statistics/).

Exhibit 17 Source: World Bank, *World Development Indicators, 2008* (http://books.google.com/books?id=O67oDJW01pwC&printsec=frontcover&dq=%22World+Development+Indicators:+2008%22#PPA310,M1).

the United Kingdom is developing significant renewable energy resources, particularly wind and wave power; renewable energy is an issue we would wish to explore in considering the long-term future of any country. In all, primary energy production contributes no less than 10 percent to the nation's GDP, which is one of the highest shares among the industrialized nations. It would be nice to know how long that oil can be expected to last, but we will ignore that issue for now.

The United Kingdom has a solid base in technology. Its scientists have won 79 Nobel prizes, compared with 233 for the United States and 84 for Germany. (This information is presented in Exhibit 9, which includes scientists born in other countries but working in the country where they are counted.) It ranks twentieth in the number of Internet users (for the percentage of Internet users in selected countries, see Exhibit 11), and is among the top ten for number of personal computers per capita (Exhibit 12). There have been news stories, too, in the last few years that many American scientists are emigrating to Britain, where they can experiment with cloning and perform stem-cell research without the restrictions placed on them in the United States. In the number of patents granted per capita, however, it falls somewhere behind Finland and Slovenia; in fact, it ranks only eighteenth in this category (see Exhibit 10 for the top ten). This seems odd, and it might have

Cultural Indicators

Exhibit 18
Feature Film Production, 2006

Rank	Country	Films
1	India	1,091
2	Nigeria	872
3	United States	485
4	Japan	417
5	China	330
6	France	203
7	Germany	174
8	Spain	150
9	Italy	116
10	South Korea	110

Exhibit 19
Exports of Books, 2002

Rank	Country	U.S. dollars (millions)
1	United States	1,921
2	United Kingdom	1,805
3	Germany	1,257
4	Spain	685
5	France	519
6	Italy	510
7	China	409
8	Canada	396
9	Belgium	362
10	Singapore	349

Exhibit 20
Movie Attendance (most recent data)

Rank	Country	In millions
1	India	2,860
2	United States	1,421
3	Indonesia	190
4	France	155
5	Germany	149
6	Japan	145
7	United Kingdom	139
8	Spain	131
9	Mexico	120
10	Canada	113

Exhibit 18 Source: United Nations Educational, Scientific and Cultural Organization. Accessed November 4, 2008, at www.unesco.org/culture/.

Exhibit 19 Source: "International Flows of Selected Cultural Goods and Services, 1994-2003," UNESCO Institute for Statistics, 2005. Accessed November 4, 2008, at www.uis.unesco.org/template/pdf/cscl/IntlFlows_EN.pdf.

Exhibit 20 Source: UNESCO Institute for Statistics, Custom Table Viewer. Accessed on November 5, 2008, at http://stats.uis.unesco.org/unesco/TableViewer/document. aspx?ReportId=136&IF_Language=eng&BR_Topic=0.

something to do with patent law rather than inventiveness. It might also be that whoever compiled the data from which Exhibit 10 was abstracted supplied defective information for the United Kingdom. Depending on the purpose of our study, this could be worth more research.

==================== **Security Indicators** ====================

Exhibit 21
Opacity Index of Selected Countries

Exhibit 22
Trouble-Prone Young Men in Selected Countries (2010 estimate)

Rank	Country	Index
1	Finland	9
2	Hong Kong	12
3	Singapore	14
9	United Kingdom	17
9	Germany	17
12	Canada	22
13	United States	23
14	France	24
16	Japan	25
19	South Africa	26
22	Israel	30
24	South Korea	31
28	Taiwan	34
31	Thailand	37
31	Mexico	37
34	Italy	38
35	Indonesia	41
35	Russian Federation	41
38	Argentina	43
38	Pakistan	43
40	India	44
41	China	45
42	Brazil	46
43	Saudi Arabia	47
45	Venezuela	48

Country	Males, Age 15–29	Total population	% Population
Afghanistan	4,774,218	34,504,794	13.8
Algeria	4,488,735	34,586,184	13.0
Argentina	5,037,111	41,343,201	12.2
Brazil	25,803,694	201,103,330	12.8
China	169,756,656	1,347,563,498	12.6
Cuba	1,188,758	11,477,459	10.5
Egypt	11,788,558	84,440,272	14.0
Greece	925,946	10,749,943	8.6
India	163,390,842	1,184,090,490	13.8
Indonesia	31,971,656	242,968,342	13.2
Iraq	4,380,053	29,672,191	14.8
Iran	11,671,137	67,037,517	17.4
Israel	879,811	7,353,985	12.0
Japan	10,289,917	126,804,433	8.1
Kazakhstan	2,242,902	15,460,484	14.5
Kuwait	577,712	2,787,656	20.7
Mexico	14,965,819	112,468,855	13.3
Occupied Palestinian Territories	619,499	4,119,083	15.0
Pakistan	27,473,235	179,659,223	15.3
Russia	15,841,369	139,390,205	11.4
Saudi Arabia	4,604,638	29,207,277	15.8
Somalia	1,283,238	10,112,453	12.7
South Africa	8,138,189	49,109,107	16.6
Sudan	6,251,957	41,980,182	14.9
Turkey	9,959,639	73,322,470	13.6
United States	32,995,927	309,162,581	10.7

Exhibit 21 Source: *Opacity Index 2007–2008: Measuring Global Business Risks,* Milken Institute, April 2008 (www.milkeninstitute.org/publications/publications.taf?functio n=detail&ID=38801146&cat=ResRep).

Exhibit 22 Source: Population Division of the Department of Economic and Social Affairs of the United Nations Secretariat, *World Population Prospects: The 2008 Revision,* medium variant; accessed November 8, 2008, at http://esa.un.org/unpp/index. asp?panel=2. U.S. Census Bureau International Data Base; accessed November 8, 2008, at www.census.gov/ipc/www/idb/summaries.html.

The United Kingdom also may have the kind of social base that contributes to a stable, economically successful society. With roughly two rooms per person, it ranks in fourth place for its housing supply. However, the UN Human Development Index does not rate its quality of life among the top ten (Exhibit 16), and a quick data search reveals that it lags in the number of university students per capita. For some purposes, these issues also may justify more study.

Militarily, the United Kingdom is the world's fourth-largest spender (Exhibit 1); yet the budget for its armed forces is much less than one-tenth that of the United States. It is the third-largest weapons exporter (Exhibit 3), though only 30 percent as large in this market as the United States and a bit more than one-third as large as Russia. And with approximately 200 warheads, it owns a significant nuclear deterrent (Exhibit 2).

Diplomatically, the United Kingdom is a permanent member of the United Nations Security Council, which gives it much more power than its size would suggest. It also ranks fourth among the world's donors of foreign aid (Exhibit 13), which confers some status of its own. It is third in the number of environmental treaties by which it is bound (see Exhibit 15). In most cases, it is a party to a treaty rather than a signatory, but what that indicates will not be clear without further study.

The United Kingdom's opacity index is only seventeen (Exhibit 21), signifying that its business and political operations are relatively open to public scrutiny. This tends to be a sign of basic stability, as the governments of volatile countries seldom want anyone watching their actions too closely.

Our table of young male populations does not include the United Kingdom (see Exhibit 22, which is not a top-ten list, but a group of countries that interested us when we compiled it). However, the U.N.'s World Population Prospects database (http://esa.un.org/unpp/index.asp?panel=2) reports that in 2010 there will be 6.15 million males in the violence-prone ages between fifteen and twenty-nine, or about 10 percent of the total population. This is roughly the same as the United States and Cuba, which are among the world's most stable places. Given the history of terrorist attacks in Britain, this may be one place where the indicator should be weighted less heavily than in other countries.

Culturally, data from the movie industry suggest that Britain consumes the good-life fantasies of Hollywood more than it exports its own. It ranks seventh in the number of movie tickets sold each year (Exhibit 20), but it is not among the top ten producers of feature films (Exhibit 18).

Without going into depth, the data we have collected thus far paint a picture of the United Kingdom as a significant economic, military, and diplomatic power in the world. The data also suggest that we can expect the United Kingdom to remain economically comfortable, stable, and influential for some time to come. In a formal research project, we would collect much more data and try to fill in the details of this quick impression.

However, even this extremely brief study raises some interesting questions. How long will that North Sea oil last? And how will the economy react when it runs out? Will the United Kingdom's environment suffer if the country reverts to burning coal? Will the United Kingdom become as dependent as the United States on oil from the Middle East? We clearly have more work to do in this area.

How long can Britain remain a global economic leader? The world increasingly depends on technology, and the United Kingdom does not seem to be producing all that many college graduates. Can it maintain a strong technology base without them? Does Britain have some alternative way of training engineers and technicians that does not show up on college data? Perhaps a system of technical schools, possibly supplemented by on-the-job training? Or does it rely on technologically sophisticated immigrants from India and other lands? For a serious study, we would have to know.

And what does that modest population of young males indicate when compared with Britain's history of terrorist attacks? Recent news reports have said that militant religious leaders in Britain may be attracting young Muslims to the *jihad* against the West, and even against their adopted homeland. How many of Britain's young men are potential converts to Muslim extremism? Flag this area for much more research! It could be critical to the economic and political stability of the United Kingdom, and to the safety of the hospitality industry there.

We see in these questions the power of trend data. Some of them would be answered if we were working with trends, rather than looking at single data points. The question of how long the North Sea oil will last is an obvious example.

We see also the value offered by even a cursory look ahead. In a few minutes of thinking about the most basic data, we have identified several important issues that must be examined further before we can feel confident that our image of the United Kingdom will not change significantly with relatively little notice. Forecasters often carry out such preliminary studies to learn whether a subject merits greater attention.

Most of us learn best by doing something, not by reading about it. So for a more valuable introduction to forecasting, why not try this on your own? Pick a country and make your own forecast. Gather the necessary data, see what the trends and indicators imply for it, and evaluate that nation's stability and future. Then see how things are likely to evolve over the next ten years and try to figure out the merits of opening a new hotel or resort there. This exercise will give you a far better sense of how much can be accomplished using publicly available data and relatively simple methods of analysis.

If you want a really interesting challenge, try looking at India. It is a huge country with an extraordinarily varied population and culture, and it is changing rapidly in ways that are likely to be felt around the world. Compare India with China, and you will have seen the future of one of the world's most important bilateral relationships, two of its largest and fastest growing markets, and 40 percent of its population.

It will take considerable effort. Some years ago, FI examined India in depth for a government client. Since then, we have carried out smaller comparisons of India and China. It was fascinating work, and we would love to investigate these neighboring giants in much greater depth. However, such an evaluation will have to wait for a client with a serious interest in this region since our study of India alone occupied much of our staff for nearly a year.

Looking Ahead

In a fast-changing world, the cost of being unprepared seems to grow every day. The memory of buying stocks just before the market crashed in 2008 should be enough to convince anyone that we all need better information about the future.

It is available. With a little effort, we can diagnose the future as a doctor diagnoses a patient. The vital signs are there to be read.

This chapter provides only a brief sample of the ways in which forecasting methods can be used to anticipate developments affecting the hospitality industry and, in turn, many aspects of our lives and careers. It should be a good place to start your own study of the subjects that concern you and a guide to the kind of reasoning that can give you a leg up in many other fields as well.

"If only I had known then what I know today." How often have you heard it said? How often have you said it yourself? Learn to look ahead as forecasters do, and you may never say it again.

In the remaining chapters, FI uses its forecasting expertise to examine the issues currently facing the hospitality industry and explain the relevant trends associated with each area of focus. In the Key Trends section of each chapter, we discuss each trend that is applicable to the subject of that chapter and explain the implications of that trend for the area under discussion.

2

The World Economy: Today's Pain Is Tomorrow's Gain

T HE WORLD ECONOMY has been on our list of trends for more than twenty years. We have rephrased our description occasionally to clarify our intent, but the trend has never changed: continuing growth, with only brief, relatively minor interruptions, for at least the next five years. That continues to be the case today.

At the beginning of 2009, this trend seemed in doubt. Around the world, economies were contracting and major financial institutions were sinking into bankruptcy. Trade had shrunk so severely that many cargo ships had been taken out of service for the duration; at its worst, the Baltic Dry Index, a common measure of shipping prices, had fallen 89 percent in six months. Even the mighty Chinese economy was expected to grow by only 5 percent or so in 2009, down from an estimated 8 percent the year before and nearly 12 percent in 2007. Most observers were calling this the worst financial chaos since the Great Depression of the 1930s. In this, they were correct.

Yet, unlike some commentators, we have never been convinced that another Great Depression is at hand. In fact, we believe that our perpetual forecast will survive intact. The current downturn is painful, especially for the hospitality and travel industry, but it will not last as long as some pessimists fear. The global economy will begin to grow again before the end of 2009. In five years, the chaos that began late in 2008 will be remembered as a necessary purge that readied the world for another round of solid growth.

Before we examine the crisis itself, it is worth looking at how this broad recession has affected the hospitality and travel industry. After housing, which triggered the decline, hospitality was one of the first sectors to feel the effects of the 2008 downturn.

Awash in Bad News

Even before economists agreed that a recession had begun, the global airline industry was seeing its largest drop in traffic since the SARS epidemic of 2003. Worldwide passenger traffic was off 2.9 percent in September 2008, compared with the previous year, and another 1.3 percent in October. By March 2009, passenger traffic was 11.1 percent below the previous year, when the decline had already begun. (This includes an estimated loss of 2 percent because the high-travel Easter weekend shifted from March in 2008 to April in 2009.) The International Air Transport

Association lost 24 of its 230 members to bankruptcy in 2008 and expected that number to grow in 2009.

The world's hotels also were feeling the pain. In the United States, revenue per available room (RevPAR) was off by 8 percent by mid-October 2008, with luxury hotels down by 14 percent. PKF Hospitality Research, revising an earlier forecast, predicted a drop in U.S. occupancy rates of 4.4 percent in 2009 to a level of 58.3 percent, the lowest in twenty years except for the few weeks immediately after September 11. Even that gloomy outlook proved too optimistic. By the end of May 2009, occupancy in the United States was down to 51.6 percent, off some 10 percent from twelve months earlier. RevPAR was only $47.96, off nearly 19 percent. In Europe a month earlier, occupancy was down to 59.4 percent, off nearly 14 percent from 2008; RevPAR was off more than 37 percent. In the Caribbean, hotel bookings varied widely, with some islands reporting losses of as much as 50 percent, while others showed small improvements. Overall, bookings were down for both the United States and Europe, which together account for 90 percent of Caribbean tourism.

Entering 2009, cruise lines were no better off. Royal Caribbean announced that bookings for the first half of 2009 were lagging behind those of 2008 and said that it would skip its quarterly dividend owing to the slowdown. Cruise Holidays reported that cancellations were up by one-third, while bookings were down by double digits. By late November, Expedia.com was listing a four-night Bahamas cruise out of Miami for just $99 per person.

Other segments of the hospitality industry were hit almost as hard.

Restaurant revenues declined in the high-end, mid-range, and even fast-casual segments as former patrons settled for home-cooked meals or supermarket takeout. Among major chains, only MacDonald's was flourishing, thanks in part to the company's new dollar menu—an innovation that many of its competitors quickly copied. As a result, American restaurants shed about 137,000 jobs in the sixteen months that began in January 2008. In the United States, industry sales were expected to grow from $552 billion in 2008 to $566 billion in 2009. When adjusted for inflation, however, that represents a real loss of about 1 percent. Full-service restaurants will be off by an estimated 2.5 percent.

Meetings and conventions have been pressed ever since American International Group got caught using federal bailout funds for an executive getaway. The Ritz-Carlton, Half Moon Bay, California, alone lost thirty-two events in the four months ending March 2009. Starwood Hotels & Resorts Worldwide reported that company-operated hotels booked 40 percent less group revenue in the first three months of 2009 than the year before. That shortfall cost the jobs of 6,000 employees, one-tenth of the firm's workforce. Roger Dow, president and CEO of the U.S. Travel Association, said his group members' hotels lost some $220 million in revenues due to event cancellations in the first two months of 2009.[1] The organization represents about one-fifth of the American hotel market.

Tourism has been lagging throughout most of the world. In Paris, the recession is tightening belts throughout the hospitality industry. International arrivals at the city's airports in February fell 8.1 percent from the previous February. Hotel occupancy was off 10 percent. Restaurants are reporting revenues as much as 20 percent below the pace of 2008.

In the United States, even the evergreen attractions have slipped. Attendance at the two Disney theme parks was off 5 percent in the first quarter of 2009, and company profits dropped by 32 percent. Analysts at Goldman Sachs were predicting a decline of 10 percent for the year. Orlando was particularly depressed, with overall hotel occupancy off by 26 percent in the final week of March and revenue per room down by 35 percent, to $68.15. Travel through Orlando International Airport slipped by 11.1 percent in February.

In Las Vegas, airline and car traffic are off, and room rates at major hotels are being discounted by 20 percent or more. In the six weeks ending February 20, would-be visitors reportedly canceled 50,000 room-nights worth of stays. In March, RevPAR was reported down 38 percent from the previous year.

In all, the UN World Tourism Organization reports global tourism down by 3 percent in Europe and Asia in the second half of 2008. It foresees a further decline of 1 to 2 percent worldwide in 2009.

Certainly, it has not been the kind of performance anyone would have expected to see when the world economy still seemed sound. It has not been the kind of performance anyone would like to see repeated. And it was not what we expect to see in 2010 and beyond.

Financial Epicenter

When the global economy is growing, it forms a benevolent cycle. Prosperity in each country expands markets for the exports of all its trading partners; the partners' export profits spur their demand for imports, which in turn generates still more wealth at home. Since the end of World War II, this cycle has begun in the United States, the world's most powerful economy and the engine that drives the rest.

Since early 2008, the process has been running in reverse. At first, weakness in America was offset to some extent by the strength of China, whose voracious appetite for raw materials supported the world's commodity producers almost single-handedly. That ended with the collapse of the American financial system, which had grown vastly overexposed to losses from securities backed only by high-risk mortgages. Many banks in Europe had made the same mistake. Even China had a few hundred million dollars' worth of exposure. So when America's real estate market plunged and people began to default on those mortgages, banks began to go belly-up. The survivors hoarded their capital, unwilling to lend it to anyone whose finances might be shaky—which was to say anyone at all. Credit markets dried up, which meant that ordinary businesses could no longer get the capital they required to fund their daily operations. Many cut back. Some failed. Unemployment grew. Profits shrank. As the major economies followed the United States into recession, their trading partners followed. The benevolent cycle turned vicious.

Since the collapse began, governments around the world have been scrambling to rescue failing institutions, get money moving again, and keep a painful recession from turning into an outright depression. We all have watched the process in great detail in the news media, so there is little point in recounting it here. Instead, we will look at the health of the world's major economies, consider what remains to be done, and try to anticipate what this economic turmoil will mean for the future of hospitality and travel. We will begin with the United States—the epicenter of the financial earthquake that is now shaking the world.

According to the most common definition, a recession begins only when a country's GDP has declined for two consecutive quarters. By that standard, the United States still had not entered a recession as of September 2008. In the second quarter of the year, the economy was still growing at an annual rate of 2.8 percent. It began to shrink only in the period from July through September, when it was off by 0.5 percent. By this standard, the United States was not really in recession until the fourth quarter of 2008.

Yet it had been clear for most of the year that the economy was in trouble. Employment fell continuously beginning late in 2007. Through November 2008, about two million jobs had disappeared since January, and the losses were accelerating. More than four million people were collecting unemployment compensation, the most in twenty-six years. Unemployment had crept up to 6.7 percent, according to the official numbers.

Yet this may not have been the full extent of the problem. Skeptics point out that the government has changed the way it calculates unemployment over the years, and the old way may be more accurate. According to the standard used until the early 1980s, that 6.7 percent unemployment reported for November really meant that 12 percent of workers were jobless. The definition of discouraged workers—people who are willing and able to work but have given up looking for a job—has changed as well. Add them in, as they were calculated until the mid-1990s, and unemployment would have been almost 16 percent.

Since then, the American economy has continued to shrink, while unemployment has grown. According to the federal Bureau of Economic Analysis (BEA), the GDP contracted at an annualized rate of 6.1 percent in the last quarter of 2008 and by an estimated 5.7 percent in the first quarter of 2009. If it follows the traditional pattern, first quarter 2009 losses will grow by a few tenths of a percent when the BEA reworks its calculations based on complete data. New jobless data were grim as well. In May, employers laid off an estimated 345,000 workers. The arrival of new graduates in the job market brought the nation's official unemployment rate to 9.4 percent, the highest it had been since July 1983. In all, some six million jobs have been shed from the American economy since the downturn began.

Looking at the long-term unemployed, the situation is grimmer still. These are people who have been out of work for more than six months. Their numbers have grown to about four million, up from just 1.4 million at the beginning of the recession. Upwards of 16 percent are college-educated, more than in any previous recession. On average, they once held relatively well-paid, stable jobs. If this recession follows the pattern of 2001, many of them may never work again, except in low-wage service positions that lack health insurance, retirement plans, and other benefits.

Other data confirm the depth of the economy's distress. Begin with the housing market, where the trouble first appeared:

- The collapse in home prices, which touched off the general economic decline in the United States, accelerated in the first three months of 2009, the latest data available as this is written. On average, the cost of an existing home was about 20 percent lower than a year earlier. The S&P/Case-Shiller twenty-city index of home prices in major metropolitan areas was off 32 percent from its July 2006 peak. It had fallen for thirty-two straight months. Losses were worst in Phoenix and Las Vegas, where prices had fallen 36 and 31 percent, respectively. At the end of 2008, about twelve million homeowners owed more on their mortgages than their homes were worth, up from only three million at the end of 2006, with the number expected to reach 14.6 million in 2009. One in eight is either behind on mortgage payments or in foreclosure, which is a record high.

- Sales of existing homes rose 2.9 percent in April, to an annual rate of 4.68 million per year. That was the good news. The bad news was that up to half of those homes were in foreclosure.

- New home starts in April were down to an annual rate of 458,000, down 12 percent in just a month. It was the fewest monthly starts in the fifty years the government has been tracking them.

- New home sales rose a scant 0.3 percent to an annualized rate of 352,000. This was the second increase in three months, but slightly less than the 360,000 that economists had expected. The number of new homes on the market fell to an estimated 291,000, the fewest since May 2001. Yet, at that rate of sales, it would take more than ten months to unload the inventory of new homes.

Consumers make up about two-thirds of the American economy, so their contribution will be critical to any recovery. Thus far, the data are mixed.

- Retail sales were off 1.3 percent in March, 0.4 percent in April, down again in May. Among major retailers, only bottom-end Wal-Mart prospered. At other major retailers, same-store sales plummeted—off an estimated 18 percent among women's clothiers and about 20 percent at department stores. Overall, same-store sales were down 4.8 percent in May, when a decline of 4.1 percent had been expected. All this was particularly disappointing because the Memorial Day weekend sales had drawn 5 percent more shoppers than in 2008.

- The auto industry was hit hardest of all. New car sales in May came in 34 percent below 2008 levels. Ford sales were off by 24 percent from twelve months earlier—and that was the bright spot in the market. GM was down more than 29 percent, Chrysler 30 percent, Toyota 38 percent, and Honda 39 percent. Perversely, this was good news because sales were even worse in April. For some makers, May represented the best sales month for the year.

If all this seems almost unrelievedly grim, you get the picture. The United States is in its longest recession since World War II, and by some measures, perhaps its worst. At one point last October, six out of ten Americans believed an all-out depression was likely.

Before we explain why Forecasting International has never shared this gloomy outlook, we need to find out how much help the United States can expect from its trading partners.

World Tour

Although the 2001 recession in the United States was painful, it remained shallower and briefer than it might have been. The credit goes largely to China, which had grown so large and continued to expand so rapidly that its demand for raw materials helped to prop up America's trading partners until the world's largest economy got back on its feet.

China will not save the day this time. Economic activity already has plunged throughout the world. In November 2008, the JPMorgan Global All-Industry Output Index sank to 35.4, its lowest reading in the eleven years it has been tracked. This is consistent with a global GDP that is contracting at a seasonally adjusted annual rate of –1.5 to –2 percent. Global output, new orders, input prices, and employment were falling at the fastest rate JPMorgan had ever seen. All this suggested that the first quarter of 2009 also would be down, officially putting the world into recession.

A look at the state of some important trading nations confirms this assessment.

China

The world's largest country has also been its fastest-growing. Over the last twenty-five years, this largely rural land has transformed itself into the fourth-biggest industrial producer, after the United States, Japan, and Germany. It manufactures half of the world's cameras, one-third of its cell phones, and 60 percent of its buttons. A single city, Wenzhou, produces 40 percent of the shoes sold on earth. As a competitor, China has a big advantage over other nations: Even in the comparatively well-paid industrial area of Guangzhou Province, wages still average just $0.77 an hour, less than one-fourth the price of labor in Mexico. It also has a government that is solidly behind capitalism. The National People's Congress, once devoted to Mao's austere brand of communism, now includes many members who formerly headed private companies rather than government departments.

All of this, plus a currency that generally has been undervalued on foreign exchange markets, has turned China into a trading powerhouse. In 2007, it exported $1.22 billion worth of merchandise, up more than 25 percent on the year. Roughly $233 billion of that went to the United States, more than eight times the $28.4 billion worth of Chinese products the United States imported as recently as 2003.

Exports, however, are just one piece of the Chinese economy. The country's GDP totals about $3.25 trillion at the official exchange rate or $7.1 trillion when measured according to local purchasing power. Exports account for only one-fifth of that. The rest comes from internal growth. China's economy has been expanding by more than 9 percent annually since 2003, peaking at 11.9 percent in 2007.

But this is changing rapidly. In the second half of 2008, China's economy slowed sharply. Much of its expansion since 2004 has depended on a high level of investment. Worried that soaring real estate prices would trigger uncontrolled inflation, Beijing tightened credit and throttled it back. Real estate development plunged, cutting demand for concrete, steel, and other construction-related products.

Since America's financial problems have infected the rest of the world, demand for Chinese exports has shrunk as well. In January and February 2009, they came in more than 26 percent below the level a year earlier. March was off just 17 percent, but April showed a 22 percent decline. It does not help that the renminbi is significantly more expensive on the world's currency exchanges than it used to be, making the country's products a bit less attractive to foreign buyers.

As a result of these changes, GDP growth is expected to come in at around 7.5 percent in 2009, after being up only 6.1 percent in the first quarter of the year. For any other country, this would be a solid expansion. But China needs to find jobs for nearly twenty million new workers each year, which requires growth near double-digit rates.

The situation has become even more troubled because of Beijing's recent focus on shifting manpower and investment from relatively low-profit industries such as textiles and shoe-making to high-value-added fields in high technology. This policy was causing growing unemployment in light industry even before the global recession shrank demand from China's export markets. Officially, the unemployment rate is only 4 percent, although this omits rural areas. In practice, economists estimate that urban unemployment is closer to 12 percent and could reach 14 percent as the global contraction continues.

China has responded strongly to the worldwide recession. The country has about $1.87 trillion in foreign reserves and the highest peacetime savings rate anyone can remember—a staggering 50 percent of GDP. This enabled President Hu Jintao to enact a stimulus plan of four trillion yuan, or about $585 billion, in infrastructure spending. It is the largest such package to date.

These factors limit China's ability to put a floor under the world economy as the United States falls deeper into recession. It also means that the 100 million Chinese tourists expected to flood the world by 2020 may be a year or two late.

India

The world's second-most-populous country once was viewed as a perpetual beggar state, but no longer. For the last decade, it has radiated economic health. India's GDP expanded by an average of 9 percent annually for the four years ending in 2007. Goldman Sachs forecasts that it will continue to grow by an average of 5 percent annually *for the next half century.* According to the investment bank's estimates, the Indian economy will be bigger than Japan's by 2032. By 2050, the country's per capita income will grow by 3,500 percent!

Yet, there are signs of trouble even in this golden economy. Inflation peaked at 13 percent in August 2008, leading the Reserve Bank of India to hike interest rates to the highest levels in seven years. By the first months of 2009, inflation had fallen below 1 percent. Unfortunately, industrial production was slowing as well. For the year ending in April 2009, it was 2.3 percent below its level a year earlier. And in October 2008, exports were off for the first time in seven years. By January 2009, overseas shipments were down nearly 16 percent from a year earlier. This is significant, because about 27 percent of India's GDP comes from exports of goods and services in roughly equal amounts. The global recession has not yet put an end to India's growth, but it has slowed it down.

Economic forecasters say India's GDP will continue to expand despite the worldwide downturn. On average, they foresee more than 7 percent growth in 2008 and 6.5 percent or better in 2009.

This can only come as good news to the world's hospitality and travel industry. More than ten million Indian tourists were expected to visit other lands in 2008. In 2009, if the country's economy holds up, those travelers could represent one of the few hospitality markets that continue to grow through hard times.

Japan

After a dozen years of stagnation, this one-time powerhouse was finally back on track. Japan's economy grew at a yearly rate of 7.3 percent in the fourth quarter of 2003 and 6.1 percent in the first quarter of 2004. This compares to an average of only 0.4 percent per year from 1998 through 2002. By 2007, however, growth had slowed to just 2 percent, and toward year's end the consensus held that Japan was headed back into recession.

By 2009, that recession had arrived. Japan's GDP shrank a catastrophic 3.3 percent (12.7 percent annualized) in the fourth quarter of 2008. In the first quarter of 2009, it was off another 4 percent for an annual rate of 16 percent. The critical export sector was off by 26 percent for the quarter.

The Conference Board's leading economic index for Japan confirms that the downturn has a way to run. For the six months ending March 2009, it fell by 26.4 percent, the worst decline recorded in the forty-four years the index has been tallied. This strongly suggests that Japan will follow its trading partners out of recession, not lead the way.

Europe

The European Commission was predicting economic stagnation throughout its region as early as March 2008. By 2009, the outlook had deteriorated. In May 2009, the Commission predicted that the European Union would shrink by 4 percent in 2009, with contractions of 5.4 percent in Germany, 3 percent in France, 4.4 percent in Italy, and 3.8 percent in the United Kingdom. Performance to date suggests that these estimates may be slightly optimistic. In April 2009, Germany's GDP was 6.9 percent below its level a year earlier. France was off by 3.2 percent, the United Kingdom by 4.1 percent, and Italy by 5.9 percent.

There was a little good news as well. The Conference Board's leading economic index for the Eurozone gained 2.2 percent in the first four months of 2009, but this followed a drop of 15 percent between June and December the previous year. The European economy may be reaching bottom, but it has a long way to go before substantial growth returns. Even in 2010, the Commission expects the regional GDP to expand by just 0.1 percent.

Russia

Economically, Russia had been faring pretty well. After years of post-Soviet malaise, the country ended 2007 with its ninth straight year of growth, peaking at a heady 8.5 percent in the fourth quarter of 2007. Growth continued through the first half of 2008, the most recent data available as this is written. Russia's balance of trade was strongly positive, thanks largely to oil exports of more than five million barrels per day. Triple-digit oil prices were making Russia rich.

Then oil prices collapsed, as did Russia's stock markets. MICEX, the country's largest exchange, lost 17.5 percent in just one day, while RTS lost 64 percent in the two months beginning in mid-July. Much of that stock had been used as collateral for more than $500 billion in loans from Western banks; many of those loans were called in. Foreign investment, which totaled $81 billion in 2007, was expected to come in at $50 billion for 2008; by 2009, it is likely to be lower still. More than $150 billion in foreign funds has already been pulled out of Russia. The middle class reportedly has shrunk from 25 percent of the population to just 18 percent as nearly ten million Russians have fallen into poverty in the span of a few months. None of these developments were cause for optimism.

By early 2009, it was clear that Russia had entered a severe recession. By April, its GDP was off 9.5 percent in twelve months. By early June, the country's Economy Ministry was predicting a GDP loss of 6 to 8 percent for the year, and other data suggested an even worse decline. Looking at the government's budget, the Ministry predicted deficits of 10 percent in 2009 and 6 percent in 2010. Economists say this is consistent with a drop of 15 percent in GDP for 2009.

Now the Good News

As badly as the recession has hit the hospitality industry, it could have been a lot worse. Operators that have managed to streamline their operations and cut costs have been making the best of a bad situation. Some are running in the black.

In the air, most large American carriers have posted losses. Yet the red ink is shallower than industry observers feared. Delta Air Lines and UAL Corp., parent of United Airlines, lost $1.2 billion between them in the first quarter of 2009. AMR Corp., the parent of American Airlines, lost $375 million. Some low-cost carriers, such as JetBlue and AirTran, managed to post profits. It has helped a lot that fuel prices are well below their 2008 peak.

Even the losers are seeing improvement. Continental Airlines logged 9.7 percent fewer passenger miles in March than the previous year, but just 3.8 percent fewer in April. American's passenger traffic was off nearly 11 percent in March, year on year, but only 4.7 percent in April. AirTran's traffic was down a scant 0.3 percent in April, with more than 80 percent of its seats filled.

On the water, Carnival Cruise Lines general manager Hans J. Hahn reports that profits were flat, at best, because filling ships required an average cut of 60 percent in ticket prices. Yet those deep discounts did keep passengers on the firm's vessels. Although January and February are traditionally losing months for the industry, passenger numbers for the first two months of 2009 were up 60 percent over last year. Carnival carried 32,000 cruisers to Caribbean islands in the period. Profits may soon begin to recover, as the line bumped prices back up for the spring break in March 2009. Results for the month are not yet available.

Restaurants also seem to be recovering. Some sit-down chains, such as the Cheesecake Factory, have racked up better-than-expected profits. And the National Restaurant Association's comprehensive index of restaurant activity rose in April

2009 for the third consecutive month—its Restaurant Performance Index stood at 97.7 in March, up 0.2 percent from February and 1.3 percent over the quarter. The Expectations Index, which measures restaurant operators' six-month outlook, stood at 99.4 in March—up 0.9 percent from February for its fourth consecutive monthly gain. This was its strongest level in 14 months.

Hotel revenues are still down, thanks to sharp cuts in room rates, but for most segments occupancy appears to have bottomed out in January 2009. According to Smith Travel Research, upscale hotels saw room demand off by about 9 percent in January. By the first week of April, it was down by only 2 percent. The "midscale-with-food-and-beverage" segment was up from a trough of −16 percent to −13 percent. Only the lower-end chains hovered near their January low, about 10 percent below the previous year. As performance goes, it was not great, but at least most segments were moving in the right direction.

The recession has even given a boost to a few niche hotels. With traditional sites foundering, occupancy is way up at super-cheap facilities with plush accommodations but tiny rooms. The Jane Hotel, in New York City, offers 350 thread-count sheets and state-of-the-art audio systems in 150 single rooms just seven by eight feet across. Bathrooms are shared, except in some higher-priced rooms, but at $100 per night, the Jane has no problem attracting guests. So too at The Pod Hotel, in midtown Manhattan near the United Nations, where the 350 bunk-bed rooms go for $89 per night. Occupancy at The Pod Hotel is 90 percent, a level that most traditional hotels can only envy.

Foreign investors also are creating new options for short-term stays in New York City and Washington, D.C., but only for certain elite guests. According to our contacts in China and Russia, their countrymen are buying up cheap houses in those cities and converting them to living quarters for government workers on temporary assignment to the United States. The houses are staffed by couples from the home country. Investors see this as a win-win proposition. The diplomats get comfortable lodgings at prices well below hotel rates. The investors receive guaranteed bookings and the promise of spectacular profits when real estate prices recover.

Looking Ahead

These first signs of new life in the hospitality industry reflect what looks like a spring thaw in the American economy. Speaking in early May 2009, Federal Reserve Chairman Ben Bernanke told Congress the economy should start growing again later that year. It was his most optimistic assessment since the downturn began. There are in fact signs that the bottom may already be in. In diverse corners of the economy, some important indicators are picking up.

Leading Indicators Improving

Real estate, of course, has been the economy's weakest sector. In March 2009, economists expected construction spending to drop 1.5 percent for its sixth straight monthly loss. Instead, it rose by 0.3 percent. In April, it jumped by 0.8 percent. It was the largest one-month increase in eight months. In January, the National

Association of Realtors index of pending home sales hit an all-time low. In March, it climbed 3.2 percent to 84.6, the second monthly increase. That was 1.1 percent above last year's levels.

In some places where home prices crashed first and worst, they are recovering strongly. With home prices now down to half their peak levels, sales in Sacramento County, California, have been climbing since the end of 2007. By March 2009, they were up 45 percent over the previous year, to 2,254 homes. In Las Vegas, the most depressed market in the country, they were up 35 percent. Prices were up as well, if only slightly.

Nationwide, pending sales of existing homes rose 6.7 percent in April from March, according to the National Association of Realtors. This was up 3.2 percent from a year earlier.

People's second favorite investment is even stronger. By early June, the stock market had recovered nearly everything it had lost since the previous November. The Standard and Poor's Index was up nearly 250 points in three months. On June 4, the Dow Jones Industrial Average touched 8,900, the highest it had been since January and within about 300 points of its December high. On average, the stock market in early June was 40 percent above its recession low. No one is certain that the bottom is behind us, but the signs are promising.

Manufacturing was still shrinking, but not as fast as it had been. The Institute for Supply Management's manufacturing index rose 2.7 points in May, to 42.8. That was the fifth straight gain and the best reading since September 2008. According to Scott Brown, chief economist at Raymond James, "Recent data suggest that the worst part of the economic decline is behind us."[2]

The grimmest statistic in the economy has been the number of job losses. Yet even in this area, there was what passed for good news. That loss of 345,000 nonfarm jobs in May, though nasty in any other economic season, was actually a good deal better than the 600,000 most economists had expected. Many observers greeted it as the first robin of a much-delayed spring.

It is also worth remembering that there is a difference between unemployment and the other indicators. Construction, manufacturing, and especially the stock market lead the economy. When they go up, the rest of the economy can be expected to improve in the months ahead. Employment is a lagging indicator. It seldom begins to grow until well after GDP has done so. On balance, the indicators suggest that the economy is beginning to bottom out. Better times probably lie ahead.

The American public seems to be convinced. Consumer confidence readings appear to have bottomed out in February 2009. Since then, they have been rebounding sharply. An increase of 14.1 percent from April to May brought the index to 54.9, its highest level in eight months.

Consumers were spending more as well. Even though the U.S. economy shrank in the first quarter of 2009, consumers began to open their wallets. Spending was up by 2.2 percent after falling in the two previous quarters. Disappointingly, March and April brought slight declines. Yet personal income unexpectedly rose 0.5 percent in April, its largest increase since May 2008. Real disposable income shot up by 1.1 percent. This seems a good omen for future spending. In all, economists generally expect consumer spending to grow at an annualized rate of at least 1 percent through 2009. By the end of the year, this new consumption should lift the economy out of recession. Ben Bernanke was right.

The Conference Board's Leading Economic Index confirms this assessment. It rose a sharp 1 percent in April 2009, the latest revision currently available. This was the first good news from the index in seven months. As confirmation, the index's positive components outweighed the negatives for the first time in sixteen months. Stock prices, the interest rate spread, consumer expectations, initial unemployment claims, the average workweek, supplier deliveries, and manufacturers' new orders for consumer goods and materials all helped to lift the index in April. They more than offset the three negative contributors: real money supply, building permits, and manufacturers' orders for nondefense capital goods. In all, it was welcome news.

Cause for Optimism

There are more positive items to factor in as well. The early publicity about Washington's stimulus package has long passed, but the spending itself has barely begun. Over the next few months, the money slated for infrastructure maintenance and other such projects should create much-needed construction jobs. In addition, President Obama vowed in early June to add still more new spending, enough to create or save 600,000 more jobs. Combined, these developments at last give economists sound cause for optimism.

In mid-2009, it seems that Washington's tentative, undersized, but nonetheless incredibly expensive interventions in the economy have done their job. Economists such as Princeton's Nobel Laureate Paul Krugman have complained that the government has spent no more than half enough to head off a severe recession, and in this they are correct. However, that clearly was never the Obama administration's goal. Instead, the President and his advisors set out to prevent a severe recession from becoming an all-out economic rout. In this, they have been effective. Thus far, the recession of 2008–09 shows no sign of becoming a depression. By most measures—including loss of GDP, decline in major stock indices, and even new and continuing unemployment claims (all measured as percentages)—it is not even the worst recession since World War II.

Clearly, growth will not return immediately. Neither will jobs recover without delay. Yet, by the end of 2009, it will be clear that the worst of the recession has passed, and that it did so several months earlier. Once more, the world will follow the United States back to prosperity.

Hospitality Will Recover

This has been a lengthy preamble in support of a much briefer message: For hospitality, the good times are not over. They are simply on hold for a while. The downturn will be endurable, and the recovery gradual but inevitable.

This conclusion is based on many factors. The most significant include economic trends as this is written and the stated policies of President Obama and other national leaders, both in the United States and in the other major trading nations. It should help also that U.S. federal budgets are prepared in September and October—just after the crash in 2008 and after the beginning of the recovery in 2009. Preparation of the budgets after any major economic surprises should add needed stability to federal spending.

Although any of these factors is subject to change, we remain confident that the current recession has much less time to run than many observers fear. The path out of economic downturns has been clearly understood since the days of the New Deal. There is no acceptable excuse not to deal effectively with this one. For any elected leader, or even the Chinese government, the political consequences of delay or failure would be intolerably dire. Thus, the response to recession in Washington, Beijing, and the world's other major capitals will continue to be swift, and it will be effective.

The world has been set back about three to four years. So look to 2005. At the worst of the recession, air travel, hotel occupancy, international tourism, meals served at full-service restaurants, and many other measures of the hospitality industry will return to the levels of three years past. Having three years of progress erased is an unpleasant blow, but it is one the industry can survive. The year 2005 seemed comfortable and prosperous at the time.

Profits may take a bit longer to recover, particularly in non-luxury markets. Attracting middle- and lower-income guests in a down economy is likely to require substantial discounts. This will trigger some consolidation in hospitality and travel. Weak players will be absorbed by their stronger competitors. Some may leave the business entirely. But the leaner, stronger, more adaptable providers will survive until prosperity returns.

Since we expect another "jobless recovery," it could be some time before hospitality and travel returns to its pre-recession peak. We expect to reach the profit levels of 2007 and early 2008 by 2011.

Thereafter, the world and the industry will return to the path they were on before the downturn. As global wealth begins to grow again, business executives and tourists again will fill airline seats, hotel rooms, and resort facilities. American, European, Chinese, and Indian travelers will ensure the continuing expansion of hospitality and travel. By 2015, the fears of 2008 and 2009 will be no more than fading memories.

Key Trends for the Economy

As mentioned in Chapter 1, FI has developed a tool to help with trend analysis (see Appendix A). It is a list of fifty-five major trends in world politics, technology, national and international economies, and other important aspects of global society. In this section, we look at the key trends for the economy, using entries from Appendix A. We list each relevant trend and our assessment of it, and then detail the specific implications of this trend for the world economy.

1. THE WORLD'S POPULATION WILL GROW TO 9 BILLION BY 2050.

Assessment: Demographic trends such as this are among the easiest to recognize and most difficult to derail. Barring a global plague or nuclear war—wildcard possibilities that cannot be predicted with any validity—there is little chance that the population forecast for 2050 will err on the low side.

Implications for the Economy: Rapid population growth will reinforce American domination of the global economy, as the European Union falls to third place behind the United States and China.

To meet human nutritional needs over the next forty years, global agriculture will have to supply as much food as has been produced during all of human history.

Unless fertility in the developed lands climbs dramatically, either would-be retirees will have to remain on the job or the industrialized nations will have to encourage even more immigration from the developing world. The third alternative is a sharp economic contraction and loss of living standards.

Barring enactment of strict immigration controls, rapid migration will continue from the Southern to the Northern Hemisphere, and especially from former colonies to Europe. A growing percentage of job applicants in the United States and Europe will be recent immigrants from developing countries.

7. SOCIETAL VALUES ARE CHANGING RAPIDLY.

Assessment: This trend will continue for at least the next two decades in the industrialized lands and two generations in the developing world.

Implications for the Economy: Narrow, extremist views of the left and right will slowly lose their popularity in the developed lands. This should bring more pragmatic government that will provide consumers greater security and thereby promote economic growth.

Growing demand for quality and convenience is creating many new niche markets. This will be a prime field for entrepreneurs over the next ten years in hospitality and many other industries.

The demand for greater accountability and transparency in business will be crucial, not only in the U.S. business community, but also in countries that wish to attract international investors.

Reaction against changing values is one of the prime motives of cultural extremism, particularly in the Muslim world and in parts of India. As values change in those lands, terrorism is likely to proliferate, slowing economic growth and raising the cost of doing business.

9. TIME IS BECOMING THE WORLD'S MOST PRECIOUS COMMODITY.

Assessment: This trend is likely to grow as changing technologies add the need for lifelong study to the many commitments that compete for the average worker's time. As this trend matures in the United States, it is likely to survive in other parts of the world. It will not disappear until China and India reach modern post-industrial status, around 2050.

Implications for the Economy: Stress-related problems affecting employee morale and wellness will continue to grow. Companies must help employees balance their time at work with their family lives and need for leisure. This may reduce short-term profits but will aid profitability in the long run.

As time for shopping continues to evaporate, Internet and mail-order marketers will have a growing advantage over traditional stores.

China, India, and other developing countries can expect consumer trends similar to those in the United States as workers seek out convenience foods, household help, and minor luxuries to compensate for their lack of leisure time.

12. TOURISM, VACATIONING, AND TRAVEL (ESPECIALLY INTERNATIONAL) CONTINUE TO GROW WITH EACH PASSING YEAR.

Assessment: Travel seems to be in the DNA of the middle and upper economic classes. This trend will continue as long as national economies continue to generate new prosperity for the formerly poor.

Implications for the Economy: The current global recession will cause a rare contraction in the tourism market. It will be temporary, but tourism will lag behind the economic recovery, not help to bring it about.

Once the present recession has passed, the hospitality industry will grow at a rate of at least 5 percent per year for the foreseeable future.

Tourism offers growing opportunities for out-of-the-way destinations that have not yet cashed in on the boom. This will make it an important industry for still more developing countries.

Soon after the recession ends, the number of people whose jobs depend on tourism will approach 14 percent of the global workforce.

16. YOUNG PEOPLE PLACE INCREASING IMPORTANCE ON ECONOMIC SUCCESS, WHICH THEY HAVE COME TO EXPECT.

Assessment: This trend appeared with the Baby Boom generation and has strengthened with the later cohorts. It will be interesting to see what changes the current recession brings about and what develops among the children of the Millennials, something we find difficult to predict with confidence.

Implications for the Economy: Gen X and Dot-com entrepreneurs are largely responsible for the recent economic growth in India and China, where they are becoming a major force in the Communist party. In India, the younger generations dress and think like their American counterparts, not their parents. Throughout the world, these generations will lead their economies out of the 2008–09 recession and build a stronger foundation for future prosperity.

If younger-generation workers find their ambitions thwarted, they will create growing pressure for economic reform. If reforms do not come fast enough in the developing world, unmet expectations will cause more young people to emigrate to the developed lands.

Disappointment will also drive underemployed young men in the developing world into fringe political and religious movements. This could cause a new wave of terrorism and instability in the coming years, with profound effects on the economies of the United States and other target countries.

17. GENERATION X, THE DOT-COMS, AND THE MILLENNIALS ARE GAINING SOCIAL AND ORGANIZATIONAL INFLUENCE.

Assessment: As trends go, this is an evergreen. In a few years, we will simply add the next new generation to the list.

Implications for the Economy: Younger consumers tend to be extremely well informed about their product choices, thanks in large part to their comfort with the Internet. Net-savvy travel marketers have a strong advantage in reaching this market.

Marketing to Generation X and the Millennials requires a light hand, with strong emphasis on information and quality. Brands credibly positioned as "affordable luxury" will prosper.

Any perceived inadequacy of service will send them to a competitor. Under-forty customers make few allowances for other people's problems. However, they are relatively tolerant of impersonal service. What they care most about is efficiency.

These generations also will be industry's future employees. The good news is that they are well equipped to work in an increasingly high-tech world. The bad news is that they have little interest in their employer's needs and no job loyalty at all. They also have a powerful urge to do things their own way.

19. THE ECONOMY OF THE DEVELOPED WORLD IS GROWING STEADILY, WITH ONLY BRIEF INTERRUPTIONS.

Assessment: These trends have been revised many times since they were first codified in the late 1980s. Some trends have fallen out of the list as they matured or as circumstances came along to change them. Others have been added as they were recognized. This trend has remained a constant, and with each revision its effective period has been extended. To invalidate this trend would take a catastrophe on the order of the permanent loss of Middle Eastern oil from the Western economies. Not even the recession of 2008–09 rises to that level of destruction.

Implications for the Economy: Barring another terrorist incident on the scale of September 11 or some equivalent shock, the world's recovery efforts should reinforce each other, with each trading nation helping to generate the continued well-being of its partners. By 2011, business profits and GDP growth will return to the peak levels seen before the recession of 2008–09.

Labor markets will remain tight, particularly in skilled fields. This calls for new creativity in recruiting, benefits, and perks, especially profit sharing. This hypercompetitive business environment demands new emphasis on rewarding speed, creativity, and innovation within the workforce.

In the United States, the growing concentration of wealth among the elderly, who as a group already are comparatively well off, creates an equal deprivation among the young and the poorer old. This implies a loss of purchasing power among much of the population; in time, it could partially offset the forces promoting economic growth.

20. THE GLOBAL ECONOMY IS GROWING MORE INTEGRATED.

Assessment: This trend will continue for at least the next two decades.

Implications for the Economy: The growth of commerce on the Internet makes it possible to shop globally for raw materials and supplies, thus reducing the cost of doing business. In niche markets, the Internet also makes it possible for small companies to compete with giants worldwide with relatively little investment.

Demand for personnel in distant countries will increase the need for foreign-language training, employee incentives suited to other cultures, and aid to executives going overseas. As Eastern Europe integrates more fully with the European Union, a major investment in personnel development will be needed over the next few years.

Western companies may have to accept that proprietary information will be shared, not just with their immediate partners in Asian joint ventures, but with other members of the partners' trading conglomerates as well. In high technology and aerospace, that may expose companies to extra scrutiny, due to national security concerns.

21. CONSUMERISM IS STILL GROWING.

Assessment: This trend seems likely to remain healthy for at least the next fifteen years.

Implications for the Economy: Growing demands for product quality and safety will inhibit the profits of companies that cannot adapt to them, but will add to the bottom line for companies that can make the necessary adjustment efficiently. By opening new markets for information, quality assurance, and other products and services, these companies will add a modest increment to the GDPs of developed lands.

This is a mandate for quality. Brands with good reputations will have a strong market advantage over lesser competitors and unknowns. A second-rate or poor reputation will be even harder to overcome than it is today. It will take very few mistakes to undermine a reputation for quality.

22. RESEARCH AND DEVELOPMENT PLAY A GROWING ROLE IN THE WORLD ECONOMY.

Assessment: This trend is stabilizing as developed nations, particularly the United States, devote more of their resources to less productive activities. Although R&D spending is likely to decline slightly during the current recession, we believe this is a temporary phenomenon. The trend will regain momentum in the years ahead and will not fall off the list before the middle of this century.

Implications for the Economy: The demand for scientists, engineers, and technicians will continue to grow, particularly in fields where research promises an immediate business payoff.

Low-wage countries such as China will continue to take low-wage jobs from advanced industrialized countries such as the United States, but those jobs will be replaced by higher-paid jobs in technology and service industries.

Countries such as India, China, and Russia may continue to suffer a "brain drain" as those with high-tech skills emigrate to high-demand, high-wage destinations. However, there is some evidence that growing numbers of technology students and professionals are spending time in the West to learn cutting-edge skills, and then returning to their native lands to work, start companies, and teach. This trend may promote the growth of some developing countries while reducing the competitive advantages of the developed world.

By inhibiting stem cell research, the United States has made itself a less attractive place for cutting-edge biomedical scientists. The United Kingdom is capitalizing on this to become the world's leader in stem cell research. In the process, it is reversing the brain drain that once deprived it of top scientists. However, America is likely to become more hospitable to research under the Obama administration.

Washington's neglect of basic science is being felt in the declining fraction of patents, Nobel Prizes, and other awards going to American scientists. As other countries become more skilled in critical high-tech fields, the United States is fast losing its edge. If this trend is not reversed, it will begin to undermine the American economy and shift both economic and political power to other lands.

23. Services are the fastest-growing sector of the global economy.

Assessment: We foresee no obvious end to this trend.

Implications for the Economy: Services are now beginning to compete globally, just as manufacturing industries have done over the last twenty years. By creating competitive pressure on wages in the industrialized lands, this trend will help to keep inflation in check.

The growth of international business will act as a stabilizing force in world affairs, as most countries find that conflict is unacceptably hard on the bottom line.

32. When not perturbed by greater-than-normal political or economic instability, oil prices average around $65 per barrel.

Assessment: The long-term trend toward stable energy prices can only grow stronger as new refineries open between 2010 and 2012, the West reigns in consumption, and alternative energy technologies become practical.

Implications for the Economy: One of the major costs of doing business should remain under control. This will make it possible for companies to earn acceptable profits while keeping prices relatively affordable.

Inflation also should remain under control, with benefits for disposable income and consumer confidence.

34. Technology increasingly dominates both the economy and society.

Assessment: Technology-related changes in society and business seen over the last twenty years are just the beginning of a trend that will accelerate at least through this century.

Implications for the Economy: New technologies should continue to improve the efficiency of many industries, helping to keep costs under control. However, this increased productivity has retarded job creation in the United States. It was largely responsible for the so-called "jobless recovery" that followed the recession of 2001. Other developed countries are likely to feel the same effect in the future.

New technologies often require a higher level of education and training to use them effectively. They also provide dozens of new opportunities to create businesses and jobs.

Automation will continue to cut the cost of many services and products, making it possible to reduce prices while still improving profits. This will be critical to business survival as the Internet continues to push the price of many products to the commodity level.

New technology also will make it easier for industry to minimize and capture its effluent. This will be a crucial ability in the environmentally conscious future.

Consumers are increasingly shopping on the Internet and posting their reactions there. One dissatisfied customer's negative report on the Internet can influence the buying decisions of potential customers for years.

38. The Internet continues to grow, but at a slower pace.

Assessment: Internet growth will continue until essentially no one in the world lacks easy access to e-mail and the Internet, about thirty years by our best estimate.

Implications for the Economy: Internet-based commerce will continue growing rapidly.

Business-to-business (B2B) sales on the Internet are dramatically reducing business expenses while giving suppliers access to customers they could never have reached by traditional means.

Internet-based operations require more sophisticated, knowledgeable workers. People with the right technical training will find a ready market for their services for at least the next fifteen years, as major businesses compete to hire them. However, the specialties required in any given country will change as some skills are outsourced abroad.

39. TECHNOLOGY IS CREATING A KNOWLEDGE-DEPENDENT GLOBAL SOCIETY.

Assessment: This trend will not reach even its halfway mark until the rural populations of China and India gain modern educations and easy access to the Internet.

Implications for the Economy: Knowledge workers are generally better paid than less-skilled workers, and their proliferation is raising overall prosperity.

Even entry-level workers and those in formerly unskilled positions require a growing level of education. For a good career in almost any field, computer competence is mandatory. This is one major trend raising the level of education required for a productive role in today's workforce. For many workers, the opportunity for training is becoming one of the most desirable benefits a job can offer.

New technologies create new industries, jobs, and career paths, which can bring new income to both developed and developing countries. An example is the transfer of functions such as technical support in the computer industry to Asian divisions and service firms.

For some developing countries, computer skills are making it faster and easier to create wealth than a traditional manufacturing economy ever could. India, for example, is rapidly growing a middle class, largely on the strength of its computer and telecom industries. Many other lands will follow this example.

40. PEOPLE AROUND THE WORLD ARE BECOMING INCREASINGLY SENSITIVE TO ENVIRONMENTAL ISSUES AS THE CONSEQUENCES OF NEGLECT, INDIFFERENCE, AND IGNORANCE BECOME EVER MORE APPARENT.

Assessment: A solid majority of voters throughout the developed world, and even some in the developing lands, now recognize the need to clean up the environment and especially to control greenhouse warming. They will keep this trend intact for at least the next thirty years.

Implications for the Economy: Demands for still more environmental controls are inevitable, especially in relatively pristine regions. This will limit industrial development in these areas, but will leave them open to controlled tourism.

Manufacturers throughout the developed lands will have to spend more on pollution controls and recycling. This will eat into their net profits in the short run, but eventually will make them more efficient and more profitable.

In compensation, antipollution equipment and other "green" technologies will spur the growth of new companies and perhaps even new industries. This will help to drive future economic growth.

The developed countries will have to subsidize antipollution efforts in many of the developing lands, which view the environmental movement as a devious way for their rich, industrialized neighbors to deprive them of their fair share of the world's resources.

Relatively unspoiled environments will enable the development of "green" tourist industries and will be a significant economic asset to countries that manage to protect them.

43. Preference for industrial development over environmental concerns is fading slowly in much of the developing world.

Assessment: View this as a countertrend to Trend 40. It will remain largely intact until the poor of India and China complete their transition into the middle class, around 2040.

Implications for the Economy: Broad regions of the planet will be subject to pollution, deforestation, and other environmental ills in the coming decades. These will reduce GDP growth, particularly in many resource-based economies.

Diseases related to air and water pollution will spread dramatically in the years ahead. Already, chronic obstructive pulmonary disease is five times more common in China than in the United States. Illness is one of the factors that most damages GDP growth in developing lands. As citizens of the developing countries come to expect modern health care, the medical sector will become a much more important part of these economies.

This is just a taste of future problems, and perhaps not the most troublesome. Even the U.S. government now admits that global warming is a result of human activities that produce greenhouse gases. It now seems that China and India soon will produce even more of them than the major industrialized nations. Helping the developing lands to raise their standards of living without causing wholesale pollution will require much more aid and diplomacy than the developed world has ever been willing to devote to this cause.

46. More entrepreneurs start new businesses every year.

Assessment: This is a self-perpetuating trend, as all those new service firms need other companies to handle chores outside their core business. It will remain with us for many years, not only because it suits new generation values but because it is a rational response to an age in which jobs can never be counted on to provide a stable long-term income.

Implications for the Economy: This trend is driven by the attitudes and values of Generation X and the Millennials and by the rapid developments in technology, which create endless opportunities for new business development.

Specialty boutiques will continue to spring up on the Internet for at least the next twenty years.

This trend will help to ease the poverty of many developing countries, as it is already doing in India and China. In turn, this will add to the demand for goods and services, further accelerating economic growth.

53. Institutions are undergoing a bimodal distribution: the big get bigger, the small survive, and the mid-sized are squeezed out.

Assessment: Thanks in part to technology, this trend is likely to be a permanent feature of the business scene from now on. It will accelerate significantly during the recession of 2008–09.

Implications for the Economy: Thus far, industries dominated by small, regional, often family-owned companies have been relatively exempt from the consolidation now transforming many other businesses. Takeovers are likely even in these industries in the next decade.

This consolidation will extend increasingly to Internet-based businesses, where well-financed companies are trying to absorb or out-compete tiny online startups, much as they have done in the brick-and-mortar world.

No company is too large to be a takeover target if it dominates a profitable market or has other features attractive to profit-hungry investors.

55. INTERNATIONAL EXPOSURE INCLUDES A GROWING RISK OF TERRORIST ATTACK.

Assessment: This trend is unlikely to change in the next decade and relatively unlikely to change in the next twenty years. A permanent end to the international terrorist threat would require a broad philosophical and cultural change in Islam that makes terrorists pariahs in their own communities. No such change is on the horizon.

Implications for the Economy: Until the terrorist problem is brought under control—probably not soon—the more volatile parts of the world will find it difficult to attract outside investment capital. The exceptions will be developing oil states, such as Kazakhstan.

American-owned facilities and those where Americans congregate will have to devote more of their budgets to security. This is rapidly becoming true for companies from other Western lands as well.

Some of the most important security measures will be invisible to customers, but highly intrusive for staff. These may include comprehensive background checks for new hires, much as airports need to screen such behind-the-scenes personnel as baggage handlers and fuel-truck drivers.

The economies of the industrialized nations could be thrown into recession at any time by another terrorist event on the scale of September 11. This is particularly true of the United States. The impact would be greatest if the attack discouraged travel, as the hijacking of airliners to attack the World Trade Center and Pentagon did in 2001 and 2002.

The U.S. economy is being affected already by American anti-terrorism measures. Washington's decision to photograph incoming travelers and require more extensive identification from them significantly depressed tourism to America. The number of foreign students coming to American universities declined by some 30 percent.

Endnotes

1. Susan Stellin, "Hospitality Industry Suffers as Corporations Cut Back," *Miami Herald* 6 April 2009. Accessed June 10, 2009, at www.miamiherald.com/business/tourism/story/983381.html.

2. Scott Brown, *Monthly Economic Outlook*, 11 May 2009, Raymond James & Associates, Inc. Accessed June 12, 2009, at www.raymondjames.com/pdfs/monit/mnth090511.pdf.

3

"Bang! You're Dead!" Hospitality in the Age of Terror

LASHKAR-E-TOIBA'S COORDINATED ASSAULT on Mumbai November 26, 2008, was a terrorist spectacular. It required just ten fighters, who arrived by boat from Pakistan. Working in pairs, they attacked ten targets across the city, killing 174 people and injuring more than 800. It took Indian security personnel three days to ferret out the last of the assailants. Second only to the September 11 attacks in the United States, it may have been the most complex and effective terrorist incident ever mounted.

Predictably, the largest and most effective assaults were aimed at the hospitality and travel industry. Terrorists occupied the five-star Taj Mahal and Oberoi hotels, popular gathering places for both Western tourists and the city's elite. Also attacked were the Leopold Café, a restaurant popular with American and British visitors, and the Chhatrapati Shivaji rail terminal.

For the world's terrorists, this was business as usual. They like "soft targets"— relatively undefended locations where they can find masses of unwary victims. As a result, many of the most destructive terrorist incidents have struck at hospitality, tourism, and travel, which by their nature must remain as inviting as possible. Since the invasion of Iraq, these have included:

- The truck bombing of the Islamabad Marriott Hotel in September 2008, which killed at least fifty-three and wounded 266.

- The January 2008 suicide bombing of the Serena Hotel in Kabul, attributed to Taliban fighters, with eight dead and others wounded.

- The bombing of the Mansour Melia Hotel in Baghdad, July 25, 2007, with twelve dead, just before a meeting of local leaders.

- A failed restaurant bombing in Exeter, England, by Mohammad Sadaam-Alim, a Muslim convert, in May 2007.

- The London subway bombings of July 2005, which caused fifty-six deaths and some 700 injuries.

- The railway bombings in Madrid, with 202 fatalities, on March 11, 2004.

We can expect many attacks like these in the future. They are part of a continuing wave of violence that began with al-Qaeda but is now being carried on independently by sympathizers around the world. These attacks differ from the terrorism of the 1970s and 1980s in a number of key ways:

- They aim less to promote specific political goals than to wage a cultural war of Muslim extremists against—well, anyone who attracts their attention, but especially the United States and its allies.

- They no longer aim for limited destruction that makes a point and allows the terrorists to fight another day; instead, they are designed for mass blood-letting, to intimidate and destroy the terrorists' chosen enemies, even when that means "martyrdom" for the perpetrators.

- Since government targets are becoming increasingly well defended, these terrorists very often aim at places where civilians congregate.

This is important for hospitality providers, not just because of the threat itself, but because of the effect it has had on many of the industry's customers. In late 2003, a poll asked more than 2,300 tourists in Southern California what factors were most important in planning a vacation or convention. On a scale of one to ten, with ten being the most significant, domestic visitors gave safety an average rating of 8.9. Two-thirds of international visitors said that safety was their single most important concern. In choosing a hotel, 62 percent of domestic visitors and two-thirds of international travelers put safety and security at the head of the list. That fraction probably has declined somewhat as the memory of the September 11 attacks fades, but it would take only one incident to renew the traveler's concern with personal security.

In fact, the Mumbai attacks have had much the same effect on travel intentions, according to a survey conducted by the Association of Corporate Travel Executives.[1] Nearly half the organization's members reported that they often travel to and within India. Of these, 48 percent said that they were curtailing travel to India "until the situation became more settled." Seven percent said they would avoid India "indefinitely." Fully 78 percent of travel managers said they would be reviewing contracts with Indian hotels to ensure security and guest safety. Thirty-one percent said they would be looking for specific improvements, such as better staff training, improved surveillance systems, or backup communications systems for guests trapped in their rooms.

Under the circumstances, it seems necessary to weigh the industry's vulnerabilities and figure out what can be done about them.

In the Crosshairs

Terrorists are targeting the hospitality industry for sound tactical reasons. People gather with their guard down at hotels and restaurants in every city in the world. They pack into trains and planes. Often, they segregate themselves into convenient groups—American military personnel in this restaurant, Western tourists in that hotel, and no devout Muslims at all in the local bars and night clubs. And with the exception of airlines and to some extent cruise ships, security measures at potential targets tend to be lax or nonexistent. No other sector of business offers easier or more conspicuous victims than hospitality.

Let's look at some of the more obvious vulnerabilities.

Hotels Are Popular Targets for Good Reason

There are many points of access in a hotel—or resort or casino—and each one offers opportunities for attack. Hotel lobbies are large, open spaces with multiple entrances and hundreds of people moving through them every day. Driveways make it easy to bring a car bomb right up to the door. Loading docks, garages, delivery vehicles, and luggage storage areas all present risks of their own. Ventilation systems and water supply are vulnerable. And few hotel operators really want to provide effective security for fear that airport-style lines and metal detectors will put off customers even more than the fear of terrorism does.

Transportation Is a Prime Target

Attacks on the transportation system can be devastating for the hospitality industry, as we know all too well. The bombing of Pan Am Flight 103 over Lockerbie, Scotland, in 1988; the 1995 sarin gas attack on the Tokyo subway system; and the rail bombings in Madrid and London rattled nerves around the world. But it was the hijacking of four airliners for use in the September 11 attacks that best demonstrated what terrorist incidents involving transportation could do. September 11 all but put an end to elective travel for months. By September 21, hotels in New York City that are accustomed to being fully booked were running at 40 percent occupancy. Restaurants in European tourist centers quickly saw their business drop off by 40 percent or more. And over the next year, eight airlines either went out of business or filed for bankruptcy protection. So did eight cruise lines.

Since then, security has been tightened dramatically for airlines and cruise ships. Airline passengers and their carry-on luggage are routinely searched. Airport personnel must survive rigorous background checks and soon will be required to carry biometric ID cards. Cruise lines now forbid anyone but passengers to board their vessels. Cruise ships pick up half a dozen sea marshals along with the harbor pilot to protect the bridge and engine room and patrol the rest of the ship for signs of trouble. In the port of Miami, divers even meticulously scan the hull for attached mines before the vessel is allowed to enter the harbor, and a Coast Guard cutter accompanies the ship to the dock.

Yet more travel-related attacks are sure to come. Months after the devastating bombing of commuter trains in Madrid in 2004, Spanish authorities found a partially completed bomb under railroad tracks running between Madrid and Seville. A week later, a French railroad worker discovered a bomb under the line from Paris to Basel. India has seen a series of rail bombings—in July and November 2006, February and December 2007, and October 2008—with nearly three hundred dead in all. It seems only a matter of time before another railroad bombing is successful.

Travel in the United States may be even more vulnerable than it is in Europe. New York City alone has 468 subway stations, all of them inviting targets for a terrorist bomb. Much of the transportation on the East Coast is routed through tunnels into New York City, Baltimore, Norfolk, and other cities. Much of the rest travels over major bridges. Al-Qaeda leader Khalid Sheikh Mohammed reportedly instructed a subordinate in the United States to look into blowing up the Brooklyn Bridge. On the West Coast, bridges form a series of choke points for most of the highway traffic from Seattle to San Diego. A single bus full of explosives could disrupt or block traffic for months. And, of course, al-Qaeda has long been rumored to be planning another spectacular attack using hijacked planes to destroy American targets. That could cause an all-out depression in the hospitality industry for years to come. By early 2004, approximately $11 billion had been spent on air security in the United States, but only $110 million on security for subways and commuter rail.

Major Sporting Events Are Terrorist Magnets

The assassination of eleven Israeli athletes at the Munich Olympics in 1972 set a precedent that today's extremists must long to follow. Over the next twenty-nine years, until the September 11 attacks, no other assault garnered so much publicity for the terrorists' cause.

Any major athletic event offers yet another opportunity for mass slaughter. As a result, these have become some of the most highly policed gatherings in the world, as evidenced by the examples below.

- Greece reportedly spent almost $1.3 billion on security for the 2004 Olympics. It even installed sonar to scan the Athens harbor for underwater threats.

- China's security budget for the 2008 Olympics is believed to have been about $2 billion. More than 100,000 security personnel massed in Beijing for the event—not counting the military and a vast network of informers and intelligence agents.

- Antiterrorism plans for the 2012 Olympics in London originally were budgeted at £500 million (upwards of $760 million). Estimates in late 2008 say the final security bill will total more than £1.5 billion.

- The comparatively tiny Super Bowl XLII, the 2008 edition of America's annual football (not soccer) spectacular, had a security budget of $6 million, and that was just the National Football League's contribution. Approximately fifty local, state, and federal public safety agencies descended on Glendale, Arizona, for the event. Even the FBI Critical Incident Response Group was on hand to deal with possible terrorist incidents, hostage takings, or other high-risk violent crimes.

As long as masses of sports devotees gather, the risk of terrorism associated with major sporting events will continue to be a major concern. However, the kind of security precautions these events now receive suggests that the next major incident may not occur at the venue itself. Instead, the target could be a hotel that houses the athletes or their fans, a restaurant in the host city, or even the streets of the victor's home city. Managing this kind of risk should be a priority for hospitality providers in the affected cities.

Financial Infrastructure Could Be Vulnerable

An attack on the financial infrastructure could cripple the hospitality industry, at least temporarily. About 80 percent of bills in this sector are paid by credit card. And in a recent study of terrorist risks to credit card issuers, Forecasting International (FI) found some methods of attack that could be orders of magnitude more destructive than the worst case of credit card fraud ever recorded to date.

In the United States, just ten data processing centers transmit everything from huge corporate transfers to Social Security deposits to personal utility payments—more than $3.5 trillion per day. (It could be worse; before 2001, there were just three such centers.) The equivalent systems in Europe and Asia also are highly concentrated. An assault on those centers—by destroying their telephone lines, detonating readily available (or easily made) electromagnetic-pulse bombs to wipe computer memories, or simply filling janitorial jobs and carrying pipe bombs to work—could create a liquidity crisis that would disrupt the global economy for weeks or months.

Destroying Data Could Be Safe, Easy, and Disastrous

Thus far, cyberterrorism has been more fantasy than reality. Most terrorists probably find it easier to build bombs than to learn about computers and networks. Yet the risk is real. A virus that destroyed reservations or billing records could cost a company millions of dollars immediately, and the inconvenience to thousands of customers might ruin existing relationships and future sales. And we know of at least one case in which a malicious hacker encrypted a company's data and offered to sell the key for a hefty price. At this point, most firms have installed at least rudimentary firewalls and antivirus software, but we doubt that many could withstand the attention of a skilled and determined cyberterrorist. The attack could be even worse if the hacker were an employee or disgruntled former employee familiar with the company's security systems.

Weighing the Risk

Anyone with a morbid imagination can spin frightening scenarios air. This can in fact be a worthwhile exercise for hospitality executives trying to identify their own facilities' risks. Nonetheless, it is important to keep the threat in perspective. The whole point of terrorism is to create a maximum amount of fear with a minimum of resources so that small, weak forces can win out over an enemy they could not hope to defeat in a head-to-head battle. Only a few of the potential targets will ever be directly attacked.

In creating fear, terrorism clearly succeeds. Late in 2003, polls found that 70 percent of people in Italy and Germany were "somewhat worried" or "very worried" about terrorism. In Spain, where a native Basque terrorist movement is blamed for killing more than 1,000 people over a period of four decades, 85 percent of respondents were similarly concerned in the months before the train bombings in Madrid.

Yet consider this: According to Alan B. Krueger, professor of economics and public affairs at Princeton University, an American's chances of dying because of terrorism in 2005—a reasonably average year—were one in five million.[2]

Even in the obvious hotspots, the fear of terrorism is much greater than the actual threat. In Israel, 219 people died in terrorist incidents between 2005 and November 2008. (This number excludes the terrorists themselves.) This is fewer than three for every 100,000 people over a four-year period, or about one-eighth the 2007 death rate from homicide in the United States.

Unfortunately, the impact of a terrorist attack can be all out of proportion to the event itself. As horrifying as the September 11 attacks were, they killed only 7 percent as many people as traffic accidents did in the United States that year. Yet, as stated earlier, ten days after the attack, normally full hotels in New York City were running at 40 percent occupancy and several airlines and cruise lines went out of business or filed for bankruptcy protection. Before it was all over, the world's airlines lost an estimated $25 billion and cut some 100,000 jobs.

In forecasting, we often distinguish among several different categories of event. There are high-probability, high-impact events for which we all must plan. There are also low-probability, low-impact events that can safely be ignored. The remainder fall somewhere along the spectra of probability and impact.

Even for the hospitality industry, terrorist attacks in almost any individual location are very low-probability events. Yet their impact is so high that we must plan for the possibility and avoid it as best we can, just as we avoid standing under trees during a lightning storm.

Dangerous Ground

The Motel 6 on the outskirts of Rock Springs, Wyoming, is probably safer from terrorist attacks than the Marriott in Islamabad, Pakistan—but you probably could have figured that out on your own. Fortunately, there are more useful things to be said about where terrorists are likely to strike.

As we have seen in the United States, Spain, Britain, and too many other countries, nowhere in the world is entirely safe from terrorism. In addition to the Middle East and India, Africa and Latin America clearly deserve special caution. Africa is rife with revolutions, insurgencies, and border conflicts that obviously make travel dangerous. Latin America has a long history of kidnapping for profit. And while some kidnap victims are returned once the ransom is paid, many are killed instead. We can avoid vacationing in high-risk places today simply by watching the evening news.

For investment and other longer-term planning, the task is harder. Nonetheless, the most unstable, terror-prone lands have some characteristics in common. We will look at three factors that are particularly worth considering.

How Rich Are the Very Rich? How Poor Are the Very Poor?

A wide gap between the richest and the poorest members of a society is one of the most reliable indicators of the social and political instability that can inspire terrorism.

To measure this gap, compare the share of total household income received by the richest tenth of a country's population with the share received by the poorest tenth. For example, in Brazil, the richest tenth of the population receives 44.8

percent of the nation's total household income, while the poorest tenth receives only 0.9 percent. That is, the rich receive about fifty times as much income as the poor. Countries with an index over 45 are likely to be highly unstable.

FI developed this indicator many years ago, and it is the most valuable clue we have that a country may be on the brink of chaos. Several years ago, the CIA began to publish it in the *CIA World Factbook*, available online at www.cia.gov/library/publications/the-world-factbook. Unfortunately, figures are available only for a limited number of countries. For the rest, you will have to dig out the data yourself.

How Many Young Men Are There?

Throughout the world, the people most prone to violence, whether political or otherwise, are males between the ages of fifteen and twenty-nine. This group provides the majority of terrorists, rioters, and mujahideen.

This indicator clearly shows differences between the prosperous industrialized countries, where birth rates are low and young men are a relatively small part of society, and the developing lands, where birth rates are high and this troublesome group is larger. In the United States, men of this age make up about 10.7 percent of the population; in Japan, they are only 8.1 percent. In contrast, 14.0 percent of the population in Egypt consists of men in their prime troublemaking years. In Iran, the figure is 17.4 percent.

This information on young male populations was detailed in Exhibit 22 in Chapter 1. The exhibit contains estimated 2010 data for twenty-five countries of interest, plus the United States for comparison.

Of course, there is more to the analysis process than statistics. In almost any society where there are enough young men, a few will commit political violence. Witness the bombing of the federal office building in Oklahoma City. Other dynamics such as government policy, as in Sudan, or the absence of an effective government, as in Somalia, can bring chaos even more efficiently than other factors.

There are two factors, however, that can dramatically affect the risk of terrorism. These are employment and education. Where most young men have jobs, they have a stake in "the system" and are much less likely to become terrorists. There also is a good chance that they will be too tired after work to bother with activism in any form. But high levels of unemployment among young men create a reservoir of potential troublemakers ready to be exploited by unscrupulous leaders.

The situation is even more volatile in places where those young men have a good education. The poor and illiterate know they are likely to remain poor; they may consider this unjust, but they have grown up with limited expectations and generally have come to accept their conditions. But throughout the Middle East and in some other areas, there are hundreds of thousands of young men who were educated for a middle-class life that is no longer available to them. Without prospects and deeply embittered, they are the most ready of all to take up arms against a world they feel has closed them out. In the most terror-prone countries, large numbers of literate, unemployed young men face a life of poverty.

How Large and Influential Is the Muslim Community?

It goes against the grain to single out any religion as a source of trouble. Yet it has been clear for years that the Muslim lands face major problems with religious extremists who are dedicated to advancing their political, social, and doctrinal views by any means necessary. In our 1994 study of terrorism, the spread of militant Islam was the single most obvious factor we found that would increase both the frequency and the intensity of terrorist violence in the years ahead. With deep reluctance, we gave in and added this to FI's list of major trends shortly before the September 11 attacks.

Islam has never undergone the equivalent of the Protestant Reformation or the Jewish Reform movement. The clergy remains the ultimate authority in all matters, civil as well as religious. Thanks to the apparently liberal tenet that Muslims can disagree in matters of dogma, yet remain true to the faith so long as they subscribe to a few core principles, there is no religious doctrine or authority to weed out leaders whom other faiths would reject as vicious lunatics. And the idea of *jihad*—religious war against "enemies of Islam"—remains strong in the Muslim world.

This combination of factors—the availability of young men to act as foot soldiers, the disappointed expectations of a middle class that has lost its future, an untempered tradition of zealotry and religious war, and unscrupulous leaders willing to exploit them—creates the primary source of terrorism in the world today. The most unstable and often dangerous countries in the years ahead will combine all these factors. Anyone willing to do a little research when making long-term plans can easily identify, and steer clear of, such locations.

Future Shocks

Terrorism is evolving in at least four ways: it is gaining a wider base of support, it is becoming decentralized, it is diversifying, and it is aiming increasingly at civilian targets. In the years ahead, these trends will increase the terrorist threat to the hospitality industry throughout the world.

Recruitment Tools: Middle East Wars

Whatever else the Iraq war has accomplished, it has been a boon for the cause of terrorism. Iraq has played much the same role for terrorism in the early twenty-first century that Afghanistan did a generation earlier. It has been an inspiration, a recruiting tool, and a training ground for the global terrorists of the future.

The occupation of Afghanistan by the Soviet Union in the 1980s was a cause that radical Islamists could rally around. All over the Muslim world, extremists picked themselves up and hurried to the front, where fellow Islamists trained them in the ways of terrorism and the U.S. Central Intelligence Agency provided weapons and supplies that are being used against the West to this day. This is where both Osama bin Laden and the Taliban's Mullah Omar got their start, as clients of the CIA.

Afghanistan gave terrorists another useful tool as well: a global population of sympathizers willing to look the other way as they go about spreading fear and death. For every Muslim who went to Afghanistan, many others could not make that commitment yet were sufficiently radicalized to view the terrorists as heroes, even when they continued their attacks after the original cause was won.

It is worth remembering that terrorists and their sympathizers represent only a minority of the world's Muslims. Over a period of six years ending in 2007, the Gallup Organization carried out the largest survey of Muslim opinion ever conducted. The poll included direct interviews with tens of thousands of people in more than 35 countries that in the aggregate are home to 90 percent of the world's Muslim population. In this massive research study, only 2 percent of Muslims turned out to be true radicals. Another 7 percent were "politically radicalized"; that is, they had a negative view of the United States and believed that the September 11 attacks were fully justified. And in 2006, the Pew Research Center found that 17.7 percent of Muslim respondents believed that violence against civilian targets in order to defend Islam can "often" or "sometimes" be justified. At most, then, fewer than 20 percent of Muslims might qualify as terrorist sympathizers. Unfortunately, one-fifth of 1.4 billion people still represents a very large number.

After the battle to drive Soviet troops from Afghanistan, Osama bin Laden concerned himself with three issues: the presence of "infidel" troops in the religiously important Arab land of Saudi Arabia; the West's failure to deal effectively with the ethnic cleansing of Muslims in Bosnia, Croatia, and Kosovo; and the bombing of Iraq by the United States and its allies in the original Gulf War. As an afterthought, he added American support for Israel to the list in an effort to attract followers from sympathizers of Hamas, Hezbollah, and other extremists in and around Palestine. These grievances resonated widely enough to bring al-Qaeda an estimated 5,000 members worldwide.

Some fifteen years later, American troops remain in Saudi Arabia, and the United States has occupied Iraq, gone to war in Afghanistan, and struck at suspected Taliban strongholds in Pakistan. The second Iraq war inspired a new generation of terrorists, just as the first Afghanistan and Gulf wars did, and as Afghanistan continues to do. Iraq may have trained and equipped them as well. Foreign fighters are known to have entered Iraq through Iran and Syria early in that war, and reports say that before the relative calm of 2008, insurgents were using weapons the Americans had supplied to the Iraqi police.

During the 2008 campaign, President Obama declared his intent to remove most American troops from Iraq within sixteen months of taking office. We therefore believe that the Iraq war will effectively be over by mid-2010. At that point, Afghanistan and the adjoining areas of Pakistan once more will be the world's primary inspiration and training grounds for the next generation of Muslim terrorists. Terrorists bloodied by these parallel wars against Americans and their allies will launch many of the attacks that batter the world in the next ten years.

Decentralization

Terrorist incidents are likely to become even harder to prevent because the structure of the terrorist community is changing. When al-Qaeda and its associated groups were still largely unchallenged, there was at least some recognizable structure to it. The 1998 attack by American cruise missiles on an al-Qaeda compound in Afghanistan may have failed, but at least it had an identifiable target. Security officials still monitor thirty to forty groups affiliated with al-Qaeda in Southeast and Central Asia, the Caucasus, North Africa, and Europe. Yet those groups are losing their significance. More and more, terrorists take inspiration from bin Laden and his cohorts, but specific incidents are carried out more or less spontaneously by small groups of like-minded individuals who may have known each other for years. These cells are difficult to detect before it is too late, and virtually impossible to infiltrate.

In addition, terrorist groups that once focused on local goals, such as undermining the stability of oppressive governments, are heeding the call to *jihad*. The Pakistan-based Lashkar-e-Toiba used to concern itself only with "liberating" Muslim Kashmir from India. Late in 2003, Australian authorities arrested a member of the group believed to have been scouting out targets for attacks Down Under. And since the Iraq war began, the radical Ansar al-Islam has spread out from its base in the northern part of that country into Europe, where members are believed to be recruiting suicide bombers for attacks not only in Iraq, but also on the Continent. The group's founder, Mullah Krekar, now lives in Norway and is believed to have been involved in the bombings in both Morocco and Madrid. (An attempt to deport him failed in 2008, after years in court, because Norwegian law forbids sending foreign exiles back to countries—in this case Iraq—where they might face execution.) This move away from local goals toward *jihad* will add to the difficulties of combating international terrorism. For antiterrorism specialists, the world is becoming more complicated every day.

Diversification

This broader base of support is allowing terrorists to diversify in other ways. A few years ago, security specialists had to worry only about men from Muslim countries. If they watched out for that one obvious group of potential attackers—like the men who carried out the September 11 attacks—they had done their job. Today, women and Western-born converts have joined the terrorist cause, which is making it still more difficult to defend against attack.

Female Recruits. The trend toward recruitment of women is easy to see in Iraq. In 2003, only two suicide attacks involved a female bomber. In 2005, women carried out five suicide bombings. In 2007, the number rose to eight. In the first seven months of 2008, no fewer than sixteen women died as suicide bombers. A few similar attacks have been seen in Afghanistan as well.

The idea of encouraging women to blow themselves up seems at odds with Muslim claims that Islam is the last bastion of feudal chivalry, in which the role of men is to protect women from the world's harsher aspects. Yet it makes sense in a culture that has no place for women outside the protection, or domination, of men. Some female bombers seem to be motivated by revenge. One who killed fifteen in late 2007 had been a member of Saddam Hussein's Baath Party; two of her sons had joined al-Qaeda in Iraq and had been killed by Iraqi security forces. Others are widows who have no way to earn a living and may face unwanted forced marriage. In this context, being told that they will be striking a blow for Islam may provide not only a welcome escape, but a sense of honor that is otherwise unavailable to women.

One other category of female suicide bomber also deserves mention. According to reliable reports, extremists have been recruiting from long-term care facilities, sending out mentally handicapped women to act as suicide bombers. It is a lot easier to talk someone into wearing a vest full of explosives if they cannot really understand what they are doing!

The rise of female terrorists has proved inconvenient for security forces. For one thing, the all-covering burka is an ideal place to hide an explosive vest. For another, female security personnel have been uncommon, and in the strait-laced Muslim world it is unthinkable for a male officer to search female suspects. This rise in female terrorists has required police in Kirkuk to recruit 112 female officers, while the military set up a police training program for women in northern Iraq. Predictably, officers in this male-dominated society have not welcomed their new female colleagues.

Western-Born Converts. Middle-Eastern women are not the only new recruits to the terrorist cause. Al-Qaeda reportedly has been deploying would-be terrorists who look and sound like native Westerners—which is exactly what they are. Some of the new recruits in the training centers along the Afghan border with Pakistan are second- and third-generation Muslims who have grown up in the West. Others are Europeans who have converted to Islam. They speak English, French, Danish, or German as natives and carry legitimate documents from their native lands. This could make them extraordinarily difficult to apprehend.

The list of incidents involving terrorists born or raised in the West is growing rapidly:

- Three of the four terrorists who carried out the London subway bombing of July 7, 2005, were from West Hampshire. The fourth had been born in Jamaica.

- Of the four terrorists arrested in the copycat bombing on July 21, 2005, two had been brought from Africa to Britain by their parents and had been raised in the United Kingdom. Two others had arrived as adults and had lived in the country for at least five years; one was a naturalized subject.

- In 2007, German authorities arrested members of a jihadist cell believed to be associated with the Islamic Jihad Union of Uzbekistan. The group had been noted studying American facilities as part of a bomb plot. Its leader turned out to be a man named Fritz Gelowicz. He was a native-born Caucasian German who had converted to Islam, become radicalized, and trained in Pakistan.

- In France and Australia, authorities have arrested on terrorism-related charges a number of Western converts to Islam, many of whom are believed to have joined al-Qaeda or associated organizations since the invasion of Afghanistan. A report by French intelligence officials estimated that there were between 30,000 and 50,000 such converts, and by implication potential terrorists, in that country alone.

The rise of terrorists born and raised in the West is of particular concern for the hospitality industry, which depends on large quantities of low-level workers with a high turnover rate. Any of those workers could be Muslim extremists with legitimate documentation and a local job history. This may be a special concern for hotels and restaurants in Britain, where between 400,000 and 500,000 people reportedly travel to and from Pakistan in an average year.

Civilian Targets

The final development in contemporary terrorism—the growing focus on hospitality-related targets—is the most worrisome of all. It is taking place in part because government security efforts have become much more vigorous in recent years. They have had reason. In 1996, a truck bomb at the Khobar Towers near Dhahran, Saudi Arabia, killed nineteen American peacekeepers attached to the United Nations and wounded 372 others. In 1998, terrorists associated with al-Qaeda used truck bombs to destroy the American embassies in Dar es Salaam, Tanzania, and Nairobi, Kenya. In 2000, another al-Qaeda team killed seventeen American sailors and damaged the *USS Cole* in the harbor at Aden, Yemen. Though it took much too long, the lessons of those events have been learned.

Military bases and other government installations today are much harder to attack than they were in the 1990s. Wherever possible, major buildings are located well away from local roads, and would-be car and truck bombers must pass through multiple checkpoints and drive slowly around concrete barriers.

As a result, terrorists have been forced to seek out softer targets. And the softest targets of all belong to the hospitality industry, which exists specifically to welcome strangers into comfortable, relaxed surroundings. With the exception of some pipeline bombings in the Middle East and South America and the occasional embassy or consulate, nearly all of the facilities attacked in the last ten years have belonged to the hospitality industry. Hotels, restaurants, and transportation systems are likely to remain in the crosshairs for as long as the battle against terrorism continues. *Hospitality is still the softest of targets.*

Safety First

Despite the horrifying headlines that regularly arrive from around the world, many companies seem to have shrugged off the risk of a terrorist attack. According to a survey by the Business Roundtable, 85 percent of American firms have increased their spending on security since the terrorist attacks of September 11, 2001. Yet their budgets for this purpose have risen by only 10 percent, on average, in nearly three years. Even in this time of relatively stable prices, about half of that increase has gone toward keeping up with inflation only.

The situation is little better in the hospitality industry. Though some hotels have added security cameras to their lobbies and installed electronic locks on guestroom doors, many more have done nothing at all. A survey of hotels in the volatile Pacific Rim, location of the bombings in Jakarta and Bali, found that only 25 percent had made any effort to bolster security.

That really is not good enough. Small facilities such as independent hotels and restaurants, which cannot afford to set up their own security operation, will find it increasingly necessary to hire a competent security firm to do the job for them.

While that mandate applies to everyone in the hospitality industry, there are places where it is particularly important. Las Vegas almost goes out of its way to offend the sensibilities of fundamentalist Islam, which bans gambling, alcohol, and any form of sexual activity by women that is not rigidly controlled by their husbands. If terrorists strike at the hospitality industry inside the United States, they are likely to hit Las Vegas first.

A hint at what even a small terrorist attack could accomplish there came in April 2004, when a power line failed at the Bellagio, causing a cascade of problems that eventually burned several thousand feet of cable. The resort was shut down for more than three days at a cost of about $3 million per day in lost revenue. A deliberate attack, calculated to cause as much damage as possible, could have been far worse.

Identity Concerns

Security begins with people. This is especially true for the hospitality industry, where large numbers of workers are needed to serve even larger numbers of guests. Being absolutely certain who all those people are is the first step in defending against terrorism.

For any business, the most likely security threats come from disgruntled employees and former employees. Before people are hired, they should be screened thoroughly, not only to confirm their identity but to weed out those with significant criminal records, suspicious associations, or other potential risks. The screening procedure should be as rigorous at a hotel or restaurant as it is at an airport or airline. This will be particularly difficult for companies that hire large numbers of non-citizens, and especially undocumented workers. Yet no company that skimps on this process can hope to be safe from attack.

In a world of terrorism, this requirement extends not only to the firm's own employees, but to those of suppliers, builders, and service contractors. Someone who comes to repair the air conditioning could also release anthrax into the system, and no one would find it easier to contaminate food than the people who deliver it. Suppliers and contractors who cannot guarantee that their employees have been screened as rigorously as the facility's own workers should be replaced by firms that can.

Having once screened their new hires, large-scale employers need to make certain each day that anyone presenting an employee ID really is that worker and not an imposter. Since photographic identity cards can be tampered with, something more secure is required.

That probably means biometrics, the use of automated systems to match people with their known physical attributes. Available technologies include fingerprint and retinal scanners, facial recognition software, and pen-sized accelerometers that can measure the precise hand movements used to sign one's name—data far more difficult to disguise than the signature itself. These techniques have undergone rapid development since September 11, and many are now deemed reliable enough for practical application. Installing a biometric identity system and training security personnel to use it is expensive, but it is by far the best guarantee now available that someone who appears to be an employee really is who he or she claims to be.

Identifying guests with any certainty is still more difficult. For restaurants and other businesses where customer turnover is extremely rapid, it may be impractical or impossible. However, hotels, resorts, and conference centers all need to be certain who is staying with them. This will be simpler now that most foreign visitors need machine-read visas, fingerprints, and photo IDs to enter the country. A national identity card, if one is ever issued in the United States, could make the process easier still. These changes will be especially welcome for international meetings, where asking guests for fingerprints or other reliable identification has been an especially frequent and difficult challenge.

On an industry-wide level in the United States, working with the Department of Homeland Security to identify potential problems could help to ease the process of "people security." The U.S. Citizenship and Immigration Services (formerly the Immigration and Nationalization Service), U.S. Immigration and Customs Enforcement, and U.S. Customs and Border Protection all can provide valuable information about security threats such as known terrorists who are believed to have entered the country. The U.S. Travel Association, the American Hotel & Lodging Association, and other leading industry groups should make developing close working relationships with these agencies a priority.

Site Safety

As we have observed, nearly all hospitality facilities are soft targets. The only exceptions we can think of are a few major resorts at those times when major meetings of political and business leaders are held on-site.

Given the history of terrorist attacks, this has to change. Ideally, no one could enter a hotel, restaurant, plane, or train before his or her identity had been confirmed and he or she had passed through a metal detector. Then security guards would monitor all public spaces to make certain that no one had slipped through inappropriately. That will never happen, of course, but most hospitality locations could do a much better job of protecting their premises than they do today.

We can see evidence of this in the amount that hospitality venues spend on security. With all that they have to protect, average American hotels spend just 1 to 2 percent of their payroll on their security force. Contrast this with hotels in Israel, which spend, on average, about 8 percent of payroll on the security force.

In Israeli hotels, there is none of the chaos typical of hotels elsewhere. Guests are processed in an orderly, efficient, and security-conscious manner. They are likely to enter through a single lobby entrance that is protected by an airport-style metal detector. Guards patrol inside and out. At the most security-conscious hotels in Israel, identity checks are performed outside the hotel itself, and no one other than guests is allowed in at all.

Yet when it comes to hotel security, American casinos probably set the standard. At the state-of-the-art Borgata Hotel Casino & Spa in Atlantic City, more than two thousand video cameras constantly watch the 125,000-square-foot casino floor, 70,000 square feet of event space, 50,000-square-foot spa, 7,100-car parking lot, employee areas, and access routes to more than two thousand guestrooms. There even is an automatic face-recognition system to screen for known cheats (and to identify VIP guests so that they can be quickly targeted for special service). If the government ever provides a database of terrorist photographs—an idea that has been suggested but not yet acted upon—the system might be able to identify them as well.

At The Venetian in Las Vegas, uniformed guards patrol the public areas, while others are stationed at the entrances and at a security booth in the lobby. Even before a major expansion, there were more than two hundred guards in all, at least forty on duty at any time; since then, both the number of rooms—now about four thousand—and the number of guards have doubled. If these casinos simply added metal detectors at each entrance, they would be ready to face the worst that the age of terror is likely to throw at them.

It is easy to argue against that kind of security. Setting up the systems requires a big investment, and operating them involves substantial continuing costs. Guests at a luxury hotel might be more put off by the presence of armed guards and metal detectors than they are by lax security.

And there have been occasional excesses. For a time, the Bellagio in Las Vegas reportedly blocked driveway access with a vehicle parked across a blind corner. When guests stopped their cars, aggressive security guards dressed in black and without visible identification approached and demanded to look in their car trunks. Those who refused were rudely turned away. It was a bad mistake, and it lives on in harshly negative customer satisfaction reports that are widely available on the Internet.

At the first International Conference on Terrorism, held in Lisbon in 2007, one of the lecturers was Walter Laqueur, a highly respected specialist in international affairs. He offered a number of "theses" about terrorism, and one is particularly significant to the hospitality industry: "It would be wrong for governments to venture too far ahead of public opinion," he said, "for it will not gain the necessary support for more stringent measures aiming at the prevention of terrorism." Similarly, the hospitality industry cannot adopt more intrusive security measures than its guests believe is necessary. Getting too far ahead of them would only drive patrons to the competition.

Yet hospitality security need not be taken to extremes in order to accomplish its purpose. The most important components of casino security—the cameras and the people to monitor them—are nearly invisible; they provide safety without inconvenience or anxiety. In the future, hotels, resorts, and even restaurants and cruise lines will follow the gaming industry's lead, screening employees much more stringently and carefully monitoring both public and private areas in their facilities.

Security need not be perfect. It just has to be good enough to discourage would-be terrorists. That, at least, is possible. And there is every reason to believe that most guests would be willing to put up with a little inconvenience in return for the knowledge that they are as safe as they can be in an increasingly unsafe world.

Key Trends for Security

In this section we look at the key trends for security using entries from Appendix A. We list each relevant trend and our assessment of it, and then detail the specific implications of this trend for security in the hospitality and travel industry.

1. THE WORLD'S POPULATION WILL GROW TO NINE BILLION BY 2050.

Assessment: Demographic trends such as this are among the easiest to recognize and most difficult to derail. Barring a global plague or nuclear war—wildcard possibilities that cannot be predicted with any validity—there is little chance that the population forecast for 2050 will err on the low side.

Implications for Security: Rapid population growth will reinforce American domination of the global economy, as the European Union falls to third place behind the United States and China. Among the poor nations, this will foster still more resentment of the world's most prosperous land.

Unfortunately, when populations grow faster than resources do, the general quality of life inevitably declines. Since the wealthy are largely immune to this loss, the poor and middle class not only suffer, but see that their rulers do *not*. And because political leaders the world over find it convenient to blame their problems on others, much of the resulting hostility will be aimed at the wealthy industrialized lands, which will be reviled as exploiters of the developing countries. Terrorist movements are one expression of the unrest that can be expected to grow as the world population does.

Barring enactment of strict immigration controls, rapid migration will continue from the Southern to the Northern Hemisphere and especially from former colonies to Europe. Culture clashes between natives and immigrants are likely to destabilize societies throughout the developed world. Germany, Britain, and other lands traditionally welcoming to refugees and other migrants already are experiencing strong backlashes against asylum-seekers.

7. SOCIETAL VALUES ARE CHANGING RAPIDLY.

Assessment: This trend will continue for at least the next two decades in the industrialized lands and two generations in the developing world.

Implications for Security: Reaction against changing values is one of the prime motives of cultural extremism, particularly in the Muslim world and in parts of India. As values continue to evolve in those lands, becoming more materialistic and Westernized as the younger generations achieve more influence, terrorism is likely to proliferate. It will be exported to the Western countries that radicals blame for the "contamination" of their traditional culture.

17. GENERATION X, THE DOT-COMS, AND THE MILLENNIALS ARE GAINING SOCIAL AND ORGANIZATIONAL INFLUENCE.

Assessment: As trends go, this is an evergreen. In a few years, we will simply add the next new generation to the list.

Implications for Security: Radical conservatives in the Muslim and Hindu worlds view the materialism of younger generations as proof that the West is contaminating and degrading their society. The backlash against this perceived influence is one of the most powerful tools that unscrupulous leaders can use to motivate potential terrorists to "defend their faith" by attacking Westerners.

19. THE ECONOMY OF THE DEVELOPED WORLD IS GROWING STEADILY, WITH ONLY BRIEF INTERRUPTIONS.

Assessment: These trends have been revised many times since they were first codified in the late 1980s. Some trends have fallen out of the list as they matured or as circumstances came along to change them. Others have been added as they were recognized. This trend has remained a constant, and with each revision its effective period has been extended. To invalidate this trend would take a catastrophe on the order of the permanent loss of Middle Eastern oil from the Western economies. Not even the recession of 2008–09 rises to that level of destruction.

Implications for Security: After a relatively brief interruption, the gap between the world's have and have-not nations will continue to widen. In the Middle East and the developing countries, resentment against the prosperity of the West, especially the United States, will inspire terrorist incidents with growing frequency. Many of these attacks will strike at the hospitality industry.

The gap between haves and have-nots within the United States is growing as well. This could eventually inspire protest movements against business and government, but there is little possibility that they will resort to violence to gain their ends.

32. WHEN NOT PERTURBED BY GREATER-THAN-NORMAL POLITICAL OR ECONOMIC INSTA-
BILITY, OIL PRICES AVERAGE AROUND $65 PER BARREL.

Assessment: The long-term trend toward stable energy prices can only grow stronger as the West reigns in consumption and alternative energy technologies become practical.

Implications for Security: Young men in Saudi Arabia and some other oil-rich states once grew up knowing that government subsidies guaranteed them a comfortable life. Today, they must earn a living on their own, often with inadequate preparation, in a troubled economy. Poverty rates are rising, even while the Saud family and its hangers-on remain extremely rich—this in the land of Mecca, dominated by the ultra-conservative Wahhabi Islam movement, and host to American troops, some of them female. This is a recipe for terrorism and revolution. Recent attacks linked to al-Qaeda are likely to be only the first in a long and bloody series.

34. TECHNOLOGY INCREASINGLY DOMINATES BOTH THE ECONOMY AND SOCIETY.

Assessment: Technology-related changes in society and business seen over the last twenty years are just the beginning of a trend that will accelerate at least through this century.

Implications for Security: As technology brings extra productivity, it retards job creation. We saw the effects in the slow recovery of employment in the United States from 2002 through early 2004. The world is likely to feel the same effect as the recession of 2008–09 passes, and again in the future whenever an economic contraction provides an opportunity to cut employment. This will increase the number of disaffected people who feel they have no place in society. In rigidly conservative countries, and in immigrant communities in more liberal industrialized nations, resentment toward the prosperous will grow.

New technologies often require a higher level of education and training to use them effectively. This, too, will limit opportunities for the unprepared.

Technology brings vulnerabilities of its own. Dependence on computer data systems and telecommunications networks means that a single virus or hacker attack can cost one company many hundreds of thousands of dollars. The Melissa virus in March 1999 reportedly shut down the computer systems of between ten and twenty-five *Fortune* 500 companies. There is no widely accepted way to measure the cost of virus attacks, but at least one estimate suggests that computer viruses cost up to $55 billion in 2003 alone. In mid-2008, *Consumer Reports* put the cost to the U.S. economy at $8.5 billion over the previous two years.

On the other hand, new technology is one of the most valuable tools against terrorism. Improved detectors for metal and explosives will make it increasingly difficult to plant bombs on aircraft and ships and in government buildings.

54. Militant Islam continues to spread and gain power.

Assessment: This trend may wax and wane, but it seems unlikely to disappear for any reason short of a Muslim reformation comparable to those that transformed Christianity and Judaism.

Implications for Security: Virtually all of the Muslim lands face an uncertain and very possibly bleak future of political instability and growing violence. The exceptions are the oil states, where money can still buy relative peace, at least for now.

The West, particularly the United States, is likely to face more, and more violent, acts of terrorism for at least the next twenty years.

Both Europe and the United States ultimately may face home-grown Muslim extremist movements. Thanks largely to waves of immigration during the 1980s and 1990s, Islam is the fastest-growing religion in both regions. There are credible reports that extremist clerics in Europe are successfully recruiting young Muslims to the cause of *jihad* against their adopted (and in some cases native) homes.

Western interests also will be vulnerable in many countries outside the Muslim core. The strong international ties formed among Islamic militants during the anti-Soviet war in Afghanistan have produced an extremist infrastructure that can support terrorist activities almost anywhere in the world.

This development must be taken even more seriously because, for the first time, a Muslim country—Pakistan—has nuclear weapons, which Muslim extremists view as an "Islamic bomb" available to promote their cause. As the world has learned, some high-ranking Pakistanis already have been willing to donate nuclear technology to other Muslims. From here on out, the possibility of nuclear terrorism is a realistic threat.

55. International exposure includes a growing risk of terrorist attack.

Assessment: This trend is unlikely to change in the next decade and relatively unlikely to change in the next twenty years. A permanent end to the international terrorist threat would require a broad philosophical and cultural change in Islam that makes terrorists pariahs in their own communities. No such change is on the horizon.

Implications for Security: The growth of international business brings new opportunities and targets for terrorism. The presence of Western-owned facilities in Muslim lands also provides some extra motivation for terrorism. This is particularly important for resorts and nightclubs where men and women mingle in ways not approved by radical Islam.

Western corporations may have to devote more of their resources to self-defense, while accepting smaller-than-expected profits from operations in the developing countries.

Like the attacks on the World Trade Center and Pentagon and the American embassies in Kenya and Tanzania before them, any attacks on major corporate facilities are likely to be designed for maximum destruction and casualties. Bloodshed for bloodshed's sake has become a characteristic of modern terrorism.

Countries where terrorism is most common will find it impossible to attract foreign investment, no matter how attractive their resources.

Though Islamic terrorists form only a tiny part of the Muslim community, they have a large potential for disruption throughout the region from Turkey to the Philippines.

The economies of the industrialized nations could be thrown into recession at any time by another terrorist event on the scale of September 11. This is particularly true of the United States. The impact would be greatest if the attack discouraged travel, as the hijacking of airliners to attack the World Trade Center and Pentagon did in 2001 and 2002.

The U.S. economy is being affected already by American anti-terrorism measures. Since Washington began to photograph incoming travelers and required more extensive identification from them, tourism to America is significantly off and the number of foreign students coming to American universities has declined as well.

Endnotes

1. "Business Travel to India On Hold for Many Companies: New Hotel Security Parameters a High Priority According to ACTE Survey," Association of Corporate Travel Executives, 4 December 2008. Accessed April 27, 2009, at http://www.acte.org/resources/press_release.php?id=377.

2. Alan B. Krueger, *What Makes a Terrorist: Economics and the Roots of Terrorism* (Princeton, N.J.: Princeton University Press, 2007).

4

Tourism Trends: If This Is Tuesday, It Must Be Kuala Lumpur

AROUND THE WORLD, the cost of travel is falling, while the middle class is becoming generally more prosperous and eager to go places. At the same time, demographic trends, changing values, and other developments are helping to bring both turmoil and highly profitable new opportunities to the travel and tourism segment of the hospitality industry.

Two longstanding trends will remain unchanged as far into the future as we can see: growth and globalization. Tourism is expanding rapidly, with more travelers every year and a wider variety of destinations and activities.

Expanding Travel

The world's travel and tourism industry is going through some grim times of late. The worldwide recession that began in 2008 has consumers frightened, and frightened people cut back on elective travel. In the United States, hotel occupancy rates for 2009 are expected to come in at just 58.3 percent, the lowest in two decades. In the Caribbean, hotel bookings were off 30 to 50 percent by November 2008, with even grimmer results expected in 2009. Cruise bookings are down, and cruises are going at fire sale prices. Even Disney says early 2009 reservations are off 10 percent at its theme parks. Managing director Simon Hargreaves of the Travel Trust Association estimates that the travel sector has shrunk by 1 to 5 percent in 2008 and will do so again in 2009.[1]

Fortunately, bad times never last. As we have said, the recession should be passing by mid-2009. Travel will take a while longer to recover because consumers will need some time to be sure the worst is over and because job growth will lag GDP growth. By 2010, however, they will be climbing out of their storm cellars and beginning to explore the world again.

That is important, not just to the industry, but to the global economy. Travel and tourism is the fifth or sixth largest industry in the world, adding more than $2 trillion to the global GDP in 2008, according to the World Travel & Tourism Council (WTTC), and providing jobs for nearly 73.7 million people—and that is just the industry's direct impact. Add in suppliers and other industries that depend on travel and tourism and the total impact is closer to $6 trillion—nearly 10 percent of the world's GDP—and 238 million jobs, or more than 8 percent of global employment.

Those numbers will be rising rapidly in the years ahead, just as they have for most of the last half-century. Once the recession is over, travel and tourism are expected to grow by more than 4 percent annually. In a pre-recession forecast, the WTTC predicted that by 2018 the global travel market would add nearly $10.9 trillion annually to the world's GDP. Employment will not grow quite as quickly, but the WTTC predicted that travel and tourism should support some 296 million jobs around the world by 2018. Given the recession, we would put these targets back to 2021. It still represents solid growth after the lean times have passed.

Looked at another way, in 1950 the travel industry recorded just twenty-five million international arrivals. (That includes both business and vacation travel, but personal travel regularly makes up about 80 percent of the total.) In 2007, arrivals were up to 898 million, a jump of 100 million in just two years—and even that is just the beginning. By 2020, forecasters predict that there will be 1.5 billion arrivals, a solid majority of them vacationers. If the recession delays that target by a year or two, this will still be a time of steady, profitable growth. And the grimness of 2008 will be long forgotten.

Places to Go, Things to Do

The tourism market expands when potential travelers have more disposable income, and throughout the developed world and much of the developing world, they generally have had it. In the United States, more than 20 percent of households had annual incomes over $100,000 in 2007. These households spend nearly half again the national average. And 57 percent of these affluent consumers have purchased a luxury travel product over the last year. The number rises with income. Among households with incomes over $150,000, 64 percent have bought luxury travel products; over $200,000, the number is 68 percent. Similar trends are seen throughout Europe, Japan, and other relatively prosperous regions. When people have money, they spend it on travel.

Given so many economically comfortable travelers, countries from Brazil to Malaysia and Chile to Yemen have been working hard to attract their share of tourist dollars. On the whole, they have been extremely successful, not just bringing in the wealthy, but attracting middle-class travelers as well. Heavy promotions, together with the spread of lower-cost tour packages and discounted airfares, have opened elite destinations to less wealthy tourists. Middle-class travelers are now flocking to Fiji, Tahiti, and—for more adventurous tourists—the Antarctic, which were once exclusive playgrounds of the rich. Cruise lines, too, are seeking middle-class customers and experiencing great success. At the same time, relatively untraveled lands are rapidly building tourist industries. Nepal, Vietnam, Malaysia, Dubai, and South Africa are all drawing visitors, especially from within their own regions.

This ability to spend has inspired a host of new tourism products aimed at the relatively well-off. "Theme" and "total immersion" travel experiences aim to provide guests with a complete escape from their daily routines. Old-fashioned dude ranches have been joined by French cooking classes in French châteaux, so-called "adrenaline vacations" such as race-car driving schools and bungee jumping in New Zealand, sailing on a clipper ship, and research expeditions to tropical rain forests. One of the hottest markets is for "destination weddings," where the entire wedding party flies to Mexico or the Caribbean for an all-expenses-paid marriage celebration. With American weddings now averaging $22,000, a three-day marriage weekend for $2,500 (guests pay their own way) can be awfully attractive.

Travel Markets

Not all regions benefit from these trends equally. Europe and America remain the world's favorite travel destinations, while Africa is at best an also-ran. Here is a brief look at prospects for major regions of the world.

North America. Not long ago, conventional wisdom in the industry held that travel in this region would follow its accustomed patterns. Nearly half of all international tourism would occur between the United States and either Canada or Mexico, while most of the rest would be made up by a steady flow of American tourists to Europe and Europeans to the United States. North America would remain secure in its place as the second-largest travel destination in the world.

It has not worked out that way. Travel to and from the United States has remained depressed by the fear of terrorism and by the high cost of going to Europe when the dollar does not buy nearly as much as it once did. Recent demands by American security officials have further suppressed travel to the United States. Entry rules now require that most visitors submit to being photographed and fingerprinted; eventually most will also have to carry a "biometric" passport that includes copies of their fingerprints and iris patterns. Since American authorities made it harder to enter the country, tourist arrivals have fallen 30 percent since 2001.

This too shall pass. Once the recession is over, growing prosperity in the United States, Canada, and Mexico will sustain the expansion of travel within North America at about 3 percent per year. Eventually, the United States will find its way out of the morass of Iraq, the dollar will regain its exchange value, and the tourists will find their way between North America, Europe, and points east. Overall, international travel will grow by a bit less than 4 percent per year in this region, somewhat below the global average. Yet the United States will continue to lead the world in spending on and earnings from travel.

Europe. The Continent also is in for slower growth than its tourist industry has been accustomed to, even after the current downturn has passed. Tourist arrivals are expected to expand by only 3 percent per year, bringing the total to 717 million arrivals in 2020; the recession will delay some of them to about 2022. Many of those visitors will bypass western Europe, the traditional destination of choice. Both northern and southern Europe are in for faster-than-average growth, as Asian tourists flock to Germany and Scandinavia, while others seek out the beaches of the Mediterranean. The fastest growth will be in travel to and from central and eastern Europe, where Soviet domination crippled economies and kept travel demand bottled up for more than forty years. By 2020, both Russia and the Czech Republic will join the world's top ten destinations for international tourism.

The Caribbean. Although this area makes up only a small piece of the travel market, with just 3 percent of international tourist arrivals, it is the overwhelming leader among cruise destinations, receiving nearly half of all cruises taken in the world. Credit this to balmy weather, spectacular beaches, a highly competitive travel industry, and proximity to the United States, which provides 80 percent of all cruise passengers. None of these factors is likely to change, so tourist arrivals in the Caribbean should double between 1997 and 2013, and may nearly double again by 2022 or so. However, there are natural limits to how many tourists can be packed onto relatively small islands. Sustaining this growth rate will require the speedy development of resorts on relatively untapped islands. In the end, this could homogenize the Caribbean experience and send vacationers looking for less heavily traveled waters.

Central and South America. Recognizing the economic benefits of greater tourism, these regions have been positioning themselves as the natural destination for eco-tourists. This strategy will serve the region well in the next twenty years. From the lush rain forests of Costa Rica to the Amazon River Basin to the preserves of sea elephants, seals, and penguins of Tierra del Fuego, Central and South America offer wonders to delight nature-minded vacationers. Cultural attractions also abound in pre-Colombian ruins and Andean villages far off the beaten path.

Developing these resources will not be easy, however. This region's attractions have survived to be worth visiting largely because they are so hard to reach, and many of them will be unable to accommodate large numbers of tourists without being changed in essential ways. Nonetheless, once the world economy recovers, tourism to South America can be expected to grow by nearly 5 percent per year at least through 2020.

The Middle East. For an area with such a reputation for volatility and danger, the Middle East does remarkably well on the international tourist market. Among all the world's regions, it was the second-fastest-growing tourist destination throughout the late 1990s. It will continue to grow in the years ahead, from 19 million tourist arrivals in 2000 to roughly 69 million in 2022.

Part of this growth can be attributed to the development of attractions, such as the spectacular Bibliotheca Alexandrina and the Burj Al Arab hotel in Dubai, where the seafood restaurant is reached by submarine. And even European tourists have begun to make their way to resorts on the Red Sea. The single biggest asset the region has to offer is Islam. Around the world, 1.4 billion Muslims look to the Middle East for inspiration and spiritual leadership. Many of them are beginning to look there for luxury vacations as well. In 2001, some 42,000 Indonesian tourists visited Qatar, Yemen, and other destinations in the region, and the flow of Indonesian tourists to the Gulf States is expected to grow by about 7 percent per year.

Africa. South of the Sahara has it all—all but tourists, that is. Sun-baked, surrounded by beaches, with a continent full of exotic wildlife, Africa still manages to attract only 4 percent of the world's international tourists, and nets just 2.5 percent of the profits—and more than a third of these go to the desert lands of Morocco, Tunisia, and Algeria in North Africa, not the lush southern region. Even with natural resources to recommend them, the combination of deep poverty and political instability is a hard sell.

This will be slow to change. Even though Kenya has Beijing's approval as a destination for Chinese tour groups, and South Africa's Sun City is building a market among Asian tourists seeking a resort vacation closer to home than more traditional destinations, overall growth in tourism to Africa will average about 5.5 percent over the next fifteen years, according to the World Trade Organization, and nearly all of that will occur north of the Sahara, where growth rates are in double digits. Our research found no one who even bothers to estimate the growth of tourism in equatorial and southern Africa.

Asia. Asia merits close attention. There is just so much of it, and the outlook for tourism there is changing dramatically.

Just a few years ago, the international tourism industry in effect served less than 20 percent of the world's population: the roughly one billion people who lived in the United States and Europe and about 120 million Japanese. Other regions might provide interesting destinations for wealthy tourists from the industrialized countries, but as *sources* of international tourism, they might as well have not existed.

China and India in particular had more than two billion potential tourists in theory—populations of about 1.1 billion people in China and just under 1 billion in India—but essentially none in practice. Both national economies had been virtually stillborn, thanks to excessive regulation and centralized planning by governments philosophically opposed to free enterprise. As a result, neither country had a viable middle class to pay for vacation travel and related services. China also heavily restricted its citizens' movements outside the country; no international tourism was allowed until 1978.

In both countries, these conditions are changing rapidly. In 1978, China opened its economy to small private ventures such as crafts operations and family-owned restaurants. Over the years, a vibrant market economy has evolved, the Communist Party has begun to admit the capitalists it once despised, and China has joined the World Trade Organization. India, for its part, has been chopping away at the endemic red tape and corruption that has hobbled business development throughout the world's largest democracy ever since it gained independence in 1947.

The results have been remarkable. Between 1978 and 2000, China's GDP quadrupled. It is now growing—according to Beijing's official figures—at between 8 and 10 percent every year. The Indian economy has grown by an average of about 6 percent per year since 1990. In both countries, the middle class is expanding rapidly. At the end of 2003, one study found that 19 percent of the Chinese population—247 million people—qualified as middle class, and their numbers were growing by 1 percent per year. In India, there were more than 300 million in the middle class, and their numbers were growing even faster. "Middle class" does not mean quite the same thing in Asia as it does in the West—a net worth of $18,000 to $36,000 makes a Chinese family middle class, while in India this group spans yearly incomes with local purchasing power equivalent to anywhere from $20,000 to $600,000. In any case, many of them can afford to travel abroad—an estimated 85 million in China alone.

To date, these are still relatively small markets. Yet tourism from China and India is growing far more rapidly than the tourist market from other countries. The Pacific Asia Travel Association estimated that Chinese spending for international travel would reach $100 billion by 2008. By 2020, according to the World Trade Organization, 100 million Chinese will fan out across the globe, replacing Americans, Japanese, and Germans as the world's most numerous travelers. That same year, fifty million Indians are expected to tour overseas.

In Europe, castles, the autobahn, and snow are clearly big draws for many Chinese tourists. Scandinavia is hosting waves of Chinese tourists, as is Germany. In Europe, nearly all Chinese tourists belong to approved tour groups; Beijing still forbids individual tourism there without a personal invitation and a local visa. Indian tourists are spreading out a bit farther. Shopping holidays in Dubai, which is duty-free, and packaged tours to Paris, London, Switzerland, and Austria are attracting visitors from the Subcontinent in large numbers.

Nor is all this travel one-way. China soon will be not only the world's largest source of tourists, but the most popular destination as well, with 130 million arrivals in 2020. The 2008 Olympics in Beijing hastened this trend, but were only part of a massive effort to improve China's attractions and infrastructure. Both the government and many private tour operators are working to develop scenic, cultural, historical, and religious sites as tourist destinations, and Beijing has announced a plan to train 100,000 tourism specialists over the next ten years. The reward for all this effort will be an estimated forty million new jobs in the tourist industry.

Chinese and Indian vacationers are beginning to reshape the map of world tourism. Although Europe remains the planet's favorite travel destination and the top draw for Asian tourists with time on their hands, those out for a quick shopping trip or just a few days off are heading for places much closer to home. More than seven million mainland Chinese sought R&R in Hong Kong in 2007, roughly as many people as the territory's native population, and that probably is just the beginning. Chinese tourists are also visiting Thailand, Malaysia, and Vietnam in large numbers. For Indian tourists, Hong Kong, Singapore (duty-free), and Malaysia all attract shopping trips and quick getaways. Nepal has been a major draw for cultural tourism, though the expanding communist insurgency has begun to discourage travel there. Recently, Sri Lanka has gained popularity for inexpensive beach vacations.

With so much tourist business at stake, many countries are working hard to attract the new Asian travelers. All of the Scandinavian countries have opened tourist offices in China, and Cuba has recently negotiated a memorandum of understanding that allows Chinese tour groups to visit. South Africa is marketing Sun City and other resorts to Indian customers. Nepal is promoting no fewer than five new destinations in India. And the Australia and New Zealand tourist offices have mounted campaigns to draw visitors from both India and China.

This is a trend seen throughout the world. As travel and tourism expand, new destinations and new attractions are opening up rapidly. From small villages in Bolivia to five-star resorts on the beach in Morocco, the world's tourists will have a growing smorgasbord of destinations to visit. In the years ahead, not even the most experienced and jaded travelers will be able to feel they have seen it all.

Key Trends for Tourism

In this section, we look at the key trends for tourism using entries from Appendix A. We list each relevant trend and our assessment of it, and then detail the specific implications of this trend for tourism.

2. POPULATION OF THE DEVELOPED WORLD IS LIVING LONGER.

Assessment: Demographic trends such as this are among the easiest to recognize and most difficult to derail. Barring a global plague or nuclear war—wildcard possibilities that cannot be predicted with any validity—there is little chance that the population forecast for 2050 will err on the low side.

Implications for Tourism: Older but still vigorous travelers will be a growing market for international tourism. Well into their 70s, they will retain their youthful interest in pastimes such as skin diving, hiking, and other low-impact activities with high "experience" value.

Nonetheless, facilities will require senior-oriented conveniences, such as larger signs with easy-to-read type, door handles that can be operated easily by arthritic hands, and fire and security systems that flash lights for the hard-of-hearing.

Club Med and its competitors will become "Club Medic," with nurses and emergency equipment on-site and doctors on call to care for guests who are less healthy and more fragile.

Special tours and other activities should be ranked for the amount of walking, energy, or agility they require, so that older customers can easily choose pastimes within their abilities.

It may also be necessary to increase staffing slightly in order to provide older guests with extra help in checking in, coping with luggage, arranging for local transportation, and dealing with other chores that younger patrons could handle on their own.

They also want to feel that they are recognized (especially if they are repeat customers) and catered to. Older patrons appreciate being addressed by name, and as "Mr." and "Mrs." rather than as "you guys."

Because the oldest members of society also tend to be the wealthiest, luxury cruise lines and high-end tour operators should do well as the Baby Boomers enter their retirement years.

Retirees often are willing to travel off-season, spreading their vacations evenly throughout the year. This already is helping to mitigate the cyclical peaks and valleys typical of the tourist industry. Some 62 percent of American respondents to a *National Geographic Traveler*/Yahoo! Travel poll reported planning a winter vacation of at least five days in 2004.

Despite their relative wealth as a group, many seniors are extremely careful with their money. This will further raise the demand for vacation packages that are comfortable, staffed by attentive personnel, and cheap.

Mature travelers tend to be experienced travelers. Many are unforgiving of lapses in service, facilities that are less than the best, or excessively familiar tours or activities.

7. SOCIETAL VALUES ARE CHANGING RAPIDLY.

Assessment: This trend will continue for at least the next two decades in the industrialized lands and two generations in the developing world.

Implications for Tourism: The trend is toward extreme quality and convenience. Customers want constant pampering, luxurious accommodations, and fresh meals that seem like labors of love—all at a price that will not wound the consumer's conscience.

Travelers used to focus on destinations; now they want experiences. Vacations thus are becoming more active and participatory, as tourists become less interested in "go-and-see" and more eager to go-and-*do*. This is the trend behind the growth of adventure tourism.

"Authenticity" is another key value. Tourists who go to see other lands, rather than surf their beaches, want to find unique natural and cultural features that survive as close as possible to their original form. Travel experiences that remind guests of Navajo Indian blankets with "Made in China" tags will turn a destination into one more shopping mall, leaving visitors feeling that they might as well have stayed at home.

9. TIME IS BECOMING THE WORLD'S MOST PRECIOUS COMMODITY.

Assessment: This trend is likely to grow as changing technologies add the need for lifelong study to the many commitments that compete for the average worker's time. As the trend matures in the United States, it is likely to survive in other parts of the world. It will not disappear until China and India reach modern post-industrial status, around 2050.

Implications for Tourism: Work pressure is eroding vacation time throughout the industrialized world. One-third of Americans take half or less of the vacation time their jobs theoretically allow. In Britain, 25 percent of employees take only part of their vacation time. In Japan, where employees are legally guaranteed seventeen days per year of vacation, the average worker takes only 9.5 days annually.

For those with little time but adequate funds, multiple short vacations spread throughout the year will continue to replace the traditional two-week vacation.

For well-off travelers, time pressure is a strong incentive to use travel agents and shop for packaged tours, rather than doing their own vacation planning. Less wealthy vacationers will speed the task of making travel arrangements and broaden their selection of affordable vacation packages by doing their shopping on the Internet.

Anything destinations and tour operators can do to save time for their customers will encourage repeat visits.

17. GENERATION X, THE DOT-COMS, AND THE MILLENNIALS ARE GAINING SOCIAL AND ORGANIZATIONAL INFLUENCE.

Assessment: As trends go, this is an evergreen. In a few years, we will simply add the next new generation to the list.

Implications for Tourism: These generations tend to be more conservative about money than their Boomer parents and grandparents. They will take vacations they can afford without borrowing, especially after they have absorbed the lessons of the global recession. For hospitality and travel firms, this will put still greater emphasis on delivering a high-quality travel experience at the lowest possible price.

Younger consumers tend to be extremely well informed about their travel choices, thanks in large part to their comfort with the Internet. Net-savvy travel marketers have a strong advantage in reaching this market.

Generations X and Dot-com will be major customers for tourism in the future. Marketing to them will require a light hand, with strong emphasis on information and quality. Brands credibly positioned as "affordable luxury" will prosper. Any perceived inadequacy of service will send them to a competitor for their next vacation. Under-forty customers make few allowances for other people's problems. However, they are relatively tolerant of impersonal service. What they care most about is efficiency.

These generations will be the industry's future employees. The good news is that they are well equipped to work in an increasingly high-tech world. The bad news is that they have little interest in their employer's needs and no job loyalty at all. They also have a powerful urge to do things their own way.

19. The economy of the developed world is growing steadily, with only brief interruptions.

Assessment: These trends have been revised many times since they were first codified in the late 1980s. Some trends have fallen out of the list as they matured or as circumstances came along to change them. Others have been added as they were recognized. This trend has remained a constant, and with each revision its effective period has been extended. To invalidate this trend would take a catastrophe on the order of the permanent loss of Middle Eastern oil from the Western economies. Not even the recession of 2008–09 rises to that level of destruction.

Implications for Tourism: Once the recession is over, tourism will continue to grow by at least its accustomed 5 percent per year for at least the next ten years.

Growing prosperity in China and India will quickly increase the number of international tourists from those countries. This will bring rapid expansion for destinations convenient to Asia. These include Nepal, Malaysia, Thailand, Australia, New Zealand, and parts of Africa. Many new seaside resorts are likely to appear in the Seychelles, on the eastern shore of Africa, and in Southeast Asia, much as they did in Mexico when Americans went looking for slightly exotic luxury.

The growth of tourist facilities in these far-off places will begin to draw more visits from adventurous and well-to-do Americans and Europeans. Russia and the more stable parts of the former Soviet Union will contribute growing numbers of tourists, particularly to western Europe and the United States.

21. Consumerism is still growing.

Assessment: This trend seems likely to remain healthy for at least the next fifteen years.

Implications for Tourism: This is a mandate for quality. Brands with good reputations will have a strong market advantage over lesser competitors and unknowns.

It will take very few mistakes to undermine a reputation for quality, particularly when disgruntled consumers often voice their complaints over the Internet, where vacation-shoppers may see them for years. A second-rate or poor reputation will be even harder to overcome than it is today.

32. WHEN NOT PERTURBED BY GREATER-THAN-NORMAL POLITICAL OR ECONOMIC INSTABILITY, OIL PRICES AVERAGE AROUND $65 PER BARREL.

Assessment: The long-term trend toward stable energy prices can only grow stronger as the West reigns in consumption and alternative energy technologies become practical.

Implication for Tourism: One of the major costs of tourism should remain generally under control. This will make it possible for travel companies to earn acceptable profits while keeping prices relatively affordable. This will also alleviate one factor that discouraged travel by the American middle class during the oil price spike of 2008.

34. TECHNOLOGY INCREASINGLY DOMINATES BOTH THE ECONOMY AND SOCIETY.

Assessment: Technology-related changes in society and business seen over the last twenty years are just the beginning of a trend that will accelerate at least through this century.

Implications for Tourism: New technologies should continue to improve the efficiency of airliners and cruise ships, helping to keep travel costs under control.

Tourism will benefit as Internet "virtual tours" replace printed brochures in promoting vacation destinations. Websites cover not only popular attractions, but also provide current, detailed information on accommodations, climate, culture, currency, language, immunization, and passport requirements. These sites already have proved to be a major sales asset for some hotel chains. Resorts and other destinations are likely to find them an efficient way to approach new customers.

Consumers are increasingly shopping for travel services on the Internet and posting their reactions there. One dissatisfied guest's negative report on the Internet can influence the buying decisions of potential customers for years.

For the travel industry, the move to online sales promises more efficient marketing and higher profits. Opt-in marketing campaigns online cost only $2 per sale (averaged over all industries), compared with $18 per sale for traditional direct marketing, and sellers have immediate feedback on the effectiveness of their campaigns.

Automatic translators similar to a PDA—and perhaps built into one—soon will make it possible for travelers to go off on their own in foreign lands without worrying about communicating with natives.

Technology also makes it possible to maintain information about repeat guests, who may find it increasingly tedious or difficult to provide necessary personal data. That technology, however, must be entirely transparent to customers who may find it impersonal or intimidating. Such technology will allow hotels to perform the kind of extremely personalized marketing typical of the best Internet marketers, such as Amazon.com. Whenever a return guest arrives, he or she should be gently asked a host of questions: Do you want the same breakfast as last time? Black coffee with Equal? Shall we credit your stay to the same airline-miles program? Would you like dinner at the same restaurant? Reservations to the opera again? All this information can be automatically collected on the customer's first visit. It can be retained and used transparently to make future stays as comfortable as possible.

40. PEOPLE AROUND THE WORLD ARE BECOMING INCREASINGLY SENSITIVE TO ENVIRONMENTAL ISSUES AS THE CONSEQUENCES OF NEGLECT, INDIFFERENCE, AND IGNORANCE BECOME EVER MORE APPARENT.

Assessment: A solid majority of voters throughout the developed world, and even some in the developing lands, now recognize the need to clean up the environment, and especially to control greenhouse warming. They will keep this trend intact for at least the next 30 years.

Implications for Tourism: Demands for still more environmental controls are inevitable, especially in relatively pristine regions. Many of the more popular or fragile destinations may limit the number of tourists allowed to visit them each year.

Eco-tourism will continue to be one of the fastest growing areas in the tourism industry.

China is being forced to build new resorts where Western tourists will not be exposed to power lines and cell-phone towers. Other developing countries will face the same imperative.

Destinations and tour operators with access to rain forests, wilderness areas, the ocean, and other unpolluted regions will find this trend highly profitable.

Environmental science tours and research projects with working scientists will continue to be a growing niche market.

55. INTERNATIONAL EXPOSURE INCLUDES A GROWING RISK OF TERRORIST ATTACK.

Assessment: This trend is unlikely to change in the next decade and relatively unlikely to change in the next twenty years. A permanent end to the international terrorist threat would require a broad philosophical and cultural change in Islam that makes terrorists pariahs in their own communities. No such change is on the horizon.

Implications for Tourism: Until the terrorist problem is brought under control—probably not soon—tourism to the more volatile parts of the Middle East will be a relatively hard sell for Western vacationers, despite the appeal of historic places.

This stigma is likely to spread almost instantaneously to any destination that suffers a major terrorist incident. That threat is likely to be one of the great unpredictable risks of the international tourist industry for at least the next ten years. It could last much longer.

Terrorist hazards are not limited to Muslim lands. The communist insurgency in Nepal already has inhibited vacation travel from China and India.

American-owned facilities, and those where Americans congregate, will have to devote more of their budgets to security.

Some of the most important security measures will be invisible to customers, but highly intrusive for staff. These may include comprehensive background checks for new hires, in the same way that airports need to screen such behind-the-scenes personnel as baggage handlers and fuel-truck drivers.

Disgruntled employees and former employees are the single greatest threat, because they are familiar with security procedures and weaknesses. Those recently fired are a frequent source of problems.

 Endnote

1. "Travel Market Will Shrink Next Year, Says TTA Chief," *Travel Daily News,* 10 December 2008. Accessed April 20, 2008, at www.traveldailynews.com/pages/show_page/28397-Travel-market-will-shrink-next-year,-says-TTA-chief.

5

Medical Tourism: If This Is Wednesday, It Must Be My Hip Replacement

FOR MOST OF US, getting sick is a good way to ruin a vacation. For growing numbers of people, however, seeing a doctor is the main point of going abroad. When these travelers require surgery or dental work, they combine it with a trip to the Taj Mahal, a photo safari on the African veldt, or a stay at a luxury hotel—or at a hospital that feels like one—all at bargain-basement prices. This is medical tourism, and it is one of the hottest niche markets in the hospitality industry.

Medical tourists have good cause to seek out care far from home. In some regions, state-of-the-art medical facilities are hard to come by, if they exist at all. For that reason, patients throughout the Middle East are traveling to Jordan or Asia for complicated surgery.

In other countries, the public health care system is so overburdened that it can take years to get needed care. In Britain or Canada, wait time for a hip replacement can be a year or more. And as Dr. Prathap Reddy, the Boston-trained founder of the Apollo Hospitals chain in India, comments, "If you wait six months for a heart bypass, you may not need it anymore."[1] In Bangkok or Bangalore, you can be in the operating room the morning after you get off the plane.

But for most people, the real attraction is price. The cost of surgery in India, Thailand, or South Africa can be one-tenth of the rates in the United States or Western Europe, and sometimes even less. A heart valve replacement that would cost $200,000 or more in the United States goes for $10,000 in India, including roundtrip airfare and a brief vacation. A metal-free dental bridge worth $5,500 in the States costs $500. In Thailand, a knee replacement with six days of physical therapy costs about $5,000, one-fifth the American price; LASIK eye surgery worth $3,700 is available for only $730. And a full facelift that would cost $20,000 in the United States runs about $1,250 in South Africa.

Inferior medical care would not be worth having at any price, and some skeptics warn that Third World surgery cannot be as good as that available in the United States. In fact, there have been cases of botched plastic surgery, particularly from Mexican clinics in the days before anyone figured out what a gold mine cheap, high-quality care could be for developing countries.

Yet the hospitals and clinics that today cater to the tourist market often are among the best in the world. Many are staffed by physicians trained at major medical centers in America and Europe. Bangkok's Bumrundgrad hospital has more than 200 surgeons who are board-certified in the United States. One of Singapore's major hospitals is a branch of the prestigious Johns Hopkins University, in Bethesda, Maryland. In a field where experience is as important as technology, Escorts Heart Institute and Research Centre located in Delhi and Faridabad carries out nearly 15,000 heart operations every year. Its death rate among patients during surgery is only 0.8 percent, less than half that of most major hospitals in the United States.

In some areas, these clinics are backed by sophisticated research infrastructures. India is one of the world's leading centers for biotechnology research, while both India and South Korea are pushing ahead with cell research at a level approached only in Britain.

Skilled doctors and state-of-the-art equipment are not the only benefits offered by medical centers specializing in foreign patients. In many, the doctors are supported by more registered nurses per patient than any Western facility could offer. Some facilities provide single-patient rooms that look more like a four-star hotel, with a nurse dedicated to each patient 24 hours a day. Some assign patients a personal assistant for the post-hospital recovery period. There is always the chance for a quick vacation, before or after surgery, to sweeten the deal. Many tourist clinics offer resort-like recovery facilities at a nearby beach for those whose condition or schedule does not allow for an actual vacation. And many of the Asian national airlines offer frequent flyer miles to ease the cost of returning for follow-up visits.

In some countries, there are even more benefits. Medical tourism is evolving into "wellness tourism." In this variation, the core medical clinic is surrounded by ancillary services, such as psychological counseling, exercise facilities, perhaps meditation, and more. The idea is that health-minded patients can heal their lives as well as receive treatment for a specific malady.

Under the circumstances, it is no surprise that the medical tourism market is growing rapidly. Ten years ago, it was hardly large enough to be noticed. Today, something over 250,000 patients per year visit Singapore alone; nearly half arrive from the Middle East. Perhaps half a million travel annually to India for medical care; in 2002, it was only 150,000. McKinsey & Company, a global management consulting firm, estimates that medical tourism could bring India as much as $2.2 billion per year by 2012. Argentina, Costa Rica, Cuba, Jamaica, South Africa, Jordan, Malaysia, Hungary, Latvia, and Estonia all have broken into this lucrative market or are trying to do so, and it seems that a few more countries join the list every year.

Some important trends guarantee that the market for medical tourism will continue to expand in the years ahead. By 2015, the health of the vast Baby Boom generation will have begun its slow, final decline. There are more than seventy million Boomers in the United States, and more than 150 million when Canada, Europe, Australia, and New Zealand are taken into account. They represent an overwhelming market for inexpensive, high-quality medical care.

Medical tourism will be particularly attractive in the United States, where an estimated forty-three million people are without health insurance and perhaps 120 million lack dental coverage. The number of uninsured or underinsured Americans is likely to grow as many companies cut back or eliminate their medical and pension programs. Baby Boom workers who find themselves with little or no health care coverage will welcome any chance to cut the cost of care. Patients in Britain, Canada, and other countries with long waiting lists for major surgery will be just as eager to take advantage of care that is immediately available a plane flight from home.

In the following sections we discuss the largest players in the global medical tourism industry.

Thailand

Thailand got its start in medical tourism in 1997, when the economic crash that hammered much of Asia sent canny healthcare providers looking for new markets. Today, it is the largest and best-established destination for foreign patients, and draws particularly from Japan and the United States. Some 1.3 million Japanese visited Thailand in 2006.

Major centers for medical tourism are Bangkok and Phuket. No fewer than six medical facilities in Bangkok have hospital accreditation from the United States. Bumrungrad International Hospital alone sees 850,000 patients per year, 40 percent of them from abroad. It treated 55,000 Americans in 2005, 30 percent more than the year before. As in most tourist-oriented medical communities, the major attractions are cosmetic surgery and dental treatments. However, eye surgery, kidney dialysis, and organ transplantation are among the most common specialties sought by medical vacationers in Thailand. When not pinned down by medical treatments or recovery, patients usually spend their time shopping or in local sightseeing.

In terms of vacation possibilities, Phuket boasts some of the most spectacular beaches and shorefront scenery on the planet. For a few patients, Phuket has another attraction as well: In all the world, Bangkok Phuket Hospital probably is *the* place to go for sex-change surgery. In fact, that is one of the top ten procedures for which patients visit Thailand.

India

India is a relative newcomer to medical tourism, but it is quickly catching up to Thailand. Several years ago, McKinsey predicted that the number of foreign patients seeking care in India would grow by 15 percent per year. The most recent estimates say the growth rate is already at 30 percent. One estimate suggests that at least one million medical tourists a year will obtain treatment in India by 2012.

It helps a lot that English is one of the many widely used languages in India, and the one spoken by most educated Indians, but there are other reasons for this country's popularity among medical tourists. An obvious one is the cost of care, which for many procedures is the lowest in the world. Trips for follow-up care are also relatively cheap, because Air India subsidizes them with frequent flyer miles.

Another reason for India's popularity is the range of high-level services available in such a large, technologically-advanced country. There are top-notch centers for open-heart surgery, pediatric heart surgery, hip and knee replacement, cosmetic surgery, dentistry, bone marrow transplants, cancer therapy, and just about any other specialty a patient could need.

Many of those centers are among the best in the world. Virtually all are equipped with the latest electronic and medical diagnostic equipment—and India, unlike virtually any of its competitors in this market, has the technological sophistication and infrastructure to maintain it. Additionally, Indian pharmaceuticals meet the stringent requirements of the U.S. Food and Drug Administration, while its quality of care also is up to American standards. Most of the medical centers provide accommodations that could be mistaken for five-star hotels.

Some Indian medical centers even provide services that are uncommon elsewhere. For example, instead of having the entire hip joint replaced, patients can undergo "hip resurfacing," in which damaged bone is scraped away and replaced with chrome alloy. The result is a smoothly functioning joint with less trauma and recovery time than total replacement, and at a lower cost. The operation is well tested and highly successful, but has not yet been approved in the United States.

Unlike some of its competitors, India offers a high degree of transparency. Visitors need not worry about unexpected problems with their funds or legal status.

Of course, before surgery or after, India has a broad array of unique and exotic destinations for Western tourists. From a peaceful tour of the Taj Mahal to a half-day safari in the Bandhavgarh National Park, or shopping for handicrafts in the tribal villages of Orissa and Madhya Pradesh to skin-diving in the Indian Ocean, this 4,000-year-old civilization has something to offer anyone who visits.

Costa Rica

Costa Rica has ecological wonders found in few other lands, from some of the largest, best-protected rain forests in Central America to the fire show of the Arenal Volcano. And for those with more urban tastes, the casinos of San José, Puntarenas, and Guanacaste provide all the action even a jaded Las Vegas regular could ever want.

But for North American patients, what Costa Rica really offers is inexpensive, high-quality medical care in their back yard. For plastic surgery, prices average roughly one-third those in the United States—not the prices they would find in India or Thailand, but a lot closer to home for medical vacationers with limited travel budgets.

Cosmetic surgery and dental work are clearly the specialties here. Get a face-lift and chill on the beach until the bruises go away, and the folks at home will never be quite sure why you suddenly look so good.

South Africa

South Africa is the place to go for sun, surf, and surgery within easy reach of lions, elephants, or the beaches of the Sunshine Coast. South African surgeons tend to be academically sound, but conservative, so this probably is not the best choice for the latest breakthrough in neurosurgery. Heart bypasses and joint replacements are available, but nearly all the medical tourists who visit South Africa come for cosmetic surgery. And in that arena, the many clinics in and around Cape Town excel. Most provide a personal assistant or frequent visits by a trained therapist to help out during the recovery, as well as trips to a top beauty parlor to help patients get the best from their new look. Nearly all medical tour packages include the medical procedure, post-op care in a luxury hotel or guest house, and a safari or other vacation before or after the operation. Because the South African rand is so cheap on the world's foreign exchange markets, prices tend to be lower than in some other destinations.

Other Major Players and Some Up-and-Coming Ones —————

In addition to the major centers just discussed, half a dozen other countries have significant segments of the medical tourism market, while still others are breaking into the field:

- Argentina is the fifth most popular destination in the world for plastic surgery, and the number of medical visitors there is expected to grow by 50 percent in two years.

- Cuba is resurrecting its once-renowned medical facilities in an effort to attract medical tourist dollars. Cosmetic surgery, eye care, and a well-regarded women's hospital are among the attractions.

- Hungary is drawing visitors from Western Europe, and growing numbers from the United States, for high-quality plastic surgery and dental care at prices that can be as little as half those in nearby Germany and 30 to 60 percent of American rates.

- Iran has been eyeing the success of Jordan in attracting medical tourists from other parts of the Middle East and has set its sights on pulling in patients for cardiovascular and orthopedic surgery, dentistry, organ transplants, and even psychiatric care. Given its share of the general tourist market—virtually none—Iran's prospects for success appear limited.

- A better bet is Dubai, already known as a luxury vacation paradise on the Red Sea. Dubai Healthcare City, scheduled to open by 2010, will be the largest international medical center between Europe and Southeast Asia. With a new branch of the Harvard Medical School on-site, it may also be the most prestigious.

- Malaysia offers advanced care at low prices in a variety of specialties. However, its efforts to develop medical tourism have been handicapped by an acute shortage of doctors and technicians.

- The Philippines is still an undeveloped land as far as medical tourism goes, but that may not remain true for long. Bangkok's Bumrungrad International Hospital recently made a major investment in the Asian Hospital and Medical Center outside Manila, where it hopes to clone its own success in attracting vacationing patients.

Key Trends for Medical Tourism

In this section, we look at the key trends for medical tourism using entries from Appendix A. We list each relevant trend and our assessment of it, and then detail the specific implications of this trend for medical tourism in the hospitality and travel industry.

2. POPULATION OF THE DEVELOPED WORLD IS LIVING LONGER.

Assessment: Demographic trends such as this are among the easiest to recognize and most difficult to derail. Barring a global plague or nuclear war—wildcard possibilities that cannot be predicted with any validity—there is little chance that the population forecast for 2050 will err on the low side.

Implications for Medical Tourism: If a future medical breakthrough slows the aging process and extends the health and vigor of mid-life, less care will be required for disorders such as arthritis and prostate cancer, which are strongly associated with aging.

This market may be replaced by growth in lifestyle disorders such as heart disease and lung cancer, which will have more time to develop.

In the absence of an anti-aging treatment, many geriatric diseases will be delayed, but not prevented. These patients will still need care, often at overseas facilities. They will simply need it later in life.

3. THE ELDERLY POPULATION IS GROWING DRAMATICALLY THROUGHOUT THE WORLD.

Assessment: Again, this is a demographic trend, difficult to derail and unlikely to change while the massive Baby Boom generation remains on the scene.

Implications for Medical Tourism: Seniors represent the primary market for most forms of medical care. Their growing number promises rapid expansion of medical tourism for at least the next twenty years.

Thus far, we have not heard of a medical tourist–oriented hospital or clinic specifically designed to provide a full range of services for geriatric patients. We expect many such facilities to appear in the decade ahead.

6. THE PHYSICAL CULTURE AND PERSONAL-HEALTH MOVEMENTS ARE IMPROVING HEALTH IN MUCH OF THE WORLD, BUT THEY ARE FAR FROM UNIVERSAL.

Assessment: This trend always seems a case of two steps forward, at least one step back. We expect it to continue for at least the next generation.

Implications for Medical Tourism: As long as obesity remains epidemic, the medical tourism industry will remain healthier than its customers.

Growing interest in maintaining health, rather than healing ills that might have been avoided, will propel the growth of "wellness tourism," an offshoot of medical tourism that has just begun to appear. Both tourist-oriented medical facilities and general-interest resorts will add wellness programs to their offerings.

17. GENERATION X, THE DOT-COMS, AND THE MILLENNIALS ARE GAINING SOCIAL AND ORGANIZATIONAL INFLUENCE.

Assessment: As trends go, this is an evergreen. In a few years, we will simply add the next new generation to the list.

Implications for Medical Tourism: Younger consumers tend to be extremely well informed about their options in all fields, thanks in large part to their comfort with the Internet. Though older patients are a much larger medical market, younger ones are more likely to be aware of medical facilities abroad. They will form a disproportionate segment of the tourist patient load.

In addition, younger consumers are more open to non-standard alternatives in all fields. This will promote their acceptance of medical tourism.

19. THE ECONOMY OF THE DEVELOPED WORLD IS GROWING STEADILY, WITH ONLY BRIEF INTERRUPTIONS.

Assessment: These trends have been revised many times since they were first codified in the late 1980s. Some trends have fallen out of the list as they matured or as circumstances came along to change them. Others have been added as they were recognized. This trend has remained a constant, and with each revision its effective period has been extended. To invalidate this trend would take a catastrophe on the order of the permanent loss of Middle Eastern oil from the Western economies. Not even the recession of 2008–09 rises to that level of destruction.

Implications for Medical Tourism: The United States is piling up enormous bills to dig its way out of the recession that began in 2008. So are most other Western countries. Some of this money will be repaid when governments sell their stakes in financial companies after the economic tide has turned. The rest will have to be paid down as part of their national budget deficits. This will undermine their ability to fund medical programs just as the Baby Boom generation ages into its period of greatest need. Many Boomers may face long waits for needed treatment. Many will dig into their savings to pay for care abroad, where it is more affordable.

The growing cost of insuring workers will lead many American companies to look abroad for expensive medical care at discount prices. Employee health programs will grow into a stable, profitable segment of medical tourism by 2015.

Growing prosperity in China, India, and other formerly poor lands has promoted the spread of Western-style diets, overeating, and tobacco use. Hospitals and clinics established to serve medical tourists will find a new growth market among the wealthy of their own lands who seek the best care available. This may raise demand for urgent care at facilities originally designed for patients who could afford the delay of making international arrangements.

20. THE GLOBAL ECONOMY IS GROWING MORE INTEGRATED.

Assessment: This trend will continue for at least the next two decades.

Implications for Medical Tourism: The most respected Western hospitals and medical colleges have begun to tap the market for medical tourism. Some are forming alliances with tourist facilities in India, Thailand, and other countries. Some are building their own tourist-oriented hospitals and clinics in prominent medical destinations. This practice will grow rapidly.

Eventually, facilities not allied to a major Western institution may find it difficult to compete with those that are.

35. THE UNITED STATES IS CEDING ITS SCIENTIFIC AND TECHNICAL LEADERSHIP TO OTHER COUNTRIES.

Assessment: This trend emerged from a wide variety of ill-conceived political decisions made over the last thirty years. It will take at least a generation to reverse.

Implications for Medical Tourism: There will be many opportunities for tomorrow's founders and staff of medical tourist destinations to train in the United States—if they still wish to do so.

Overseas medical facilities will have access to a growing number of new drugs and procedures not available in the United States. These assets will be a strong "draw" for many patients.

39. TECHNOLOGY IS CREATING A KNOWLEDGE-DEPENDENT GLOBAL SOCIETY.

Assessment: This trend will not reach even its halfway mark until the rural populations of China and India gain modern educations and easy access to the Internet.

Implications for Medical Tourism: The Internet is a primary marketing tool for many hospitals and clinics specializing in foreign patients. Although targeted marketing operations in Western countries will grow to supplement online information, the Internet will remain the first place most patients go to shop for medical destinations.

53. INSTITUTIONS ARE UNDERGOING A BIMODAL DISTRIBUTION: THE BIG GET BIGGER, THE SMALL SURVIVE, AND THE MID-SIZED ARE SQUEEZED OUT.

Assessment: Thanks in part to technology, this trend is likely to be a permanent feature of the business scene from now on. It will accelerate significantly during the recession of 2008–09.

Implications for Medical Tourism: This trend will reach the medical tourism industry no later than 2015 and will be well established by 2020.

We will see the rise of multinational chains operating hospitals and clinics that specialize in care for medical tourists. Their primary assets will be a reputation for quality care and an advertising budget capable of global reach. Many of these chains will be established or affiliated with "name" institutions in the West.

54. MILITANT ISLAM CONTINUES TO SPREAD AND GAIN POWER.

Assessment: This trend may wax and wane, but it seems unlikely to disappear this side of a Muslim reformation comparable to those that transformed Christianity and Judaism.

Implications for Medical Tourism: Hospitals and clinics specializing in the treatment of Western patients are an obvious target for terrorist attack.

The first successful attack on a medical-tourism destination will depress travel to all such facilities in the affected countries for at least two years.

This will give tourist medical facilities in Eastern Europe and South Africa a significant advantage over those in India, Thailand, and the Philippines.

Hospitals and clinics that serve Western tourists will need to devote significant resources to security. They must secure their facilities without making patients feel they are under siege. The best-defended facilities may be able to use their security as a marketing tool, particularly after a successful attack elsewhere.

Endnote

1. "Get Well Away," *The Economist,* 9 October 2004. Accessed October 25, 2008, at www.economist.com/business/displaystory.cfm?story_id=E1_PNSGQNN.

6

Away on Business: The MICE Market

MICE—MEETINGS, INCENTIVES, CONVENTIONS, AND EXHIBITIONS—used to be one of the easier, more profitable markets for the hotels and resorts that host them. Booking them took work, but each meeting signed meant a block of rooms filled, and payment for them was assured.

That has changed. Although the meetings and expositions industry has flourished and still represents a worthwhile market, it has been struggling with difficult challenges. For the host destinations, this has meant more effort, smaller profits, and much less certainty. Whereas meeting organizers once worked six to eighteen months ahead, for many that lead time has shrunk to a few weeks. Customers promise a series of meetings, then book them one at a time. They demand meeting budgets in extreme detail, complete with greens fees. Worse, most are willing to pay only for rooms actually occupied, not for the number they reserved for expected participants. The recession of 2008–09 is making meeting planners and their clients even more value-conscious.

This is a taste of things to come. In the years ahead, the global population will continue to grow and change, economies will expand and contract, science and technology will tighten their hold on business and society, and the world will knit itself ever more tightly into a single market. As a result, both opportunities and trials will abound in this segment of the hospitality market.

More and more industries are relying on MICE to accomplish a variety of important goals. Industries set up expositions or exhibitions to introduce new products and services, to gauge their appeal, and to keep existing products before the public eye. Companies use meetings to promote the exchange of ideas with co-workers and competitors and to train their people to deal with new products and procedures. They use incentives to inspire and reward better performance from their personnel. People attend meetings to establish trust and credibility with new contacts and to "press the flesh" with colleagues whom they ordinarily meet only through the impersonal media of e-mail, telephones, and text messaging.

They also attend in order to escape daily routine in a way that still counts as doing business. All of these functions are becoming more important as technology raises the pressure to increase productivity and strips away opportunities for human interaction. Contrary to early fears, high tech makes "high touch" even more necessary, not less so. The Convention Industry Council reports that more than one million meetings, conventions, and exhibitions are held in the United States every year, and the number is growing steadily.

Yet technology has its downside as well. Meetings, conventions, and expositions remain important for building new relationships, but the business world's growing reliance on e-mail has markedly reduced the need for frequent personal contact in maintaining those associations. This trend is likely to accelerate as Gen Xers and especially the tech-savvy Millennials advance into positions of authority. Thus, one primary impetus for meetings and expositions may have begun to wane.

At one time, another major reason for industry expositions was the introduction of new products. By compressing the product cycle, technology is displacing that function as well. In high tech especially, manufacturers that finalize a new product in January can no longer afford to delay its introduction for a major trade show that may not take place until June; by then, it probably will be obsolete. For this function, smaller, task-specific meetings have displaced many of the giant industry blowouts that once hosted product announcements.

Wall Street also has been a continuing problem for meeting organizers. Its relentless focus on earnings per share and its refusal to look farther into the future than the next business quarter have forced corporate executives to cut corners wherever they can, even if it means eliminating functions that could have been profitable in the longer term. Often, meetings get the ax.

Mergers and acquisitions are another major factor driven in part by investor expectations. As a result of mergers, the hardware industry now is dominated by just five major companies. Forecasting International (FI) has long predicted that there soon will be only three major airlines in the United States, a target date that now seems likely to be met under the pressure of the 2008–09 recession. And when two companies become one, there are fewer potential exhibitors for the next meeting in that industry. Merging companies also tend to shed employees in the duplicated functions, thereby reducing the number of possible attendees for future meetings.

This is one aspect of a trend that FI calls "the bimodal distribution of institutions." As large companies merge and drive mid-sized competitors out of business, thanks to their economies of scale, small "boutique" participants are cropping up to serve niche markets in almost every industry. Working to attract more exhibitors and attendees from among these micro-scale competitors may be one way to make up for the losses at the top end of the corporate food chain.

Another trend that makes life harder for meeting managers is key account selling. When companies focus their attention on the 20 percent of customers who provide 80 percent of their sales, they are in daily contact with the clients who matter to them most. Inevitably, they feel less need to see them in person at large industry gatherings. This, too, has worked to slow the growth of demand for meetings and expositions.

It also has helped to promote the growth of another important trend: Private events are quickly eroding the market for industry trade shows. Not only for key accounts, but for potential customers, companies increasingly prefer to meet their contacts in seclusion, where they need not battle competitors for attention. Some of these closed meetings are enormous, and they will continue to make up a growing part of the total market for meetings and expositions.

Although most meetings count on the local market for their success—an estimated 40 percent of attendees come from within 400 miles of the meeting site—international factors are becoming significant for many exhibition managers. In recent years, exotic meeting places have grown increasingly popular, both for small, high-end gatherings of top executives and for the promotion of international trade. Some of the developing countries are particularly in favor as venues for meetings and expositions (despite occasional problems getting equipment in and out of the country) because they have low labor costs.

Yet, with all these specific factors to buffet the market for meetings and expositions, the most general consideration for the immediate future is still the most important. This is the global economy. If the recession improves quickly, a rising tide lifts all boats, and the market for meeting and exposition space is likely to grow rapidly. If it continues and deepens, it would be a grim time for MICE.

Factors Affecting the MICE Market

A recent poll asked executives in the meetings and expositions segment what trends would be most important for the future of the MICE market. Their choices: the state of the economy, the growing use of meetings themselves, technology, the "green" movement, and the rise of Generation Y (we refer to them as the Millennials for the time in which they are coming of age). We have already considered the spread of meetings, but FI has some other trends for your attention. Following is a brief look at each of them.

Recession Worries

Although meetings in general are an essential part of the business world, most specific meetings are elective. Thus, when times get tough, they are among the first things companies think to cut.

The trimming has already begun. Late in October 2008, Meeting Professionals International (MPI) polled one thousand senior meeting professionals to determine how the recession was affecting their business.[1] The results were unsurprising:

- Fifty-seven percent said their business was off from last year. For 18 percent, it was down by more than 10 percent. Only 20 percent said it had improved, and for most the gain was 5 percent or less.

- Sixty-five percent expected their business to be off in the next few months compared with the previous year. Only 16 percent expected it to be better.

- Forty-seven percent reported that the domestic corporate segment of their business had shown the greatest decline since 2007. However, 32 percent said the same segment had shown the greatest increase.

- Fifty-eight percent said that attendance at their meetings and events had fallen off in the last year. Twenty-nine percent reported that there had been no change.

- Fifty-eight percent reported that spending on meetings and events had declined compared with a year earlier. For 17 percent of respondents, the decrease was greater than 10 percent.

The economy has deteriorated significantly since October 2008, of course. Some results of a survey of 2,740 professionals in fifty-three countries appear in MPI's *FutureWatch 2009 Survey*. According to this survey, carried out only a month after the previous one, sponsors canceled 8 percent of the meetings they had scheduled for the second half of 2008. By late November 2008, they had already canceled 7 percent of the meetings scheduled for 2009. Meeting planners anticipated a 9 percent decline in the number of events their organizations would hold in the coming year. "Meeting planners and suppliers expect that global economic uncertainty will lead to continued reductions in bookings, travel, meeting and event budgets, staffing, and event attendance," the report summarized. "The overall trend will continue, they say, until the broader economy begins to rebound."[2]

Nevertheless, FI's prediction for meetings, incentives, conventions, and exhibitions is fundamentally the same as for other hospitality markets. The worst should be over well before the end of 2009. As that year ends and 2010 progresses, the MICE market will recover. By 2011, it will return to its pre-recession peak and begin to set new records for profitability. In the long run, the hospitality industry has no bad sectors, only sectors with their own unique challenges.

Infotech Unites the World

Electronic communications has all but eliminated geographic barriers. A message e-mailed from New York to Hong Kong arrives essentially instantaneously—and costs less than a phone call to New Jersey. Copies can be sent to hundreds of different destinations all over the world with little added cost. In the next few years, when both the Internet and telephone systems are equipped to translate conversations accurately among the most common languages in real time, the process of doing business internationally will be easier still.

This has both good and bad implications for hotels, resorts, and conference centers with an eye toward MICE. The Internet makes it possible for businesses throughout the world to compete on an even footing with industry leaders. This means that smaller destinations in developing countries will find it easier to target meeting planners who would like to find novel sites for high-end gatherings. It also is increasingly possible to skip the intermediaries and market directly to clients, such as companies planning small, private meetings. And as the Internet spreads through neglected parts of Asia and Africa, some of those locations will become suitable sites for international meetings as well.

The Internet also makes it easier for business executives to keep in touch with colleagues and customers, which in turn makes it easier to spend time at a meeting thousands of miles from the office. A few years ago, guests were impressed when hotels provided a modem jack on the telephone. Today, they are demanding wireless Internet access from rooms to restaurants to poolside. This means investing in new hardware, and wireless Internet service is not even a strong competitive advantage. But the lack of it is an increasingly serious handicap when it comes to winning in the meeting market.

All this connectivity has transformed the way the hospitality industry does business. Potential customers now routinely shop for destinations, begin negotiations, register for meetings, and book their rooms on the Internet. This has forced hotel and conference center executives to change their ways, but it has made for more efficient marketing. Five years ago, marketing and managing a meeting or exhibition over the Internet was a novelty. Approaching 2010, it has become standard practice.

The downside of telecommunications for hospitality—particularly e-mail, business TV, and computerized conferences—is that it has become easier for executives to maintain contact with their customers and colleagues without actually meeting them in person. "Virtual" meetings have begun to replace travel and face-to-face meetings. This is especially true of trips by one or two executives from site to site within big companies, which account for an estimated 80 percent of business travel. Virtual meetings are also having an impact on conferences, which people have traditionally used to reinforce their existing relationships. Now they can meet someone in person the first time and then "meet" them online whenever they have business to discuss. So-called "face time" remains important, but to some executives it no longer seems quite as important as it once was. This is particularly true for the younger generations, who grew up with computers and may have had close online friends whom they never actually met in the real world.

Virtual meetings will be an even greater factor in the future for one obvious reason. Putting four people on airplanes to meet with a fifth costs an average of nearly $5,200. A videoconference is only $1,700. A simple audioconference runs just $689.

Not long ago, consultants Frost & Sullivan expected the global market for videoconferencing systems and services to reach $3.1 billion by 2010, a compound growth rate of nearly 21 percent per year. At the high end, where large high-definition screens can make you feel like you're in the same room as the other participants, the market was forecast to reach $1 billion by 2011, up from only $64 million in just four years. Because of the 2008 recession, those targets probably will be reached a year or two late, but they will be met.

Online conferences will not replace real-world events, but they will compete with hotels and resorts for the chance to deliver information to busy executives. At the high end of the videoconferencing market, the quality of the experience can be extraordinary—good enough that the American intelligence community now uses it to interrogate captives in Iraq and Afghanistan without leaving the comfort of their offices at home. In the long term, much of the business that still happens in person today will migrate to the Internet.

Technology is having another effect as well. Thanks to such developments as computer-aided design and manufacturing, the product cycle is becoming increasingly compressed. As recently as World War II, it took thirty years to go from theoretical idea to the release of competing products in an established market; in computing, it now takes eighteen months or less. Competition among service providers is essentially instantaneous. Companies can no longer afford to wait for giant, industry-wide trade shows to introduce new products, so they are mounting their own smaller, highly focused events. These gatherings offer another hot market for destinations able to target corporate meeting planners.

Of course, technology will continue to change meetings themselves. Not long ago, it was enough to provide attendees with wireless broadband so that they could keep in touch with their home offices, dig up information, and contact their families. This will change rapidly. Increasingly, the well-equipped household includes a home theater system, Internet and satellite radio, and a host of other electronic gadgets. It will not be long before meeting-goers expect similar conveniences to be available at their meeting sites. This will create new expenses for venues and chores for meeting planners and managers.

Meetings Go Green

For Generation X and the Millennials, the environment is a major concern. Recycling, minimizing carbon footprint, conserving energy and water, avoiding volatile solvents in paint and dry cleaning, and a host of other "green" practices and priorities are part of their daily lives. And if the Baby Boomers are a bit more concerned with their own convenience, they also bear the environment in mind when making choices. No wonder, then, that 68 percent of meeting-goers in one survey reported that they preferred to gather in an environmentally friendly venue.

To date, the pinnacle of green meetings has to be the Democratic National Convention in 2008. The party was determined to put its environmental values into practice—and, of course, to be seen doing so. The host city of Denver was on board with the idea. Planning began a year in advance. To prepare for the convention, the city and the Denver 2008 Convention Host Committee created ten green task teams, developed fifty corporate and nonprofit partners, registered 450 green business vendors, and recruited hundreds of volunteers to work together to design and implement green strategies. When it was over, the effort was intended to leave behind permanent sustainability programs for the city.

The convention center became the very model of a modern green facility. It was refitted with low-flow water fixtures. Convention delegates and reporters got reusable water bottles instead of throw-away bottles and stopped at convenient water bottle filling stations as needed. Recycling bins were everywhere, and the convention center offered recycling and composting services. Light rail and alternative-fuel buses provided mass transit. There were one thousand bicycles on loan for use during the convention. Even the key cards were made of wood.

It isn't necessary to go that far to add some eco-friendliness to your next meeting. Green practices might even have other advantages. On average, providing filtered water in reusable bottles saves $50 per attendee compared with standard bottled water. Online registration is cheaper and faster than registering on paper, and it saves trees. If you avoid putting dates on your signage, you can use it again next year. And instead of printing paper handouts and other meeting materials, try delivering them on a USB drive. It's much cheaper to prepare and easier for attendees to carry.

For further ideas, check with The Convene Green Alliance, in Arlington, Virginia. It is an association of fourteen trade organizations, major host communities such as Dallas and Atlantic City, and several trade show management groups. They all have major conventions to run and a determination to make them as eco-friendly as possible. See www.convenegreen.com for details.

New Generations Dominate

The nineteen-year Baby Boom of 1946 through 1964 was followed by an eleven-year "baby bust." Generation X thus produced the smallest pool of workers since the 1930s: There are just forty-four million Gen Xers in the United States, compared with seventy-seven million in their parents' generation. In Europe, the forty-something cohort represents just 22 percent of the population.

We should rename them "Generation E," for entrepreneurship, education, English, and e-mail, assets that members of this generation share throughout the world. Gen Xers and the Millennial generation, now in their twenties, have more in common with their peers across the globe than with their parents' generation.

Throughout the world, Gen Xers are starting new businesses at an unprecedented rate. The Millennials are proving to be even more business-oriented, caring for little but the bottom line. Twice as many say they would prefer to own a business than be a top executive. Five times more would prefer to own a business than hold a key position in politics or government.

This attitude promises new demand for the meetings and expositions market. Each new company founded by a member of Generation X or the Millennial generation will translate into rooms occupied during industry gatherings, and many will add to the market for gatherings of corporate executives, product rollouts, and other single-firm meetings.

At the same time, however, being completely "at home" on the Internet could also mean that Millennials and the generations that follow them will be more comfortable dealing with colleagues they have never met in the real world. They may feel less need for in-person gatherings, and this could partially offset the expected growth in demand for meeting space.

One more new-generation attitude is likely to have a major effect on meetings: For all their hard-nosed attention to the bottom line, Generation X and the Millennials have much less interest in their careers than their Baby Boom elders. To these younger workers, a job is just a means to an end. What really matters to them are friends, family, and fun. They are not likely to be very interested in attending meetings unless they can bring their families and put in some quality time in leisure activities.

Growing Older

At the other end of the age spectrum, we see another crucial trend. Throughout the developed world, the retirement-age population is growing at an astonishing rate. For example, the over-sixty-five cohort will rise from 12.4 percent of the American population in 2000 to more than 16 percent in 2020. The same trend can be seen in Europe, Japan, and even in some developing countries. India's over-sixty population is expanding from fifty-six million in 1991 to 137 million in 2021 and 340 million in 2051.

For destinations that host meetings and expositions, this offers one of the most vibrant markets that will be available in the next twenty years. A wide range of new goods and services will cater to the needs of the elderly, and particularly to healthy, active seniors throughout the developed world. At the same time, the healthcare industry will continue to grow rapidly to meet the medical needs of less fortunate seniors. The need to introduce these products and services and keep them before the public will provide a fast-expanding market for meeting and exposition space. Exhibitions will also be used to test-market products redesigned for older consumers—another active niche market for the hospitality industry.

At the same time, workers in the traditional retirement years represent the fastest growing employment pool in many developed countries; this is an area that has yet to be fully or efficiently tapped. Retirement-age workers are especially well suited to the hospitality industry, because they are generally polite, well-spoken, and available for part-time work.

Post-retirement workers also are likely to form a growing percentage of meeting attendees, and this will influence the meetings themselves. Venues will need to be "elder-friendly," with brighter-than-average lighting suited to dimming vision, a bit more volume on the sound system, large-type signage, and door levers rather than knobs, so that arthritic hands can operate them more easily. Younger personnel may need some training to speak with the extra formality that many elders expect. This trend will bring even greater need for precise service and quality control. Older workers, particularly those whose positions are as senior as they are, tend to have less patience with disappointment or delay than others.

Society Goes Global

Our beliefs and values are shaped by what we see and hear. Throughout the United States, people have long seen the same movies and TV programs. These media are achieving global reach. In the process, they are creating a truly integrated global society. Global migration, intermarriage, and the rapid growth of travel, for both business and pleasure, all are hastening this process. In the United Kingdom, some 21 percent of young adults answering a recent poll viewed themselves as primarily European, rather than British. Some 31 percent of French Gen Xers, 36 percent of Germans, and 42 percent of Italians also said they thought of themselves as Europeans.

Over the next half-century, growing cultural exchanges at the personal level will help to reduce some of the conflict that plagued the twentieth century. This is likely to produce a reactionary backlash in societies where xenophobia is common. Some of the most fervent "culturist" movements will spring from religious fundamentalism. Would-be dictators and strongmen will use these movements to promote their own interests, ensuring that ethnic, sectarian, and regional violence will remain common.

Thus, political risks are likely to grow in areas where there are strong religious or ethnic movements, especially when they may target Western or American interests. Anti-foreign movements are increasingly common in Europe, but anti-American sentiments are widespread throughout the developing world. Terrorism will be a continuing problem for meeting destinations in the developing world, and particularly where there are large, conservative Muslim communities.

Nonetheless, the trend toward a more homogeneous world culture is generally making life simpler for meeting planners and destination managers. In the most heavily traveled lands, it is quickly becoming easier to host international meetings and expositions with less risk of unfortunate incidents owing to cultural conflicts. The continuing spread of the English language; the development of a task-focused, profit-oriented global business culture; and the slow, steady replacement of ethnic and sectarian interests by concerns for personal security and material well-being will help to make international meetings more common and more manageable in the years ahead.

International Exposure

The growing unification of the world into a single market will bring greater demand for international meetings and expositions. Hotels and resorts with good connections to the largest international managers of meetings and expositions will be especially well positioned to benefit from this trend.

Destinations in some developing countries also will benefit from government efforts to build international trade and from the "trendiness" of exotic locales. However, the local representatives in these areas will have to reassure meeting managers about issues such as local manpower, equipment availability, and the financial risks of doing business under an unfamiliar legal system.

The threat of international terrorism will be a concern for international meetings for many years to come—and especially while American forces remain in Iraq and Afghanistan, providing extra motivation for Muslim extremists. This will require hotels, resorts, and meeting planners in many areas to take extra care in arranging security for gatherings. The Arab lands, the Middle East, and the Muslim regions of Asia are obvious high-risk areas, but Europe also has significant numbers of radicalized Muslims sympathetic to the terrorist cause. These include some converts who can pass for native Europeans—because that is exactly what they are. It will not be enough to find a venue with suitable barriers to prevent the approach of a truck bomb. For genuine security, the venue's staff must have undergone a rigorous background check. Similarly, any local personnel or services hired to help set up an exhibition also must receive clearance. In any meeting place, the greatest risk is always from the facility's own staff.

Tourism Expands

Once the current recession has passed, the hospitality industry will continue to grow by at least 5 percent per year for the foreseeable future, just as it did in the decade before 2008. Perhaps a bit ironically, this growth is likely to make the hospitality industry itself the largest single user of meeting and exposition services, both to promote its own offerings to consumers and to handle the industry's own increasingly large and frequent gatherings.

The downside of this trend is crowding, as many resort areas become increasingly packed with tourists. It will be harder for these destinations to attract major meetings, and the sardine effect will degrade the attendees' experience during leisure time at the meeting. Increasingly, meeting planners will seek out smaller hotels and resorts in out-of-the-way locations to avoid the crowds. This will open new business for destinations that until recently might have found it more difficult to attract meetings and expositions.

In order to take advantage of these opportunities, smaller venues may have to make some difficult adjustments. Lawson Hockman of the Foundation for International Meetings points out that managers of small gatherings often have to work on a tight budget and thus are extremely reluctant to commit to paying for rooms that may not be filled.[3] To gain their business, destinations may have to take on the liability of setting aside rooms for people who may never arrive. Hotels and resorts that are willing to accept that risk will have a big negotiating advantage over those that are not.

We Travel Faster

By air and by sea, passengers are getting from one place to another with higher speeds, lower prices, and greater efficiency. As a result, by 2013, air travel for both business and pleasure will triple the rate in 1985. Larger-capacity aircraft, such as the Airbus A380 and Boeing 787, will contribute to this trend. The new Airbus plane is so large that companies will be able to hold onboard meetings while on their way to meetings, just as they do on cruise ships today.

Going faster and cheaper means going farther in the same amount of time and at the same price. Thus, more distant destinations become more attractive for meetings. This trend should bring more business to hotels and resorts in developing lands with spectacular scenery and other unique attractions.

Faster, more convenient travel options also will reduce the lead time needed to arrange smaller corporate meetings and other short-notice gatherings. It will be more difficult to tap into the market to host these hasty assemblies, and hotels and resorts that can build relationships directly with companies, rather than with meeting managers, will have a significant advantage over their less-well-connected competitors.

Specialization Is Spreading

For doctors, lawyers, engineers, and other professionals, the size of the body of knowledge required to excel in a particular area precludes excellence across all areas. The same principle applies to artisans. Witness the rise of post-and-beam homebuilders, old-house restorers, automobile electronics technicians, and mechanics trained to work on only one brand of car. Information-based organizations have already adapted to this trend. Most now depend on teams of task-focused specialists to get their work done efficiently.

This trend creates endless new niche markets to be served by small businesses. It also brings more career choices as old specialties quickly become obsolete, but new ones appear even more rapidly. And each subdivision of an industry or market creates new companies and trade and professional organizations requiring meeting and exposition management services. These proliferating niche operators will provide a source of new demand for meeting space. Attracting them will require hard, continuous work in new business development.

Women Are Better Paid

Women's salaries in the United States grew from 61 percent of men's in 1960 to 74 percent in 1991. This figure soon will top 83 percent. In the future, women's average income could exceed that of men. College graduates enjoy a significant advantage in earnings over peers whose education ended with high school. Today, some 70 percent of young American women enroll in college, compared with only 64 percent of young men.

To the extent that experience translates into prestige and corporate value, older women should find it easier to reach upper-management positions. They will strengthen the nascent "old-girl" networks, which will help to raise the pay scale of women still climbing the corporate ladder.

More new hires will be women, and they will expect both pay and opportunities equal to those of men. Pay-and-benefits packages are likely to rise as women find more high-quality opportunities in other industries. Competition for top executive positions, once effectively limited to men, will intensify even as the corporate ladder loses many of its rungs.

This is nothing new for the hospitality industry, which has long provided some of the best job opportunities available to women and has paid them fairly for their skills. But it may mean that hotels, resorts, and meeting and exhibition managers will find it a bit harder to hire top candidates, thanks to growing competition from industries once reluctant to give women authority and compensation equal to that of male executives.

Work Ethic Wanes

Throughout industry, tardiness is increasing and abuse of sick leave is common. Job security and high pay are not the motivators they once were because social mobility is high and people seek job fulfillment. Some 48 percent of those responding in a Harris Interactive poll said they work because it "gives a feeling of real accomplishment." Fifty-five percent of the top executives interviewed in that survey say that erosion of the work ethic will have a major negative effect on corporate performance in the future.

For the moment, this trend may be changing. The number of unemployed in the United States recently hit its highest point in twenty years. And there is nothing like a bad job market to make people more interested in working harder to keep the paycheck they have. However, this is likely to prove a temporary reversal in a long-term trend.

The motivated self-starters on whom this industry depends will be increasingly hard to find. So will employees capable of working reliably on their own with meeting planners far from home. Finding them, grooming them for greater responsibility, and keeping them on staff will be among the hospitality industry's greatest management challenges of the next twenty years.

Seconds Count

Time is rapidly becoming the world's rarest, most precious commodity. The pressure on workers to be ever more productive grew during the recession of 2001. It will be even more intense in the deeper recession that began in 2008. As is true of many of the other trends in this chapter, this is reducing demand for large, general-purpose industry gatherings that may not repay the days, not to mention money, invested in attending them. This same trend, however, is increasing the need for small corporate retreats and other low-stress, high-productivity gatherings. These are likely to be one of the fastest-growing segments of the market for meeting space.

This offers opportunities for smaller destinations with unique attractions. In meetings of any size, many clients will appreciate cost-efficient, novel opportunities to relax in the leisure hours of their gatherings. Destinations that can supply such opportunities will have a significant marketing advantage over competitors whose primary appeal is the ability to accommodate a crowd.

Businesses Shrink

Thanks to computerized information systems, a typical large business in 2010 will have fewer than half the management levels of its counterpart in 1990, and about one-third the number of managers. This trend can be both good and bad for the hospitality industry because it means lower management expenses but fewer promotion opportunities for career-minded workers. Like many of these trends, it is a mixed blessing for the meetings and expositions market.

One reason there are fewer managers is that the work they oversaw is now being contracted out. This offers new opportunities for the firms that now handle those chores. It should translate into new growth for a variety of service industries that will need space for new meetings and their attendees.

One function that many companies are likely to farm out is the organization of MICE. This should make it easier for destinations to compete for business at those firms. Instead of trying to sell to one hard-to-identify manager who may handle meetings only for his or her division or department—and who could leave for another employer the following week—hospitality executives may be able to build a continuing relationship with a professional meeting manager who can speak for everyone at a major client firm, or for several smaller companies.

Successful Meetings of the Future ———————————

The trends suggest that the market for meeting space will grow even more challenging in the years ahead. As Francis J. Friedman, president of New York–based Time & Place Strategies, points out, "Tradeshows are the only medium where the customer pays to hear sales presentations."[4] As the business world demands ever leaner and more efficient operations, that idea is losing its appeal. And as we have seen, smaller corporate meetings face challenges of their own. Thus, questions arise: How will meeting organizers continue to flourish in this increasingly difficult environment? And how can destinations help them to succeed, and thus compete successfully for their future business?

An obvious starting point is to know what really matters to organizers charged with making their meetings a success. At FI, where we have occasionally run meetings of up to several hundred participants, we concentrate on four rewards that make it worth someone's time to attend a business gathering. Call them the "four Cs" if you want; we think of them as "C4"—an explosive combination that makes meetings work. These are contacts, contracts, certification, and clarification.

- Contacts, of course, are the people you meet. Can you impress enough of them so that they will call or e-mail you later? For most attendees, and especially for exhibitors, this is the real return on their investment in the meeting. Making first contact is the one function of meetings that is most difficult to replace by e-mail and teleconferencing.

- For the most successful attendees who do impress potential new customers or whose potential suppliers impress them, those contacts can result in contracts. Thus, large industry trade shows can have a measurable impact on the bottom line.

- Certification comes from those workshops held at many association meetings. They provide a base of common knowledge that improves the efficiency of any industry. This is particularly important in highly technical fields, such as healthcare, where any deficiency in professional skills may cost lives.

- Clarification can take many forms. It may be just a matter of asking the right question of an expert you would not have met outside the meeting. Clarification also can be more tangible: It's one thing to see a video of new equipment, but quite another to touch it and see and hear it working in person.

Skip Cox, president of Exhibit Surveys, Inc., may not use exactly those terms, but he clearly has these issues in mind when he states that successful exhibitions or conventions adhere to just two basic principles: They deliver "highly valued information to all parties attending," and they provide "an environment that fosters and promotes personal interaction for the effective exchange of information."[5] To maintain relevance, he believes at least part of the answer may be downsizing. "The highly successful exhibitions and conventions of the future," he advises, "will be more focused, vertical trade shows that are rich in content, both of formal education and of exhibitors relevant to the attendees' interests. It will be easier to deliver high-value information for a narrow field, discipline, industry segment, or area of technology." Attendees rate private corporate events as being particularly useful, Cox notes, specifically because they provide high value and specific information to meet the needs of "a very vertical audience."

Large industry gatherings also can be successful by imitating small ones. Cox adds: "Organizers will need to create well-defined vertical segments of their events and support each segment with rich content, a good representation of exhibitors relevant to each segment, and they must make it easy for attendees to 'consume' their segments of interest." An ideal mix includes large exhibitors that have a really good grasp of their field; smaller participants with diverse, highly specific viewpoints; and one or two top-notch speakers from outside the field who can set industry developments into their broader perspective. This is a good formula for panel discussions as well.

Friedman of Time & Place Strategies believes this formula may be an increasingly difficult ideal to meet. He divides meeting exhibitors into three categories: the largest companies with the biggest budgets, which make up about 10 percent of accounts; intermediate-sized companies, which represent about 40 percent of participants; and small companies with relatively small budgets, which are fully half of the meeting market. Friedman believes the importance of these latter groups to trade shows will be evolving rapidly during the remainder of this decade. Trade shows have traditionally focused on the large companies, but Friedman predicts that the focus of trade shows will shift toward intermediate-sized and smaller companies.[6]

As the most broadly knowledgeable members of their industries, large companies tend to hold the greatest interest for show attendees. As the organizers' most profitable customers, large companies merit key account selling and other targeted approaches. However, because they have many other opportunities to reach their own clients, large companies also are the least likely to be interested in attending a trade show. Their participation will continue to decline as they replace trade show exhibits with private meetings and other precisely targeted approaches to their customers. Friedman believes this trend will open up more of the large-company meeting business to destinations wishing to host the smaller meetings that are becoming more important to these most profitable clients.

In general, we are optimistic about the market for MICE in the next ten years. The global economy may be troubled, but it remains fundamentally sound. The economic union of Europe, America's stubborn refusal to slip back into recession, and many other indicators suggest that it will be stronger in the future. Thus, the number of meetings, conventions, and expositions to be hosted each year will continue to grow, even as companies find it increasingly profitable to use incentives to motivate and reward their workers.

Still, the meetings and expositions market is in for some interesting times. Growth may be more difficult to achieve than it was in the boom of the 1980s and 1990s. Yet even in a world of e-mail, videoconferencing, and the Internet, human beings will always need to meet each other; in fact, face-to-face interaction—what we think of as "high touch"—may be even more important in a world where most contact is mediated by high-tech appliances. Expositions may be smaller, meetings may shift to private venues, and even the largest gatherings are likely to focus narrowly on a few specific tracks aimed at segments of their markets; like any other industry, meetings and expositions will change with the times. However, they will still take place, and they will need hotels, resorts, and conference centers to accommodate them.

There are not only challenges ahead, but opportunities and rewards—and for savvy participants in this industry, the opportunities will be very rewarding indeed.

Key Trends for Meetings and Expositions

In this section we look at the key trends for the MICE market, using entries from Appendix A. We list each relevant trend and our assessment of it and then detail the specific implications of this trend for meetings and expositions.

2. POPULATION OF THE DEVELOPED WORLD IS LIVING LONGER.

Assessment: Demographic trends such as this are among the easiest to recognize and most difficult to derail. Barring a global plague or nuclear war—wildcard possibilities that cannot be predicted with any validity—there is little chance that the population forecast for 2050 will err on the low side.

Implications for MICE: Health services for the elderly are one of the fastest growing fields in business throughout the industrialized world. They are also the fastest growing market for meetings and expositions.

Growth in this field will continue through at least 2020, when the Baby Boom generation will finally be vanishing from the global stage. However, this is subject to change. Any dramatic breakthrough in late-life wellness could reduce demand for geriatric services and medical care and deprive MICE of its most promising market.

9. TIME IS BECOMING THE WORLD'S MOST PRECIOUS COMMODITY.

Assessment: This trend is likely to grow as changing technologies add the need for lifelong study to the many commitments that compete for the average worker's time. As the trend matures in the United States, it is likely to survive in other parts of the world. It will not disappear until China and India reach modern post-industrial status, around 2050.

Implications for MICE: The need for small, high-productivity events is growing at the expense of larger, less intense gatherings.

Though faster travel means that destinations can hope for sales to more distant customers, nearer meeting locations still have an advantage.

Destinations with a broad range of on-site leisure activities giving guests more opportunities to relax and enjoy themselves during brief leisure moments will have a strong competitive advantage over those that are merely "near" attractions. This could shift more MICE activity to cruise ships, where all of the leisure activities can be found within a few hundred feet.

11. DESPITE SOME XENOPHOBIC REACTIONS TO IMMIGRANTS, THERE IS GROWING ACCEPTANCE OF DIVERSITY.

Assessment: This trend applies most clearly to the West, where it will continue for as long as we can foresee. In other regions, including Japan and large parts of the Muslim world, it remains weak, if it exists at all.

Implications for MICE: The spread of business-oriented culture should gradually build all aspects of this market.

As English becomes the universal language of business, it is becoming easier to arrange and conduct meetings.

The risk of cultural conflicts is declining, easing one major concern for planners of international gatherings.

12. TOURISM, VACATIONING, AND TRAVEL (ESPECIALLY INTERNATIONAL) CONTINUE TO GROW WITH EACH PASSING YEAR.

Assessment: Travel seems to be in the DNA of the middle and upper economic classes. This trend will continue as long as national economies continue to generate new prosperity for the formerly poor.

Implications for MICE: The tourism industry is a growing market for MICE. Tourists are clogging many major resort areas, forcing MICE planners to seek out new destinations. For the largest gatherings, this can be a difficult challenge.

17. GENERATION X, THE DOT-COMS, AND THE MILLENNIALS ARE GAINING SOCIAL AND ORGANIZATIONAL INFLUENCE.

Assessment: As trends go, this is an evergreen. In ten years or so, we will simply add the next new generation to the list.

Implications for MICE: The younger generations are extraordinarily entrepreneurial. Their new companies will provide a fast-growing market for MICE. However, their comfort with e-mail and virtual meetings may reduce their need to meet colleagues and customers in person.

The companies started by these new entrepreneurs will include many in the hospitality industry. This promises more intense competition in all aspects of the field, including MICE.

19. THE ECONOMY OF THE DEVELOPED WORLD IS GROWING STEADILY, WITH ONLY BRIEF INTERRUPTIONS.

Assessment: These trends have been revised many times since they were first codified in the late 1980s. Some trends have fallen off the list as they matured or as circumstances came along to change them. Others have been added as they were recognized. This trend has remained a constant, and with each revision its effective period has been extended. To invalidate this trend would take a catastrophe on the order of the loss of Middle Eastern oil from the Western economies. No such dramatic reversal of global fortune can be foreseen.

Implications for MICE: A growing GDP brings prosperity and confidence to companies, encouraging them to spend on secondary activities such as meetings and expositions.

Growth in the world-leading U.S. economy should help expand the market for international meetings and expositions, as expanding trade begins to fuel further growth for all trading partners.

Fear of terrorism is likely to prevent any dramatic growth in international gatherings for at least as long as American forces remain in Iraq.

24. WOMEN'S SALARIES ARE APPROACHING EQUALITY WITH MEN'S—BUT VERY SLOWLY.

Assessment: In the United States, this trend may be in its last generation, thanks to the gender-blind values of the Millennials. In other countries, and particularly Japan, it may have another thirty years to run.

Implications for MICE: This trend will affect MICE less than it affects other industries because hospitality has always depended more heavily than most industries on female employees and has paid them relatively well in return.

In the future, however, there will be more competition from other industries for the best new hires. This will require even better pay and benefits packages, with better opportunities for training and promotion.

This gives the largest players in the market an advantage over smaller firms with fewer opportunities to move up.

25. SPECIALIZATION CONTINUES TO SPREAD THROUGHOUT INDUSTRY AND THE PROFESSIONS.

Assessment: This process will continue for at least another twenty years.

Implications for MICE: This proliferation of niche markets offers many more opportunities for meetings and incentive packages. Making these sales requires constant market development, often targeted not just to the company but directly to the department.

28. THE WORK ETHIC IS VANISHING.

Assessment: There is little prospect that this will change until the children of today's young adults grow up to rebel against their parents' values.

Implications for MICE: Finding motivated, reliable workers is likely to be much harder in the years ahead, with more competition for them from competing employers.

Keeping them motivated will require constant attention and creativity from managers and upper executives.

36. TRANSPORTATION TECHNOLOGY AND PRACTICE ARE IMPROVING RAPIDLY.

Assessment: These advances will continue at least through mid-century.

Implications for MICE: Faster, cheaper travel makes more distant destinations more practical for incentives and relatively small corporate gatherings as well as international meetings and expositions.

39. TECHNOLOGY IS CREATING A KNOWLEDGE-DEPENDENT GLOBAL SOCIETY.

Assessment: This trend will not reach even its halfway mark until the rural populations of China and India gain modern educations and easy access to the Internet.

Implications for MICE: Executives find it easier to attend meetings and other events, because e-mail and instant messaging make it easier to keep in touch with their office and customers.

"Virtual meetings" online are beginning to replace quick business trips by one or two executives. This trend is likely to accelerate as executives from generations X and Dot-com take over from their less-Internet-savvy Baby Boom predecessors.

Computer-aided design (CAD), computer-aided manufacturing (CAM), and other forms of high-tech streamlining have so hastened product development that no one can wait for the next trade show to roll out new products. This is eroding the market for major expositions, but may generate smaller, special-purpose meetings.

Smaller destinations find it increasingly easy to reach potential customers worldwide.

Faster travel and the chance to choose among more destinations also reduce the lead time required to schedule a meeting. Destinations that can market directly to customers will have a further advantage over those who must work through third parties.

48. ORGANIZATIONS ARE SIMPLIFYING THEIR STRUCTURES AND SQUEEZING OUT PERSONNEL.

Assessment: In the United States, downsizing, restructuring, reorganization, and cutbacks of white-collar workers will continue at least through 2025. The pace will not slow unless technology ceases to deliver new ways to replace human workers with faster, cheaper, more reliable hardware and software.

Implications for MICE: Arranging MICE is one secondary function that many companies are sure to farm out. This should help to support the market for meeting management.

In companies that retain this function in-house, destinations and meeting managers should find it easier to identify the right executives to approach for future contracts.

53. INSTITUTIONS ARE UNDERGOING A BIMODAL DISTRIBUTION: THE BIG GET BIGGER, THE SMALL SURVIVE, AND THE MID-SIZED ARE SQUEEZED OUT.

Assessment: Thanks in part to technology, this trend is likely to be a permanent feature of the business scene from now on.

Implications for MICE: When companies combine, they reduce the number of possible buyers for MICE and related services. They also eliminate duplicate functions, reducing the number of employees available to attend industry gatherings. At some point, the trend toward consolidation will reach meeting management companies and other segments of this industry, as it has so many others.

Endnotes

1. *MPI Business Barometer November 2008*, Meeting Professionals International. Accessed April 5, 2009, at www.mpiweb.org/CMS/uploadedFiles/Education_and_Events/Knowledge_Base/BusinessBarometer_Nov08.pdf.

2. *FutureWatch2009: A Comparative Outlook on the Global Business of Meetings and Events*, Meeting Professionals International. Accessed April 7, 2009, at www.mpiweb.org/CMS/uploadedFiles/Research_and_Whitepapers/FutureWatch2009.pdf.

3. Personal communication, February 2004.

4. Personal communication, March 2004.

5. Personal communication, June 2003.

6. Personal communication, March 2004.

7

Water, Water Everywhere: The Cruise Industry

CRUISING IS HOT, HOT, HOT, and not just when the weather turns sultry. Passenger loads have grown from a mere 500,000 in 1970 to 12.5 million in 2007 and an estimated 12.8 million in 2008. More than eighty ocean-going cruise lines with more than 250 ships now visit some 2,000 destinations, and guests can choose from more than 30,000 different cruises each year. Bookings have been expanding by 7.4 percent annually since 1990, the fastest growth rate in the hospitality industry.

Yet it has not all been clear sailing for the cruise sector. In 2001, some ten million people booked passage on the world's cruise lines. The terrorist attacks of September 11 slashed that demand. In the following weeks, seven ocean-going lines and one river cruise line either went out of business or filed for bankruptcy protection. Drastic price cuts brought business back—in the first half of 2002, ticket sales actually were up 4.3 percent over the previous year—but the discounts decimated profit.

The cruise industry entered a similar period late in 2008, when the worst chaos since the Great Depression struck the world's economies. As a luxury segment of the travel market, the cruise used to be relatively resistant to economic downturns; even in bad times, the rich can usually afford a vacation. Today, the majority of passengers are middle class, and they are not about to take a cruise when barely making ends meet and terrified that the next round of pink slips may put them out on the street. In December 2008, when it had become clear that the current recession was not just a minor downturn, Carnival Corporation reported that cruise bookings were running behind their pace a year earlier, even though prices were down.

That has changed dramatically, thanks to some of the most persuasive sales incentives the cruise lines have ever offered. Among the deals bringing timid consumers back to the ship:

- Carnival is offering discounts of up to 25 percent for bookings made up to three months in advance for cruises of up to five days and five months in advance for longer excursions.

- On the *Disney Wonder*, passengers under twelve sailed free for three-day voyages for a limited time.

- Holland America Line is offering low fares, 50 percent discounts on deposits and cruise tours, and 25 percent off the standard cancellation protection plan.

- Seabourn is giving discounts of $1,000 per suite on top of early booking savings of up to 50 percent on all seven-day Mediterranean cruises in 2009, $1,500 per suite plus early booking savings of up to 45 percent on northern Europe/Scandinavia cruises, and a host of other incentives.

All this has been remarkably successful, given the state of the American economy. January 12, 2009, was the best booking day ever for Princess Cruises, with volume up 17 percent over the previous best. Expedia CruiseShipCenters reported that bookings made in January 2009 were ahead of the previous January by 14 percent. That money-saving "staycation" does not look so good when a cruise hardly costs any more.

The industry is not out of trouble yet. All these discounts are eroding profitability, and even they may not be enough to bring passengers onboard if the recession gets much deeper. In addition, capacity is rising faster than demand is likely to; thirty-six new cruise liners are scheduled for delivery between 2008 and 2012, with several more planned but not yet in the yards.

Forces Affecting the Cruise Lines

All of this brings up obvious questions: How bad will the slump be? How long will it take the cruise industry to recover? How long will cruise prices remain depressed? How can cruise operators turn slow-growing demand into solid profits? How can they adapt to the challenges of a fast-changing world?

We have some ideas. The following sections discuss how the most important forces affecting the cruise lines will play out.

U.S. Economy

Nothing is as important to the cruise industry as the American economy. Approximately 80 percent of cruise tickets are sold to Americans. One recent study found that only 20 percent of Americans have taken a cruise, but half dream of doing so. According to the Cruise Lines International Association's (CLIA) 2008 Cruise Market Profile Study, some 51 million hoped to make that dream a reality between 2008 and 2010. Many of these potential customers may at least consider taking a cruise when they feel economically secure. But in bad economic times, the American cruise market shrinks, and it takes radical price cuts and other inducements to fill berths.

In early 2009, consumers are still afraid, and they have reason to be. GDP shrank by 3.8 percent in the fourth quarter of 2008, and most analysts expect it to keep heading down for at least two more quarters. Home prices slid 12 percent in the last three months of 2008, the biggest drop on record; they were down again in January 2009. More than 100,000 homes were in foreclosure in the first month of the year. Employment numbers were even more terrifying. Employers cut nearly 600,000 jobs in January, bringing unemployment to 7.6 percent, the highest it had been in more than sixteen years. Most forecasts say that it will reach double digits before the hemorrhaging stops. And if many working-class Americans think the economy feels worse than it sounds, they have good reason. If unemployment were still calculated as it was in the 1980s, the rate would already be about 17 percent.

We expect the economic problems to continue through much of 2009 and the slowness of the likely recovery thereafter will keep both prices and profits down until well into 2010.

So the following comes as good news: The current economic collapse should not last as long as many observers feared. In mid-February 2009, we believe that the economy will begin a new period of expansion before the end of the year. Growth will be slow at first, but by 2010 GDP growth should return to the area of 2.5 to 3 percent, where it will remain for at least the next few years.

This is important news for cruise lines, whose potential customers have been finding it hard to commit themselves to a cruise vacation even with steep discounts and other profit-killing incentives. This is one case where a rising tide floats all cruise ships.

Keep in mind, however, that this analysis presumes that the Obama administration will follow its recently enacted stimulus plan with at least one more round of government spending and a much larger program to stabilize and reform the American banking system. If the federal government does not find some way to employ several million people lost from other sectors of the economy and get the credit system working again, the downturn could be much longer and the dip in the cruise market more lasting and severe.

Aging Population

Throughout the developed world, people are living longer and, on average, growing older. (Demographically, one does not necessarily imply the other.) Life expectancy in Australia, Japan, and Switzerland is now over seventy-five years for men and over eighty for women. In the United States, every generation has lived three years longer than the previous one. An eighty-year-old in 1950 could expect 6.5 more years of life; today's eighty-year-olds are likely to survive 8.5 more years.

As a result, and because birth rates are declining throughout most of the industrialized world, older people now make up more of the population than they used to. Their numbers will continue to grow. People over sixty-five were only 8 percent of the population in the developed world in 1950, but 15 percent in 2000, and will grow to 27 percent in the next half century, according to the Center for Strategic and International Studies. In Germany, people of retirement age will climb from under 16 percent of the population in 2000 to nearly 19 percent in 2010 and 31 percent in 2050. Japan's over-sixty-five population, 17 percent of the total in 2000, will reach 22 percent in 2010 and nearly 37 percent in 2050.

This is important because older people are now the wealthiest segment of society and the most likely to have the time for an extended cruise. According to CLIA's 2008 Cruise Market Profile Study, about 24 percent of Baby Boomers, now in their peak earning years, have taken at least one cruise, compared with only 19 percent in the over-sixty group. However, well-to-do seniors generally take the longest and most luxurious cruises. Unlike younger, family- and budget-minded passengers, they tend to prefer smaller ships, giving up tennis courts and ping pong tables in return for all-out pampering. As the giant Baby Boom generation ages, the upper end of the cruise market can only grow rapidly.

The growth of the over-sixty-five market will moderate the habitual seasonality of tourism, because retirees can travel off-season and prefer to do so when it can save them some money. This should help to even out the cash flow of cruise operators.

To serve these demanding customers, some cruise lines have adapted their ships to the needs of older passengers. Others should follow their lead. Obvious features for the elderly include safety handholds in bathrooms and showers, larger signs with easy-to-read type, and large levered door handles for arthritic hands. Older cruisers also need special services such as help in moving their belongings and information about the physical demands of side trips. Such amenities will be increasingly important in the years ahead.

Growing Tourism

The number of Americans traveling to foreign countries (excluding Canada and Mexico) grew by 5 percent per year from 1981 through 1996. That expansion has slowed considerably in recent years, owing to fears of terrorism after September 11, concern about possibly hostile receptions abroad due to the Iraq war, and the weakness of the dollar on foreign exchange markets. Yet Americans continued to drive the growth of the cruise industry until the global recession took the wind out of their sails.

Those American tourists will soon be joined by the growing middle classes of India and China. By 2013, China is expected to be the single largest source of international tourists in the world, displacing Americans, Japanese, and Germans as the planet's busiest travelers. (The target date was 2010 until the recession hit.) Already, more than eighty-five million Chinese are believed to be able to afford international vacations. By 2023, 100 million Chinese tourists will fan out across the globe. (Again, the pre-recession estimate was 2020.) If just 1 percent of them take a cruise each year, they will more than double the cruise market. Long before that, cruise lines will begin to offer cruises and onboard amenities suited to Chinese and Indian tastes, while native Chinese and Indian cruise lines will appear to serve their local market.

In recent years, short-distance activities have added to the bottom line of flexible, market-savvy cruise operators. These include shipboard meetings, brief "cruises to nowhere," scenic cruises during fall foliage season, and trips to nearby destinations—for example, from the Gulf coasts of Florida and Texas to Mexico. We expect similar cruise operations to appear in the Indian, Chinese, and Japanese markets.

One more source of change is the growing number of destinations for cruises. In addition to new resorts and adventure experiences, many passengers will be attracted by unique facilities such as the extraordinarily beautiful Bibliotheca Alexandrina in Egypt, a recreation of the fabled Library of Alexandria, whose exterior walls are covered in passages from the Rosetta Stone. Another spectacular new destination is the Burj Al Arab, a literally ship-shape sixty-story hotel in Dubai where diners travel to the underwater, glass-ceilinged seafood restaurant by submarine. At least thirty new hotels were scheduled to open in Dubai in 2008 alone. One slated for 2009 is more than sixty-five feet under water and accessible only by elevator. Serving these profitable niche markets will require small, luxurious ships suited to shallow ports and discerning cruisers.

High Tech, High Touch

The more dependent we become on technology, the more we require the attention of a friendly, courteous human being to soothe our jangled nerves. Fortunately, that very high-tech environment increasingly brings us the human contact we crave. The finest cruise ships now provide the best of both worlds, using technology to provide comfort, connectivity, and entertainment at sea and a large, well-trained staff to tend the passengers' every need.

For example, Hapag-Lloyd's opulent, German-speaking *Europa* offers a state-of-the-art "Cruise Infotainment System" that combines a capable PC and Internet connectivity with twenty-four-hour video and audio on demand in all suites. Outboard power pods pull the ship through the water with absolutely no vibration or noise. The two suites for the disabled provide electronically oper-ated beds with hydraulic lifts. High tech all the way.

Yet the vessel's most spectacular features are the appointments provided for guests, including the attention of 1.7 highly trained crew members per passenger. Cabin stewardesses serve nearly every stateroom; the twelve premium accommo-dations have a butler. Deck stewards spritz sunbathers with cooling Evian water. Fresh flowers abound. Penthouse guests enjoy a fully stocked bar, hand-made chocolates, and caviar on request. No wonder *Berlitz Ocean Cruising & Cruise Ships* gives *Europa* five-stars-plus, the only ship in the world to attain that rating.

However, what may be the epitome of high touch is found on the Seabourn line, where every member of the staff begins each cruise by studying photographs of the passengers. By the end of the second day, they can address every guest by name. It is a courtesy that astonishes many first-time passengers and is appreci-ated by all.

In the future, computer data mining will enable cruise lines to do the kind of personalized marketing to cruise passengers that is now being pioneered in hotels and resorts. Crew members will not only be able to recognize guests, but will "remember" what meals and entertainment cruisers enjoyed on previous voyages and be able to suggest appropriate activities for their current trip.

Not every vessel, nor even every line, can hope to provide guests with that level of luxury and attention. Yet this is the balance all must work toward, a com-bination of high-tech conveniences with personal attention that leaves passengers feeling pampered—and eager for their next voyage.

Energy Economy

Cruise ships will never be cheap to run, but at least they will not be burdened by high oil prices. The $140+ per barrel oil of mid-2008 was an aberration, brought on by a combination of rising demand from China and India, inadequate global refin-ing capacity, and rampant speculation. New oil supplies are coming online in the former Soviet Union, China, and other parts of the world, and several new refiner-ies will come online in Saudi Arabia and Russia by 2012. In all, oil will generally remain in the neighborhood of $65 per barrel for the foreseeable future. That is a long way from the $25 per barrel the world was accustomed to as recently as the late 1990s, but it is a price that crude operators can live with.

It helps that cruise lines worked hard to improve their fuel efficiency during the bad times. Diesel-electric ships usually are designed to run at about twenty knots, but maintaining that speed means running the engines flat-out. Cruising just one knot slower can reduce fuel consumption by 5 to 10 percent. Most cruise ships now sail just a bit more leisurely than they could. Many have added monitors to make sure the engines run as efficiently as possible. Some have installed energy management systems to even out the peaks and valleys in electrical demand. And, of course, operators are reducing drag by making sure the hull and propellers are scrupulously clean. According to industry experts, doing everything possible to save energy on a cruise ship can cut fuel use by 30 to 40 percent. Given the lessons learned in 2008 and implemented since then, fuel costs should not be a serious problem for cruise lines in the foreseeable future.

Cleaning Up

Several years ago, a research vessel crossed the middle of the Atlantic, taking samples of what it found along the way. When they reached land, the scientists told of packaging materials, clumps of tar, and even human waste floating hundreds of miles from land. The report made headlines in newspapers and magazines across the United States.

Since then, scientists have recognized that garbage collects at the center of many circular current patterns in both the Atlantic and the Pacific. One such patch of floating debris in the north Pacific holds an estimated 100 million tons of trash, most of it plastic. Some 80 percent of this material comes from land. Yet much of the remainder is believed to originate with cruise ships.

Gone are the days when vessels could casually dump their wastes near land. Yet it does happen. Ten years or so ago, Royal Caribbean International, Norwegian Cruise Line, and Carnival were all fined—in one case up to $27 million—for dumping oily bilge water, plastic trash, raw sewage, and even toxic chemicals. Crystal Cruises' *Crystal Harmony* was banned from Monterey Bay after dumping sewage and bilge water in October 2002.

U.S. regulations now ban discarding raw sewage and food wastes within three miles of shore and limit the amount of oil in dumped bilge water to just fifteen parts per million. Yet these regulations allow gray water and treated sewage to be discharged anywhere. The average cruise ship produces more than 200,000 gallons of it per day.

Many cruise lines have gone a long way to clean up their act. Royal Caribbean has long processed all its bilge water on trips to Alaska. It even carries an environmental compliance officer on each trip there. Crystal Cruises switched to more expensive, less polluting fuel years ago and voluntarily reported the Monterey Bay incident. Modern cruise ships are equipped with extensive treatment plants for bilge water and sewage and with storage facilities for other wastes, but there is clearly room for improvement.

Forecasting International (FI) believes the rules for dumping waste at sea will be tightened drastically within ten years. Those rules will be enforced by satellite surveillance and other technologies. In the future, alarms will sound if wastes are dumped near land, and discharge of raw sewage and other noxious substances will be banned anywhere at sea. Eventually, new ships may even be required to have double hulls in critical sections to prevent loss of toxic materials in a collision.

Technology Improves Transport

Outboard power pods on ships such as the *Queen Mary 2 (QM2)* are an example of a relatively recent innovation; they propel ships efficiently, quietly, and without vibration and make even the largest vessels far more maneuverable. Better stabilizers, satellite navigation, computerized controls, and even the computer-aided design systems that make it possible to build a new ship in two years instead of five are improving the business of cruising.

At the same time, design innovations are helping to better the cruise experience. On the *QM2*, which launched in 2004, one of the five pools has a retractable glass roof to combine the best features of indoor and outdoor swimming—a feature copied on MSC *Magnifica* (December 2009). Costa *Luminosa* (May 2009) has a roller skating rink and an eighteen-hole golf course "simulator." Royal Caribbean's *Oasis of the Seas*—which will be the world's largest cruise ship at 5,400 passengers and 40 percent larger than the second-place vessel, the line's own Freedom class—will have the first onboard "zipline" for the adventure-minded, plus state-of-the-art lofts and a levitating bar that ascends and descends over three decks. Seabourn's *Odyssey* will provide the greatest luxury of all: elbow room. The first new "six star" ship in six years, it boasts one of the highest space-per-passenger ratios at sea; 90 percent of its 225 suites offer full-sized balconies.

Many other new technologies will be less noticeable, but equally appreciated by guests. Radio frequency identification (RFID) chips will make it possible to track every item in the ship's inventory, so the purser will never run short of delicacies or consumable items for the passengers. Computers and other devices are making it possible to personalize customer experiences in the grocery, retail, and food service markets. Cruise passengers will expect that same level of technology-driven personal care onboard ship.

In the years ahead, these and many other novelties will continue to make cruising more economical for operators and more pleasurable for their passengers. Expect to see floating islands that act as artificial ports, even more efficient engines and waste management systems, more small and modern coastal vessels optimized for the run to Alaska and the New England foliage season, and all manner of new amenities for guests.

Cyber-Cruising

These days, you *can* take it with you and pretty much have to. The Internet, that is. It's a rare user of e-mail who can stand to be away from his or her inbox for more than a day or two at a time, and many cruise passengers love being able to share vacations with friends and relatives almost as they happen. The increasingly rare hotels that do not offer free Wi-Fi for guests are losing revenues to those that do. Over the last five years, Internet access has become standard fare on nearly all cruise lines.

The exponential growth of the Internet has one more implication for cruise operators, and it is one that many cruise executives are reluctant to accept: The Internet has revolutionized the travel industry. An estimated 95 percent of travelers with Internet access now seek travel information online, and many are booking their own trips, either with online agencies or directly with the airline, hotel, or resort. This trend extends to business as well as personal travel. Expedia Corporate Travel alone reported gross travel bookings of $1.3 billion for 2007.

This development has had a predictable effect on travel agencies. The number of travel offices in the United States declined by 50 percent in the ten years through 2006. According to PhoCusWright, travel agents still booked 38 percent of the total travel market as recently as 2007. By 2010, that amount is expected to come in at just 33 percent. Of 24,000 travel agencies surviving in the United States in 2008, just sixty-five account for 47 percent of all bookings! Many of the rest are single-person "online travel consultants"—the one real growth area in the agency business. Many of these online consultants are niche operators specializing in such areas as adventure travel or ecotourism. One agent we've heard of does nothing but book trips for twins!

Thus far, the cruise industry has lagged well behind this trend. At least four out of five cruise bookings are still made through travel agents; the American Society of Travel Agents claims it is 87 percent. This cannot last. Internet users are accustomed to the convenience of shopping online. They expect the companies they do business with to provide the information they need online, where it can be browsed at will. And as cyber-wary seniors begin to leave the market, they will be replaced by Internet-savvy Gen Xers and Dot-coms who have little patience with the stately pace of offline sales. The transition to Internet-based marketing will largely bypass the luxury market, where customers prefer to have others do the tedious work of putting the travel package together. Two-earner families, those on a budget, and habitually informed consumers will take much more of the cruise shopping process into their own hands.

Eventually, there may simply be too few travel agents to meet the needs of the cruise lines. Cruise lines cannot support all the world's travel agents on their own, and it seems that no one else has much interest in doing so. This transition will be gradual, but it is inevitable. Five years from now, travel agents will be much less important to the cruise lines, while the Internet will account for a significant and growing portion of bookings.

Time Is Precious

Two-earner households just don't have much of it. Neither do affluent singles. In the United States, workers spend about 10 percent more time on the job than they did a decade ago, and that number is higher for highly paid white-collar workers. Executives and nonunionized workers elsewhere face the same trend. Even in France, which long maintained a thirty-five-hour legal workweek, the average employee spends forty-one hours a week on the job. In Korea, the average work week is forty-six hours, the longest in the world.

In this high-pressure environment, consumers are increasingly desperate for any product or service that offers a taste of luxury—and many of them can afford to pay for it. Cruises offer that taste of luxury.

Catering to this market will require some obvious adaptations: more short cruises, more three-day "cruises to nowhere," more departures from ports within driving range of their homes, still more attention to children's activities and facilities for the families of young, harried parents. (The average age of first-time cruise passengers is now under forty, thanks to industry marketing efforts aimed primarily at the twenty-five-and-over age group.) Given that Carnival Cruise Lines expects to carry more than 600,000 children in 2009, and cruise ships are now being docked at lesser ports from San José to Boston, it seems these changes are well under way.

The desire to mark the passage of time also presents opportunities for cruise operators. Older passengers often are concerned with life milestones—anniversaries, birthdays, and other opportunities for family gatherings. This is a clear market for brief, relatively inexpensive cruises. It is likely to grow as the economy improves and the retirement-age population grows.

Bang, You're Dead!

Terrorism is a long way from dead, as suicide bombings and other attacks have proved from Saudi Arabia to Bali. In fact, there is every reason to believe that al-Qaeda is reconstituting itself and a new round of large-scale attacks may not be far off.

To date, only one cruise vessel has ever been attacked by terrorists—the *Achille Lauro* in 1985. Yet commercial piracy is a growing problem, especially on routes past Africa. Somali pirates seized control of the French cruise ship *Le Ponat* in April 2008 as it returned from a trip without passengers, but the attackers released their thirty hostages under threat from elite French troops. Another band of Somalis attempted to hijack the Oceania *Nautica* in December 2008 off the coast of Yemen, but the vessel outran them. The two incidents proved harmless, but they have caused many cruise lines to change their routes to avoid the danger area.

The fact that cruise ships are increasingly being used as floating hotels is increasing the level of concern regarding terrorism. As early as February 2004, the *QM2* docked in Rio de Janeiro so that cruisers could enjoy *carnivale*, giving would-be terrorists access to a stationary target. And during the Olympics in Greece, many cruise vessels were moored in the harbor throughout the event to supplement scarce landside hotel space. Despite a $1.2 billion security program that included a new sonar system to protect the Athens harbor against attack by submarine, this was one of the most obvious opportunities for a terrorist spectacular we have ever seen. That Greek authorities managed to defend these ships successfully was a very impressive accomplishment.

For cruise lines elsewhere, many other security measures already are in place. Onboard *bon voyage* parties, once a normal part of cruising, have been eliminated because only passengers are allowed on ship. Entering port in the United States, ships now pick up six "sea marshals" along with the pilot. Two remain on the bridge, two watch over the engine room, and two patrol the remainder of the vessel. In Miami, divers from the local fire department carefully examine the ship for clinging mines, and a Coast Guard cutter leads the ship into port, watching for high-speed attackers such as the small boat that assaulted the *USS Cole* in Yemen.

In the years ahead, cruise operators will be forced to tighten security beyond current standards. They will have to screen not only passengers, but everyone who has contact with the vessel—food loaders, baggage handlers, port pilots, and their own disgruntled employees and former employees. Baggage screening will always be too expensive to handle at the individual-ship level and will be taken care of as people enter the dock by government employees, private security firms under contract to the Department of Homeland Security, or industry associations. Some cruise lines have already stopped the age-old practice of putting name tags on luggage at the airport for fear that would-be terrorists could slip a bomb or hazardous material into a bag before it ever reached the ship.

Security is as important for small inland cruises as it is for ocean-going liners. On the Potomac, tour boats glide past within striking distance of the Kennedy Center, where a bomb could endanger 40,000 people. Many ships that cruise down the Mississippi and other waterways also pass within easy reach of populous, vulnerable targets. Consequently, Coast Guard regulations now require that even tour boat passengers be screened.

Security measures are a difficult adjustment for both cruise passengers and the companies that carry them. There is something about being treated as a potential hijacker that conflicts fundamentally with the sense of luxury and pampering that cruisers signed up for and cruise operators aim to provide.

We will just have to get used to it. From now on, boarding a ship is going to look more and more like running the gauntlet at a busy airport. The alternative is even worse.

Savvy Consumers

A networked society is a consumerist society. Shoppers today can search the Internet for information about pricing, services, delivery time, and peer reviews of all manner of goods and services. Already, the monthly Internet newsletter *CruiseReports* delivers reviews of cruise ships, complete with passenger comments, directly to the reader's e-mail box. Over the next few years, this trend will sweep through the cruise industry—disappoint one passenger, and thousands of potential customers will hear about it.

Norwegian Cruise Line showed how not to handle problems in April 2003, when ice in the Gulf of Finland forced *Norwegian Dream* to cancel stops at Helsinki, Tallinn, and—unforgivably—St. Petersburg, the high point of the trip. Passengers learned of the changes only when they checked in at Dover, and they were offered compensation of only $100 to $200 each, amounts that sent irate cruisers on stage to harangue fellow passengers in a near-revolt. As one dismayed agent commented, "They've come a long way to see St. Petersburg, and $150 ain't going to cut it." The Internet carried that tale around the world, no doubt in the words of the angriest customers.

A world of savvy, demanding, networked consumers requires still greater effort to give passengers the best possible cruise. It may be even more important to soothe their frustrations when something goes wrong.

Shock and Aahs

Throughout the business world, institutions are undergoing what FI calls bimodal distribution. The big get bigger. The small survive, and some of them do quite well. But mid-sized competitors are squeezed out, because they are not flexible enough to prosper in niche markets and cannot achieve the economies of scale enjoyed by the giants of their industries.

Similarly, purveyors of high-end luxury products flourish, as exceptionally good restaurants demonstrate. The fast-food chains also make it; cheap products fill a need for those who cannot afford better. But mid-priced family restaurants eventually go broke.

We see this trend among auto manufacturers, computer makers, farms, banks, and very clearly in the airline industry. We are beginning to see it among cruise lines.

Those companies that failed or took refuge in Chapter 11 after the 2001 terrorist attack represent the vulnerable middle of the industry, underfunded and without the kind of core market it takes to survive. For the mass market, there is Carnival Cruise Lines; on the luxury end, there are Silversea and Carnival's subsidiary, Seabourn.

Carnival's ships are big, from roughly 85,000 to 110,000 tons, with stateroom capacities that range from about 2,100 to nearly 3,000 passengers. The atmosphere is relentlessly upbeat, with constant music and passenger games, but there is none of the emphasis on luxury typical of some other lines. The food is adequate, the cabins large enough, the glasses plastic—at least on deck and in the Lido Buffet. This is the McDonald's of the cruise industry, and it is spectacularly successful. Carnival's mass appeal has made it the largest cruise line in the world.

At the other end of the spectrum, we need look at only one ship—the spectacular new *QM2*, which sailed on its maiden voyage for Carnival's Cunard subsidiary in January 2004. This is the largest, fastest cruise ship ever built—150,000 tons, nearly a quarter-mile long, 100 feet taller than the Eiffel tower, able to carry 3,090 passengers across the Atlantic at speeds up to thirty knots.

Carnival set out to make the world's most luxurious cruising ship. The result, built at a cost of $780 million, is likely to provoke shock and "aahs." Even its smallest staterooms offer 194 square feet of sumptuous appointments. Its largest—two Grand Duplex apartments at the stern—can be combined with the penthouses above to create a single apartment with an unprecedented 8,288 square feet of floor space. Even the most modest accommodations, to whatever extent the concept of modesty applies to any part of this vessel, are equipped with a twenty-inch television and attached computer keyboard providing digital video, music, and audiobooks on demand with e-mail access. There are fourteen bars, ten restaurants, five swimming pools, a gymnasium, a spa with twenty-four treatment rooms, and even a putting green. In the words of one observer, "This is the ship God would have made if he had the cash flow." Carnival does, thanks to its firm hold on both the mass market and luxury ends of the cruise industry.

However, *QM2* was not the world's largest cruise ship for long. In fact, Royal Caribbean's *Mariner of the Seas*, launched late in 2003, already carried more passengers, 3,114, and the line's 1,112-foot-long, 3,634-passenger *Freedom of the Seas* was launched in June 2006. Royal Caribbean has ordered a still larger vessel for delivery late in 2009. Dubbed "Project Genesis" (to be named *Oasis of the Seas*), the ship will be 1,181 feet long, displacing 220,000 tons, with room for 5,400 passengers.

As this business grows more competitive, large and successful cruise lines increasingly will follow one of these models. Some will cater to relatively unsophisticated first-time passengers. Others will aim for discriminating cruise enthusiasts who can pay to be pampered. Smaller players will specialize in niche markets such as coastal cruises or expedition, nature, or adventure excursions. Mid-sized, mid-range operators will slowly disappear. That is just the way things are in the global economy.

Competitive Advantage

At both ends of the spectrum, the battle for market share will grow ever more challenging, which is in the nature of worldwide competition. Cruise lines will use several tools and offerings to make it in this difficult environment.

One is specialized attractions for niche markets. Theme cruises already are popular. There have been highly successful trips specializing in adventure themes, astronomy, bridge, chess, computer science, education, film festivals, gays and lesbians, murder mysteries, and nudism. We will see many more such enticements in the future. In fact, the future itself could be a marketable theme, with lectures covering technology, medicine, economics, social issues, and other important, fast-changing fields.

Well-known celebrities, entertainers, and guest lecturers fall into this same category. Whenever someone writes a best-selling book, acts on a hit television show, or sings a pop song, they create a niche market for cruise lines. We would not be surprised to learn that the winners from *American Idol* have been booked on Carnival or one of its mass-market competitors.

Yield Management

A key marketing technique still relatively new to the cruise industry is yield management. The basic idea is simple. Companies keep careful track of how their products are selling. If time is growing short and something needs to be moved out the door, it is discounted and advertised heavily until it sells.

This is basic marketing—computerized, turbocharged, and driven by up-to-the-minute sales and inventory statistics. It can work remarkably well. In one typical case, after the SARS epidemic broke out in Asia, *Crystal Harmony* was abruptly repositioned to Los Angeles. Bookings were heavily discounted and sold out in just five days.

Yield marketing cries out for the Internet, where prices can be changed around the world at the touch of a few keys. Predictably, some of its most effective practitioners in the travel industry are online discounters such as Expedia, Travelocity, and Orbitz. Profit-minded cruise lines, however, will want to bring this function in-house to route cash flow to their own bottom lines. This means that a dramatic expansion of websites and the adoption of Internet-oriented sales techniques are all but inevitable. In five to seven years, cruise operators will be every bit as dependent on Internet sales as the airline industry.

Ten Trends—Plus One

Smarter Travel (www.smartertravel.com) recently surveyed developments in the cruise industry. Many of the trends identified there paralleled Forecasting International's observations. Here is its list:

- Excitement over the enormous new *Oasis of the Seas*, even before the hype has really begun.

- The growth of *à la carte* billing with extra charges for spa treatments, Internet use, phone access, shore excursions, and so on. At least the fuel surcharges from 2008 have been dropped.

- Growing interest in exotic cruises to such places as Australia, New Zealand, Asia, Latin America, and the Middle East. For briefer trips, there is parallel renaissance in cruises to Bermuda, the Caribbean, and the Mexican Riviera for North Americans and the Mediterranean and Baltic for their peers in the United Kingdom.

- Luxury builds are returning with ships from Seabourn and Silversea, the first truly high-end vessels in a decade. Think extra space and larger spas. At least two more luxury ships are due in 2010.

- Upgrades are another major trend. Carnival, Holland America, and Princess all have made big investments to refurbish older ships. Carnival has already finished work on *Fantasy, Inspiration, Imagination,* and *Sensation,* and it has four more ships slated for modernization. Holland America has just finished one upgrade program and has announced that it will send five more ships to drydock for work. Regent Seven Seas Cruises is upgrading its three all-suite ships. And so it goes throughout much of the industry.

- Seven-night cruises are out, and three-, four-, and five-night cruises are in. Busy households just don't have the time for longer commitments these days. And in the global recession of 2008–09, they probably don't have the money, either—or, at least, the confidence to spend it.

- Shipboard dining used to be almost as regimented as military dining. You'd eat on schedule at your assigned table. No longer. Many lines, though not yet all, are opening up their restaurants so that passengers can eat whenever the impulse strikes.

- Last-minute deals are back, thanks to the weak global economy. Cruise lines with space to sell are slashing rates on trips leaving as soon as next weekend. It has never been easier to travel on the spur of the moment.

- Cruise lines increasingly want to tap local markets, so they are putting their ships where the customers are—in smaller regional ports rather than in the major travel centers. Carnival *Pride* is spending its entire year in Baltimore! If you live on one of the American coasts, there probably is at least one cruise ship within easy driving distance.

- Solo passengers used to be the Rodney Dangerfields of the cruise world: They got no respect. Suddenly, that has changed. The extra charges to occupy a single room are quickly disappearing. Fred. Olsen Cruise Lines not only reserves some cabins for lone occupants, it also decorates them with the single passenger in mind, replacing the extra bed with a settee.

We will add one more trend to this list: Cruise lines are growing either more solicitous of their well-off passengers or downright snobby, depending on which side of the velvet rope you occupy. Guests used to share all of a ship's public spaces, no matter which class of stateroom they chose to pay for. That is no longer true. Royal Caribbean, MSC Cruises, Norwegian Cruise Line, and even Carnival are setting aside exclusive restaurants, pools, and spas for their top-dollar patrons. Telling some cruisers, in effect, that they are a bit less exclusive than others marks an important change in the "luxury for all" image that cruise lines have maintained for many years. We suspect, however, that the appeal of a stress-free holiday on the sea will survive this slightly grating intrusion of the real world.

Through 2015

The next few years will be a difficult time for the travel industry in general and for cruise lines in particular. A deep global recession makes a difficult market for costly products; in 2009, even the relatively inelastic luxury market is feeling the effects. Yet the urge to travel appears to be in our cultural genes. It will not disappear simply because times are tough. Cruise lines that can provide a quality experience at the right price will continue to prosper.

"Making it" in a tight economy calls for efficiency and adaptability. Tomorrow's cruise lines will be even more flexible, even more in tune with the needs of their changing, and growing, markets. As a result, we believe they will be some of the most dynamic and profitable companies in the world.

Key Trends for the Cruise Lines

In this section we look at the key trends for cruise lines, using entries from Appendix A. We list each relevant trend and our assessment of it and then detail the specific implications of this trend for the cruise lines.

2. POPULATION OF THE DEVELOPED WORLD IS LIVING LONGER.

Assessment: Demographic trends such as this are among the easiest to recognize and most difficult to derail. Barring a global plague or nuclear war—wildcard possibilities that cannot be predicted with any validity—there is little chance that the population forecast for 2050 will err on the low side.

Implications for Cruise Lines: Older people make up a growing segment of the cruise market. Since they form the wealthiest segment of industrialized societies, retirement-age consumers are also the most likely to take cruise vacations, particularly for the longest and most luxurious cruises.

Younger travelers form a profitable market for family-oriented cruises. One of the biggest advantages of catering to them is the opportunity to build brand loyalty for their later lives, when they will be the most profitable cruisers.

Retired people are free to take trips when they wish, rather than when it suits an employer. They are beginning to even out the traditional seasonality of travel.

Older passengers need amenities suited to their physical limitations. Examples include signs with larger type, lever door handles rather than knobs, safety grips in bathrooms and showers, and extra help with their luggage.

9. TIME IS BECOMING THE WORLD'S MOST PRECIOUS COMMODITY.

Assessment: This trend is likely to grow as changing technologies add the need for lifelong study to the many commitments that compete for the average worker's time. As this trend matures in the United States, it is likely to survive in other parts of the world. It will not disappear until China and India reach modern post-industrial status, around 2050.

Implications for Cruise Lines: Harried two-earner households are eager for any luxury they can find—and many of them can afford to pay for it. Many see a cruise vacation as the ultimate luxury.

What many of them cannot afford is time. Growing numbers will take brief "cruises to nowhere," long-weekend coastal cruises, and short segments of longer cruises, preferably leaving from regional ports near their homes.

12. TOURISM, VACATIONING, AND TRAVEL (ESPECIALLY INTERNATIONAL) CONTINUE TO GROW WITH EACH PASSING YEAR.

Assessment: Travel seems to be in the DNA of the middle and upper economic classes. This trend will continue as long as national economies continue to generate new prosperity for the formerly poor.

Implications for Cruise Lines: The market for cruises will grow at least as fast as the travel market in general. If the American economy begins to expand rapidly again, cruising should grow even more rapidly. Many consumers view cruising as one of the most desirable forms of vacation, even if they have never taken a cruise themselves. In affluent times, they will be even more inclined to indulge their wish for luxury by signing up for a voyage.

Within ten years, the number of Chinese and Indian cruisers will justify providing amenities and even designing cruises specifically for their tastes. By 2020, we expect to see several new cruise lines based in China and India and catering to the needs of local vacationers.

The growth of tourism will inspire the development of many new destinations, giving cruise ships new ports of call to interest their passengers. Some of those destinations will be developed with the growing Asian tourist markets in mind.

19. THE ECONOMY OF THE DEVELOPED WORLD IS GROWING STEADILY, WITH ONLY BRIEF INTERRUPTIONS.

Assessment: These trends have been revised many times since they were first codified in the late 1980s. Some trends have fallen out of the list as they matured or as circumstances came along to change them. Others have been added as they were recognized. This trend has remained a constant, and with each revision its effective period has been extended. To invalidate this trend would take a catastrophe on the order of the permanent loss of Middle Eastern oil from the Western economies. Not even the recession of 2008–09 rises to that level of destruction.

Implications for Cruise Lines: People take cruises when they feel economically secure and take less expensive vacations when they do not. In the next few years, many more people will feel they can afford to take a cruise. This is relieving the price pressure on cruise lines, so that fewer tickets will be discounted. This should improve profitability for the next several years.

21. Consumerism is still growing.

Assessment: This trend seems likely to remain healthy for at least the next fifteen years.

Implications for Cruise Lines: This is one more force behind the disintermediation of travel. The cruise industry cannot resist this process forever.

Internet-savvy consumers will expect to find much more information online about ship facilities, prices, options, and port attractions, so they can compare possible cruising choices when planning a vacation. Disappointed cruisers will voice their complaints online, where a single negative report can influence the choices of future consumers for years.

32. When not perturbed by greater-than-normal political or economic instability, oil prices average around $65 per barrel.

Assessment: The long-term trend toward stable energy prices can only grow stronger as the West reigns in consumption and alternative energy technologies become practical.

Implications for Cruise Lines: The single greatest "disposable" expense of running a cruise ship should remain under control. This will help to keep tickets affordable and profits acceptable.

36. Transportation technology and practice are improving rapidly.

Assessment: These advances will continue at least through mid-century.

Implications for Cruise Lines: Outboard power pods, better stabilizers, improved satellite navigation, and other technologies are making cruise ships faster, more comfortable, and more efficient.

Design innovations made possible by technology are creating new experiences for cruisers. These include extensible marinas and swimming areas and retractable glass roofs, as on the *QM2*.

In the future, more ambitious innovations will be seen; artificial island ports and cruise ships the size of modest cities can be expected within twenty years.

38. The Internet continues to grow, but at a slower pace.

Assessment: Internet growth will continue until essentially no one in the world lacks easy access to e-mail and the Internet, about thirty years by our best estimate.

Implications for Cruise Lines: Vacationers accustomed to instant Internet access will be increasingly unwilling to leave their e-mail at home. High-speed Internet access in all staterooms will be standard, as it is now for business-class and luxury hotels.

This is a major force behind the growth of consumerism among potential cruise passengers.

The Internet will be an increasingly important tool for the millions of potential cruisers in the Indian and Chinese travel markets.

39. TECHNOLOGY IS CREATING A KNOWLEDGE-DEPENDENT GLOBAL SOCIETY.

Assessment: This trend will not reach even its halfway mark until the rural populations of China and India gain modern educations and easy access to the web.

Implications for Cruise Lines: Internet cruise booking will become much more important to the industry, eventually displacing travel agents in all but the luxury market.

Cruise ships increasingly will require Internet connections in every room for uninterrupted access to the guest's e-mail, either free or at a very modest price.

Data mining can provide cruise lines with an opportunity for extremely personalized marketing similar to that already being done in cutting-edge hotels and resorts.

40. PEOPLE AROUND THE WORLD ARE BECOMING INCREASINGLY SENSITIVE TO ENVIRONMENTAL ISSUES AS THE CONSEQUENCES OF NEGLECT, INDIFFERENCE, AND IGNORANCE BECOME EVER MORE APPARENT.

Assessment: A solid majority of voters throughout the developed world, and even some in the developing lands, now recognize the need to clean up the environment and especially to control greenhouse warming. They will keep this trend intact for at least the next thirty years.

Implications for Cruise Lines: Restrictions on dumping of refuse and waste will become much tighter in the years ahead and will be much more strictly enforced. Ships will be forced to use more, and more capable, antipollution technologies. These will be a significant new expense for cruise lines.

55. INTERNATIONAL EXPOSURE INCLUDES A GROWING RISK OF TERRORIST ATTACK.

Assessment: This trend is unlikely to change in the next decade and relatively unlikely to change in the next twenty years. A permanent end to the international terrorist threat would require a broad philosophical and cultural change in Islam that makes terrorists pariahs in their own communities. No such change is on the horizon.

Implications for Cruise Lines: Cruise ships are an ideal target for terrorists willing to sacrifice themselves as long as they can take large numbers of people with them. This represents a significant risk to the industry, particularly as government facilities and land-locked attractions become harder to attack.

Government mandates are likely to require even tighter security precautions on cruise ships.

A successful attack on a cruise ship could stifle the industry's growth for several years.

Clipped Wings: Troubled Times for the Airlines

IN MID-2008, with the price of oil at nearly $150 per barrel and jet fuel at similarly stratospheric levels, the world's airlines were struggling to survive. Many were failing. In 2009, with the price of oil under $50 per barrel and the cost of jet fuel comparably reduced, the world's airlines are still struggling to survive. Some seem likely to fail. The collapse of the global economy, just when the airlines finally seemed poised to make a profit, must rank as one of the bigger disappointments the industry could have suffered.

At Forecasting International (FI), we have a reputation as optimists who can see the bright side in most situations. This is undeserved. We simply go where the data lead without the emotional and philosophical biases that make habitual pessimists of some other forecasters. But in the case of the airline industry, there is no getting around it: The recent past has been grim, the future offers only modest improvements, and even these improvements may be slow to arrive.

A Few More Perfect Storms

These days, it seems that anyone who has suffered business reverses blames them on a "perfect storm"—a disastrous combination of forces and events that could not have been foreseen or defended against. If any industry has the right to use this excuse for its troubles, it is the airlines. This industry is being forced to build its future on a foundation of devastating mishaps.

When al-Qaeda terrorists hijacked four aircraft from United and American Airlines to carry out the September 11 attacks, air travel all but died. In the month after the terror spectacular, U.S. domestic passenger miles dropped 20 percent from the previous October; international passenger miles were off 37 percent. Before 2001 was over, the American airline industry shed some 79,000 jobs—one in ten of the people it had employed before September 11. Globally, industry losses in 2001 and 2002 amounted to $25 billion.

By early 2003, it had begun to seem that the worst might be past. Then Severe Acute Respiratory Syndrome, or SARS, appeared. The International Air Transport Association (IATA) estimates that in May 2003, fear of this disease cut international passenger traffic 21 percent below the level seen twelve months earlier, when post-September 11 anxiety was still near its peak. Asian carriers lost nearly 51 percent of their passengers during the worst of the period.

No sooner was SARS under control than America invaded Iraq, renewing concerns about terrorism. Transatlantic traffic in April 2003 was down just over 25 percent, while American domestic flights were off by 15 percent.

The result was predictable. Airlines filing for bankruptcy or surviving on government bailouts in late 2001 and 2002 included Sabena, Swissair, Midway, US Airways, United, Avianca, Air Canada, National, and TWA. Asked what other airlines might go under, one aviation analyst replied, "Almost any of them."

The period from 2004 through 2007 qualified as good times by the standards of the airline industry. As the global economy recovered, so did many air carriers. In North America, six emerged from bankruptcy protection, including four of the lines that had recently filed. US Airways even emerged twice. But it seems the airline industry's good times never last.

In 2008, airlines faced a catastrophic rise in the cost of fuel, as the price of crude oil soared to $150 per barrel. Every penny per gallon increase in the price of jet fuel cost American air carriers $195 million, according to John Heimlich, chief economist of the Air Transport Association.[1] There were a lot of extra pennies. In the United States, jet fuel averaged $0.90 per gallon in 2003, $1.30 in March 2004, and $4.50 in mid-2008. At some European airports, the price of Jet A topped $12.00 per gallon. Before the rise, U.S. airlines had been expected to score their first break-even year in recent memory. Instead, they lost $3.9 billion—roughly equal to the increase in their fuel bills. Carriers elsewhere brought the industry's global loss to about $5.7 billion. It could have been worse. In early summer 2008, when fuel prices were at their highest, it seemed that American air carriers alone would lose $10 billion.

Still, the toll was bad enough. No fewer than thirteen U.S. airlines filed for bankruptcy protection in 2008, including six that halted their operations. The rest of the world was equally stricken. Alitalia went under. So did XL in Britain; Sterling in Denmark; Futura, a charter carrier based in Majorca; Air Jamaica; Oasis Hong Kong; Zoom in Canada; and Nationwide in South Africa. In July, with fuel prices near their peak, airline analyst Douglas McNeil of Blue Oar Investments estimated that as many as fifty European airlines could go belly up.[2] John Kohlsatt, head of easyJet operations in Germany, suggested that when the wave of fuel-induced bankruptcies was over, there could be only five major airlines left in Europe.[3] Happily, when the price of oil declined, the threat of a bloodbath ended.

It is against this background that some longstanding trends and a few new developments will play themselves out. Here are some of the most critical issues the airline industry must deal with in the years ahead. They add up to very mixed prospects for the future.

Today's Pain Is Tomorrow's Gain

For once, we will go with tradition. We have some good news and some bad news. The bad news is that the global recession has hurt the world's airlines as severely as anything in recent memory. Industry analysts say it takes economic growth of about 2 percent for airlines just to break even. A global contraction means red ink as far as the eye can see.

The good news is that the worst may be over. It looks like consumers are ready to begin coming out of their shells to travel again. This does not mean that they will suddenly begin crowding into airline seats for vacation and business travel. It does mean that the beginning of a slow, steady recovery probably is not far off.

The United States entered its latest recession at the beginning of 2008; the world followed later that year. Then the collapse of real estate prices and overexposed banks turned what had been a slow descent into an all-out collapse. By the first quarter of 2009, the U.S. GDP was falling at a rate of 6.1 percent—and that was an improvement over the 6.4 percent rate seen in the previous quarter. It was the first time since the Great Depression that the American economy had fallen by more than 5 percent in two successive quarters. Economists estimated that the country had lost 5.7 million jobs since the recession began.

Globally, things were, if anything, even worse. "Between 40 and 45 percent of the world's wealth has been destroyed in little less than a year and a half," estimated Stephen Schwarzman, CEO of The Blackstone Group, a private equity company. "This is absolutely unprecedented in our lifetime."[4]

The results have been predictable. The world's airlines have faced their largest decline since the SARS epidemic of 2003. By March 2009, worldwide passenger traffic was down 9 percent from the previous year. It was the sixth consecutive monthly drop. In Europe, demand was off 11.6 percent. In Asia, it fell 14.5 percent. In Africa, carriers lost 15.6 percent of their passenger traffic, which was the worst showing in the world. Latin America was off just 5.9 percent, but a 2 percent increase in capacity probably made it seem worse. Only the Middle East, which was up 4.7 percent, actually gained passenger traffic; however, carriers in the region added 13 percent to their capacity.

In the United States, things have been grim. In March 2009, passenger traffic was more than 13 percent below the previous year, but revenues plunged 23 percent from their level in 2008. Declines were not limited to the domestic market, but hit the transatlantic, transpacific, and Latin routes as well.

Even travel to the evergreen attractions has slipped. Travel through Orlando International Airport sank by 12 percent in March, year-on-year, for the sixth consecutive monthly drop. A spokesman for the airport called the quarter's results "reminiscent of what we saw following 9/11." In Las Vegas, officials at McCarran International Airport reported that 3.6 million passengers flew in and out of the city in March, nearly half a million fewer than a year earlier. It was the seventeenth straight month of year-on-year declines at the airport. US Airways carried 34 percent fewer passengers in the first quarter of 2009 than in 2008 and drastically cut its flights. Even Paris was affected; international arrivals at the city's airports in March fell 9.8 percent, year-on-year, following a drop of 8.1 percent in February.

The IATA lost twenty-four of its 230 members to bankruptcy in 2008 and expects the number to grow in 2009. Responding to the release of the January traffic figures, IATA Director General and CEO Giovanni Bisignani commented, "The industry is in a global crisis and we have not yet seen the bottom. Alarm bells are ringing everywhere. Every region's carriers are reporting big drops in cargo. And, aside from the Middle East carriers, passenger demand is falling in all regions. The industry is in a global crisis and we have not yet seen the bottom."[5] In its March 2009 forecast, the IATA predicted that airlines worldwide would see revenues shrink by about 12 percent, or $62 billion, during 2009, with a net loss of $4.7 billion for the year. This was double its previous estimate and comes on top of an estimated $8.5 billion net loss in 2008.

Yet, as badly as the recession has hit the airlines, it could have been much worse. Operators that have managed to streamline their operations and cut costs have been making the best of a bad situation. Delta Air Lines and Northwest Airlines merged, with Delta eliminating 2,000 jobs in preparation for the move and closing 170 gates after both had escaped bankruptcy the previous year. Soon after the merger, Delta announced further cuts of 14 percent in transpacific flights and 13 percent in transatlantic flights for 2009. Virgin and Ryanair shed a total of 800 jobs. Scandinavian Airlines eliminated 3,000 jobs and 20 percent of its capacity. Quantas dropped 1,500 jobs in July 2008 and 1,750 more in April 2009. In May 2009, Japan Airlines announced 1,200 job cuts. American Airlines trimmed its domestic capacity by about 12 percent, United by 18 percent. Both airlines later shrank their international capacity as well. United also closed its discount operation with a loss of 1,100 jobs. Delta cut 45 percent of its service to Orlando, and several airlines reduced service to Las Vegas and Honolulu. Continental dropped service to nine cities. Oakland, California, lost 28 percent of its passenger capacity with American and Continental Airlines pulling out entirely. By May 2009, fleets in the United States alone had mothballed an estimated 500 planes and cut 29,400 jobs.

Under the circumstances, it is no surprise that most large American carriers have posted losses. At Delta and Southwest Airlines, passenger unit revenues were off about 10 percent in the first quarter of 2009. At US Airways, passenger unit revenue was down some 18 percent, and Continental reports passenger unit revenue has plunged 20 percent from a year earlier.

Because of the carriers' determined cost-cutting, the red ink has been shallower than industry observers feared. Delta and UAL Corp., parent of United Airlines, lost $1.2 billion between them in the first quarter of 2009. AMR Corp., the parent of American Airlines, lost $375 million. Some low-cost carriers even managed to post profits, including JetBlue and AirTran. Fuel prices at well below their 2008 peak have helped greatly.

And recently, even the losers are seeing improvement. Continental logged 9.7 percent fewer passenger miles in March than the previous year, but just 3.8 percent fewer in April. American's passenger traffic was off nearly 11 percent in March, year-on-year, but only 4.7 percent in April. AirTran's traffic was down a scant 0.3 percent in April, with more than 80 percent of seats filled.

These first signs of new life in the airline industry reflect what looks like a spring thaw in the American economy. Federal Reserve Chairman Ben Bernanke told Congress the economy should start growing again in 2009. This optimistic assessment came amid signs that some important economic indicators are picking up. For example, real estate home sales are rebounding after hitting an all-time low in January 2009, and by early May 2009, the stock market had recovered nearly everything it had lost since the previous November. Retail sales are also improving. Wal-Mart and many other chains reported that April's numbers came in significantly better than expected.

The government's "stress tests" of major banks also turned out better than expected. Despite all the bailouts, some of the country's biggest banks still needed more money, but the total involved only $75 billion or so—a substantial number, to be sure, but one that could be raised without another handout from taxpayers. This was comforting news for many economists and investors.

There even has been occasional good news mixed in with the bad concerning the most dismal area of the economy—the number of job losses. In May, 345,000 workers lost their jobs. In any normal year, that would have been horrendous, but it was better than the 600,000 layoffs that economists had been expecting. The lower number came as welcome indication that even this crucial segment of the economy is healthier than expected. On the other hand, job losses of 467,000 in June 2009 were higher than the 363,000 that economists expected. The June unemployment rate climbed to 9.5 percent, the highest rate in twenty-six years. This is bad news, because two-thirds of the American economy depends on consumer spending. The unemployed do not consume any more than they can avoid. They rarely take vacations, go on cruises, or eat in high-end restaurants.

In light of the mixed signs on unemployment, it is worth remembering that there is a difference between unemployment and other indicators. Construction, manufacturing, and especially the stock market *lead* the economy. When they go up, the rest of the economy can be expected to improve in the months ahead. Employment is a lagging indicator. It seldom gets better until well after GDP begins to grow again. On balance, the indicators suggest that the economy has bottomed out, or will do so soon. Better times probably do lie ahead.

The American public seems to be fairly optimistic. Consumer confidence readings have been rebounding sharply since their low in February 2009. By May, the index stood at 54.9, up nearly 15 points since April to its highest level in eight months. Consumers are also spending more, and economists generally expect consumer spending to continue growing at an annualized rate of at least 1 percent from now on. This is good news for hospitality. When consumers feel confident enough to spend at all, they spend on restaurant meals, vacations, hotel stays, and even cruises. It could be as long as two years before the hospitality industry reaches its pre-recession prosperity, but it appears that the worst is at last behind us. By the end of 2009, it will be clear that the economy is growing again. As always, hospitality profits will grow with it.

In any case, the end of the global recession is just the beginning of what is needed for the world's airlines to see good times again. We expect the next recovery to be much like the last. Corporate spending on travel and other elective expenses will recover well behind the GDP. Hiring will lag even further, and all but the most comfortable individuals and families will minimize their travel costs until a rising job market assures them that their incomes are secure. We believe that air travel will begin to grow again by mid-2010, but it will not reach pre-recession levels until 2012.

Trends in the Airline Industry

Tomorrow's Passengers

India and China are poster children for our first trend. The world's population is well on its way to doubling in forty years. Among the industrialized countries,

America is growing by far the fastest, thanks to high birth rates among Hispanic immigrants and religious conservatives. Worldwide, the fastest population growth is in the developing and undeveloped countries. In Niger and the Palestinian territories, populations will more than double between 2000 and 2050. In Yemen, Angola, and Congo, they will expand by more than 160 percent.

For the airline industry, the most important growth regions will be China, India, and the Muslim lands. According to the United Nations, China is on track to grow by some 260 million people between 1995 and 2025, bringing its population to nearly 1.5 billion; the total could be much greater if the birth rate turns out to be even slightly higher than the extremely conservative assumptions used to form the estimate. India still has a high birth rate; its population is expected to pass 1.3 billion in 2021, up nearly one-third in twenty years. By 2050, there could be more than two billion people living in India. Growth rates in the Muslim lands vary widely. In Pakistan, it is about 2.6 percent per year, enough to bring its population from 130 million in 2000 to nearly 220 million in 2020. Indonesia is growing at only half that rate. At the current rate of growth, by 2050 Pakistan could be the third most populous country in the world.

This matters to the airlines because population growth represents new passengers. It matters even more because the Indian subcontinent is the prime source of guest workers for the Middle East, and most of them travel by air. In addition, more than one million people annually fly to Saudi Arabia for the Hajj, the once-in-a-lifetime visit to Mecca required of all Muslim faithful. These markets will grow rapidly in the years ahead.

It matters still more because population growth is fastest in the cities of the developing world. Between 2000 and 2030, the global population will grow by an estimated 2.2 billion. Of this, 2.1 billion people will be added to the world's cities, primarily in places like India, China, and Indonesia. In 1950, there were just eight megacities (with populations over five million) in the world. (Newer definitions put the minimum population for a megacity at ten million.) By 2015, there will be fifty-nine megacities, forty-eight of them in less-developed countries. Of these, twenty-three will have populations over ten million, all but four in the developing lands. These vast concentrations of people in places such as Delhi, Mumbai, São Paolo, and Dhaka are likely to be among the fastest growing aviation markets in the world.

High Altitude High Tech

Not that long ago, when someone spoke of new airline technology, many people automatically thought of traveling on the Concorde and the faster, cheaper, miraculously sleeker new supersonic transports that would follow. By 2010, diplomats and the busiest executives would even bounce around the world on suborbital rocket planes, hopping from New York to New Delhi in just two hours.

Those dreams have evaporated in the heat of market reality. Now that the Concorde has been retired from service, it looks like commercial supersonic flight is an idea whose time has gone. Today's version of advanced aircraft technology is much less exciting, but more practical.

Some of the most promising developments deal with the environment, which remains a much more important issue in most of the world than it has been in the United States of late. Researchers are working hard to improve fuel economy, reduce air pollution, and cut the noise associated with jet operations.

Air travel now produces about 12 percent of global CO_2 emissions, or 1.6 percent of all greenhouse gases. That should drop significantly in the coming decade. Airlines have been making substantial reductions in their fuel use, and therefore in pollution, by relatively simple measures such as adding vertical winglets to the tips of their wings, trimming weight from food service carts, and using ground-based equipment to supply air and electricity to planes instead of running engines at the boarding gates. Alaska Airlines reports that such measures have cut its fuel consumption by 17 percent in recent years. In addition, by making engines more efficient, researchers hope to soon be able to cut aircraft CO_2 emissions by another 20 percent and nitrogen oxide emissions by 60 percent.

Newer aircraft will help as well. Most of today's jets burn about 3.5 liters of fuel per 100 passenger-kilometers. This makes them 70 percent more fuel efficient than the airliners of forty years ago, but that is only the beginning. Airbus reports that per-seat fuel consumption of its A380, which entered service in 2007, is around 13 percent lower than a Boeing 747, with total expenses per seat mile 15 percent lower. Boeing says its 787, now scheduled for delivery no earlier than 2010 (two years behind schedule), will cut fuel use by 20 percent compared with a 767, thanks to the use of highly efficient engines and much lightweight composite in its airframe. As these and other state-of-the-art aircraft slowly replace older models in the world's airline fleets, aviation's role in global warming will shrink even without further technological advances.

Noise is another important environmental issue for the aviation industry, particularly in Europe, where 7 percent of the population lives within the sound "footprint" of a commercial airport and standards are much tighter than in the United States. Today's jet aircraft are typically 20 dB quieter than the jets of 1960. That is just the beginning. Researchers hope to bring aircraft noise down another 6 dB by 2010 and perhaps 10 dB by 2020.

However, these changes are incremental advances. Some of the most sweeping changes are likely to appear not in the aircraft themselves, but in the systems that guide them from one place to another. These days, the global positioning system (GPS) keeps hikers from getting lost in the wilderness and guides drivers of luxury cars to the nearest gas station. It also enables pilots to fix their positions within a few feet of latitude, longitude, and altitude. Far more is possible.

In North America, most commercial aircraft make their way over long distances via designated air lanes, like drivers following a freeway. Straight-line flights from one point to another are relatively uncommon. This is in contrast to the situation in Europe, where most flights take the direct route and few of them are longer than ninety minutes. In large part, the American system grew out of technological limitations that no longer apply. Before GPS, air traffic controllers just found it easier to keep track of planes that moved along easily predicted paths. It has worked fairly well for the hub-and-spokes traffic system, which routes hundreds of flights per day through a few major airports.

This practice, however, has serious disadvantages. The standard airways offer limited traffic capacity, and many of them are getting crowded. And it takes more time and fuel to slip into the system and follow the airways to your destination than it would to fly in a straight line. According to a report from the UK Department for Transport, simply improving air traffic management—for example, letting planes begin their descent to an airport much earlier so that they can maintain their most efficient flying speed—could cut fuel use by another 6 to 12 percent.

GPS makes the airways pretty much obsolete. The combination of satellite navigation and air traffic computers can fix any number of airplanes within a few feet of their actual positions, making sure that two aircraft never try to occupy the same space. This makes it practical to fly point-to-point, even over the longest routes to the busiest airports.

Nav Canada, which provides air traffic control as the Federal Aviation Administration (FAA) does within the United States, believes that satellite navigation soon will allow unlimited free flight in its region. At that point, planes will fly directly to their destinations by the quickest, most convenient route, taking advantage of favorable winds. This will save still more fuel and open space for many more aircraft in the system.

Satellite navigation (commonly referred to simply as Sat Nav, Sat-nav, and satnav) could be just a tiny foretaste of the technological changes that eventually will sweep the air transport industry. Consider this: A Lockheed RQ-4 Global Hawk observation drone leaving from San Francisco could fly to Maine with up to 3,000 pounds of internal payload, loiter for twenty-four hours while surveying an area 230 miles square, fly home again, and touch down safely, all without a human hand touching its controls. The $35-million aircraft is not completely autonomous. It requires a ground-based launch and recovery element to provide differential GPS information for takeoff and landing. Yet the Global Hawk makes it clear that the day of pilotless aircraft has arrived.

To date, drones are banned from flight in congested airspace. Even with a remote human pilot, the FAA is concerned that remotely piloted vehicles (RPVs) could endanger other aircraft because they are incapable of the traditional "see-and-avoid" approach to air safety.

Yet many airliners already come close to the Global Hawk's near-independence. When using the autoland function, pilots select the approach and runway, operate flaps and landing gear, and perhaps deploy the reversers. The machinery does the rest.

Airbus has gone a step further by taking certain control decisions away from the pilot altogether. The company's newer models are hard-limited to prevent pitching up into a stall or more than fifteen degrees nose-down, banking more than sixty-seven degrees, or putting more than 2.5 G acceleration on the plane. Maneuver hard to avoid a potential collision in an A320, and the control computers automatically apply full thrust, retract spoilers, and limit the climb-out to no more than thirty degrees. The pilot is still more than an advisor, but the computers have final authority over what the plane will do.

The principle is clear. Automate the last few operations left to the pilot in an emergency or in a bad-weather instrument landing, and today's passenger-carrying aircraft would differ from the Global Hawk only in their size and cargo.

Even now, the FAA is beginning to roll out a "Next Generation Air Transportation System" (NextGen), which is scheduled to spread throughout the world by 2025. Its goal is to automate nearly every aspect of navigation and aircraft control.

By providing much more precise and flexible positioning, navigation, and timing (PNT), a raft of next-generation technologies will make it possible to confine aircraft within much narrower flight corridors. This will allow more planes to share congested airspace, speeding arrivals and reducing fuel consumption on approach.

Once experience has proved that autopilot and autoland functions based on the NextGen technologies are even more reliable than today's equipment, they are likely to ease the FAA's traditional dependence on see-and-avoid. This will bring truly autonomous aircraft one step closer.

A more radical approach comes from the Innovative Future Air Transport System (IFATS) project recently carried out by a consortium from Europe and Israel. Its goal is to provide "improved safety and efficiency of air transportation." It would do this by replacing pilots with avionics. IFATS specifically aims to develop fully autonomous passenger-carrying aircraft. The planes envisioned by the project would be far more capable than any drone yet built. They could taxi automatically from the terminal to the runway, take off and land safely in a fifteen-knot crosswind, and deliver passengers to the terminal gate. Close approach of an aircraft outside the system's control or loss of its data link to the ground would trigger an onboard collision-avoidance system capable of averting a crash with less than a minute's warning.

The automated controls would even be capable of landing safely after losing an engine during any phase of flight. On engine-out, the plane would radio the intended destination, where ground systems would automatically plan for an emergency landing. Even the decision to go around or proceed with landing would be made without human intervention.

Human beings would not be completely divorced from the airplane. Each aircraft would have a human operator—a pilot of sorts—who would oversee the computers from the ground. Under extreme circumstances, this person could even take over control of the plane, like the pilot of a contemporary RPV.

In making this kind of prediction, we always consider three questions: Is it technologically feasible? Is it economically feasible? And is it socially feasible? We believe the IFATS vision is technically feasible. It appears to be economically feasible as well. The consortium estimates that a 220-passenger airliner usually priced at $36 million would cost about $37.8 million once the necessary hardware was installed. But eliminating the cockpit would let it carry more passengers faster and more often. As a result, yearly pre-tax profits would skyrocket from $15,733,250 per airplane to $22,410,926.

That leaves the third criterion of forecasting, the one that concerns us most: social acceptability. The day probably will come when people become accustomed to leaving major parts of their lives in the invisible "hands" of computers. By 2025 or 2030, we may well spend most of our highway time reading a book or playing cards while the car steers itself. At that point, pilotless aircraft may be just one more of modern technology's welcome conveniences.

But how long would that acceptance last? At FI, we suspect it would survive until the first emergency that the automatic systems were not prepared to handle. We think especially of US Airways Flight 1549, the Airbus A320 that ditched in the Hudson River after striking a flock of birds while taking off from LaGuardia Airport. Could an automated system or a remote operator have brought that flight in to a safe landing? The only way we can see to be sure is to put autonomous planes into the air and wait for the unexpected.

Big and Small

We have written of bimodal distribution before. Giant players flourish due to economies of scale, and boutique operators prosper by delivering the kind of tailored service that mass marketers cannot. Mid-sized companies, lacking either advantage, disappear. This process has been especially hard on air carriers, which are vanishing at record rates. Globally, the number of airlines is expected to drop from around five hundred in 2002 to only sixty in 2012.

However, in this industry, the mechanism of attrition is a bit different. This is important, because it will continue to shape air travel in the next two decades as it has done for the last two.

There have been a few attempts to operate small, high-service airlines analogous to the boutiques seen in other industries. Yet, business-class-only carriers such as MAXjet, Silverjet, and EOS have foundered quickly when the economy soured or fuel prices soared.

Instead, airlines compete almost exclusively on price, and it is seldom the largest participants that compete most effectively. Discount carriers generally run tighter operations, pay their employees less, often buy used planes in good condition rather than investing in new equipment, turn them around faster between flights, and pack their passengers tighter. These efficiencies give the discounters lower costs per passenger-mile and better profits despite offering cheaper prices than their larger competitors.

As a result, discount operators are flourishing even as full-fare carriers fight to survive. Low-fare lines held just 4 percent of the American market in 1991. By 2009, discounters such as Southwest, JetBlue, and AirTran accounted for about 19 percent of the seat-miles flown in the United States. In Europe, 25 percent of passengers reportedly flew low-cost airlines in 2007, and in India discounters have captured about half the airline market. In all, discounters carry about 36 percent of the world's passengers, according to the *2008 ITB World Travel Trends Report.*

This is helping to reshape consumers' travel habits. In Europe, vacationers used to book package tours, organized and sold by major tour operators. Not anymore. In 2008, for example, roughly half of visitors arriving in Spain from other parts of Europe arrived by discount airline. Most booked their hotel rooms on the Internet. And because they paid less for airfare, many upgraded to more expensive hotel accommodations.

The global economic collapse may actually be good for the discount airlines, provided it does not last too long. In a bad economy, most people who cannot avoid flying are likely to shop for the cheapest fares available. For example, in November

2008, when British Airways already had begun to lose traffic to and from London, easyJet was up 12 percent. However, late in 2008, Ryanair CFO Howard Millar predicted that financial pressures will eventually drive nearly all of the continent's dozens of discount airlines out of business.[6] By 2018, he predicted, only the two biggest competitors—Ryanair and easyJet—will be left.

Despite the jammed seating and food choices that top out at a small bag of pretzels, low-cost carriers are winning passengers for more reasons than cheap travel. The Airline Quality Ratings, compiled by professors at Wichita State University and the National Institute for Aviation Research, rate airlines that carry at least 1 percent of American domestic passengers. Criteria measured in the survey include on-time performance, staff courtesy, baggage handling, and the number of customer complaints. The 2008 survey ranked the performance of eighteen airlines in 2006, the most recent year for which data were available. Hawaiian, Southwest, Frontier, and JetBlue—all discount carriers—were the top performers. Only three full-service carriers—Northwest, Continental, and United—ranked in the top ten.

In the United States, the discounters have one more advantage as well. United, US Airways, and the other giants exist to serve as many cities as possible. They do this by collecting passengers from smaller cities and consolidating them at about thirty major hub airports for long-distance travel. Running a hub-and-spokes system is not cheap, and it drives costs up for the major carriers by an estimated 15 percent. Discount airlines specialize in flying between cities that offer enough traffic to fill their planes and avoid the expense of hub operations.

Executives at the giant airlines argue that the hub-and-spokes model is the only way air travel can work in the United States. Of the 30,000 city-pair markets where air service is available, only 5 percent have enough traffic to support nonstop point-to-point flights. If all carriers flew point-to-point, smaller cities such as Syracuse, New York, and Stockton, California, would be lucky to get a single flight per day to half a dozen destinations. Discount airlines can offer cheap fares in part because they serve only markets that can fill planes for point-to-point travel. The top 5 percent of city-pairs that give the discount airlines their living account for nearly three-fourths of all passengers flying in the United States. The smallest 80 percent of airfields with scheduled air service provide just 11 percent of the passengers.

Economic forces are making it even harder to maintain service to the "spoke" communities. In the expensive-oil environment of 2008, both legacy airlines and discounters either cut service to many smaller markets or pulled out of them altogether. More than fifty small airports in the lower forty-eight states lost at least one-third of their seating capacity compared with a year earlier. Oakland lost 20 percent, Kansas City 16 percent, and Tulsa 13 percent. According to the Air Transport Association, at least sixty communities that had service in 2007 had lost it by mid-2008, and thirty-seven more were scheduled to do so by the end of the year.

This contraction was not limited to the United States. Sixty-one Chinese and twenty-six Russian airports lost airline service in 2008.

As we have already seen, the trend is continuing in the recession of 2009. Routes and seating capacity are likely to shrink until the economy has clearly begun to recover and airlines can begin to hope for a rebound in demand.

One more factor is at work here, and in the long run it could begin to promote a new expansion of point-to-point routes. Local populations are growing. Demand for air travel grows with them, so more markets should be able to fill planes each year. And with satellite navigation, it becomes easier for the air traffic control system to handle that kind of flight schedule. Ultimately, point-to-point air travel may be destined to make the hub system obsolete, except for the longest routes. That would open many more U.S. markets to discount service, which is not good news for the full-fare airlines.

The Bottom Line

The post-2008 downturn in air travel will have a lasting impact on the airline industry, just as the contraction after September 11 did. Boeing estimated that 5 percent fewer passenger-miles would be flown in 2020 than would have been the case if the September 11 terrorist attacks had not taken place. That put the market roughly four years behind the growth curve that analysts once expected. This fit well with FAA projections. In 2000, the FAA forecast that passenger volumes in the United States would reach 1.0 billion in 2010 and 1.1 billion three years later. After September 11, it estimated that growth would recover soon to the 5.1 percent seen annually prior to the attack. At that rate, American carriers would not fly 1.0 billion in a year until 2014.

The global recession of 2008–09 has set that back yet again. We now believe that the airline industry will recover to pre-recession levels and grow by roughly 5 percent per year by late 2012. This will mean that American airlines will not fly a billion passengers until 2017.

All this adds up to an environment much like the one that existed before the world's economic problems began. Undercapitalized, inefficient carriers will struggle to survive—and that category will include both little-known low-cost carriers and some of the biggest names in air travel. Full-fare carriers will continue to offer wider seating, in-flight Internet service, and even a few bunks for weary passengers on long flights, all in an effort to justify premium prices. They will find it a hard sell, as even business travelers put up with the discomforts of flying coach in order to save money on all but the longest routes. The number of major hub-and-spokes airlines in the United States will decline to four, and eventually perhaps to only three. The same trends will be seen in Europe and, to a lesser extent, in Asia. In each region, the most efficient, best-capitalized competitors will reap ample rewards.

Behind these forecasts are a few assumptions that we should make clear because they could prove wrong. In predicting a recovery, we assume that the cost of jet fuel will not soon head back to the stratosphere. We assume that there will not be another major terrorist event that involves hijacked airliners. We also assume that there will be no major outbreak of infectious disease, like the epidemic of SARS that inhibited Asian travel in 2003. Finally, we assume that the world's governments will recognize in time that they have not done nearly enough to stimulate their economies or to stabilize and reform their banking systems. If one or more of these assumptions proves wrong, our forecast for the world's airlines will grow considerably darker.

Key Trends for the Airlines

In this section we look at the key trends for airlines, using entries from Appendix A. We list each relevant trend and our assessment of it and then detail the specific implications of this trend for the airlines.

1. THE WORLD'S POPULATION WILL GROW TO NINE BILLION BY 2050.

Assessment: Demographic trends such as this are among the easiest to recognize and most difficult to derail. Barring a global plague or nuclear war—wildcard possibilities that cannot be predicted with any validity—there is little chance that the population forecast for 2050 will err on the low side.

Implications for Airlines: Demand for air travel will grow at least as quickly as the world's population.

19. THE ECONOMY OF THE DEVELOPED WORLD IS GROWING STEADILY, WITH ONLY BRIEF INTERRUPTIONS.

Assessment: These trends have been revised many times since they were first codified in the late 1980s. Some trends have fallen off the list as they matured or as circumstances came along to change them. Others have been added as they were recognized. This trend has remained a constant, and with each revision its effective period has been extended. To invalidate this trend would take a catastrophe on the order of the loss of Middle Eastern oil from the Western economies. No such dramatic reversal of global fortune can be foreseen.

Implications for Airlines: Thanks to the global recession, 2009 ticket sales are generally expected to be off about 15 percent from 2008.

The International Air Transport Association expects American carriers to lose about $2.5 billion in 2009—and that is the *good* news. Worldwide, all regions except the United States are expected to show larger losses in 2009 than in 2008. Industry revenues are expected to come in at $501 billion, down $35 billion from 2008.

The latest wave of airline bankruptcies has already begun. In the United States alone, thirteen lines entered bankruptcy protection in 2008, including six that terminated service. In Europe, at least fifty airlines reportedly have enough trouble on their balance sheets to threaten their survival. The situation is even worse in Asia, where not even the region's strongest airlines can be sure of weathering the bad times ahead.

Beginning in the second half of 2009, business travel will slowly recover from its low point in the current recession, bringing new demand for seats, particularly on long-distance flights. However, executives whose companies have grown accustomed to discount fares will not soon be willing to pay for business-class seats.

Leisure travel will recover approximately as it did after the last recession, with consumers returning to the market as they grow more secure in their job prospects. However, employers will put off new hiring as long as possible, just as in the "jobless recovery" after the last U.S. recession. Employment will not reach pre-crash levels until at least 2012.

Demand in the Asia-Pacific markets, particularly India and China, will gain strength much more quickly than demand in North America and Europe.

32. WHEN NOT PERTURBED BY GREATER-THAN-NORMAL POLITICAL OR ECONOMIC INSTA-
BILITY, OIL PRICES AVERAGE AROUND $65 PER BARREL.

Assessment: Given the condition of the American dollar, it might be better to denominate oil prices in euros—though this could be even more devastating for the American economy in the event of future episodes of instability. Aside from that, the long-term trend toward stable energy prices can only strengthen as the West reigns in consumption and alternative energy technologies become practical.

Implications for Airlines: While oil prices remain under control, the biggest American air carriers should at last have had the chance to become solidly profitable. Instead, they will have a better chance to survive the global economic crisis.

Airlines such as Southwest, which locked in long-term supplies of jet fuel at prices well below their peak, watched their competitors suffer while oil soared. In 2009, they are being forced to put up cash to meet the terms of their fuel contracts—some $230 million in Southwest's case. This deprives them of a significant competitive advantage.

36. TRANSPORTATION TECHNOLOGY AND PRACTICE ARE IMPROVING RAPIDLY.

Assessment: These advances will continue at least through mid-century.

Implications for Airlines: New technology should cut fuel use by as much as 10 percent per passenger-mile over the next decade.

New safety technologies, such as fuel tanks filled with inert gas, should eliminate some potential accidents in the future, saving more than 1,000 lives in the next ten years.

By eliminating the need for America's hub-and-spokes air travel network, satellite navigation will dramatically reduce the cost of air travel in the United States over the next ten years. It also will improve the profitability of the major airlines—or at least the profitability of those that survive until the transition has been made.

40. PEOPLE AROUND THE WORLD ARE BECOMING INCREASINGLY SENSITIVE TO ENVIRON-
MENTAL ISSUES AS THE CONSEQUENCES OF NEGLECT, INDIFFERENCE, AND IGNORANCE
BECOME EVER MORE APPARENT.

Assessment: A solid majority of voters throughout the developed world, and even some in the developing lands, now recognize the need to clean up the environment and especially to control greenhouse warming. They will keep this trend intact for at least the next thirty years.

Implications for Airlines: Pollution controls will continue to be a growing burden for the airlines. However, the need to cut greenhouse gas emissions eventually will help to make the air carriers more efficient and profitable.

53. INSTITUTIONS ARE UNDERGOING A BIMODAL DISTRIBUTION: THE BIG GET BIGGER, THE
SMALL SURVIVE, AND THE MID-SIZED ARE SQUEEZED OUT.

Assessment: Thanks in part to technology, this trend is likely to be a permanent feature of the business scene from now on.

Implications for Airlines: High-priced, full-service airlines have only just begun to cope with competition from the discount carriers. No-frills airlines will continue to gain market share at the expense of the full-fare lines.

Boeing's 787 is likely to find more of a market than the Airbus A380.

Competition among the discount airlines will be even more intense than competition between the discounters and the full-fare carriers.

55. INTERNATIONAL EXPOSURE INCLUDES A GROWING RISK OF TERRORIST ATTACK.

Assessment: This trend is unlikely to change in the next decade and relatively unlikely to change in the next twenty years. A permanent end to the international terrorist threat would require a broad philosophical and cultural change in Islam that makes terrorists pariahs in their own communities. No such change is on the horizon.

Implications for Airlines: No matter what else goes right, there will be a sword hanging over the industry for at least the next ten years.

New security precautions will continue to drain profits from the airlines, particularly in the United States.

It is essential that the airlines set up to screen all checked baggage before it goes onto an airplane, just as they do carry-on luggage.

Endnotes

1. John P. Heimlich, "(Oral) Statement of John P. Heimlich Vice President and Chief Economist of the Air Transport Association of America, Inc.; 'Commercial Jet Fuel Supply: Impact On U.S. Airlines;' Before the Aviation Subcommittee of the Committee on Transportation and Infrastructure of the House of Representatives, 15 February 2006." Accessed May 1, 2009, at www.airlines.org/NR/rdonlyres/B0835CD8-85B3-44B5-9B8C-4C6FB51E74EA/0/HeimlichJetFuelOral060215.pdf.

2. David Robertson, Rachel Sylvester, and Alice Thomson. "Final Call for More Than 50 Airlines," *Times Online*, 2 August 2008. Accessed June 2, 2009, at http://business.timesonline.co.uk/tol/business/industry_sectors/transport/article4446390.ece.

3. "Fuel Costs Will Trigger Airline Bankruptcy Wave—easyJet German Head," *Forbes.com*, 2 June 2008. Accessed May 12, 2009, at www.forbes.com/feeds/afx/2008/06/02/afx5068561.html.

4. Megan Davies and Walden Siew, "45 Percent of World's Wealth Destroyed: Blackstone CEO," Reuters, 10 March 2009. Accessed May 12, 2009, at www.reuters.com/article/ousiv/idUSTRE52966Z20090310.

5. "Economic Gloom Continues in January Traffic," International Air Transport Association, 26 February 2009. Accessed on May 12, 2009, at www.iata.org/pressroom/pr/2009-02-26-01.htm.

6. "Ryanair Expects Passenger Shift to Low-Cost Carriers," *Independent.ie*, 13 October 2008. Accessed May 13, 2009, at www.independent.ie/national-news/financial-crisis/ryanair-expects-passenger-shift-to-lowcost-carriers-1497280.html.

9

Tasty Trends for the Restaurant Industry

IN LOS ANGELES, which led the economic downturn in the United States, a tony restaurant known as Providence—$150 per person for dinner, on average— reported that business was off 20 percent, year-on-year, as early as October 2008. By the following February, Manhattan's mainstay Gotham Bar and Grille found revenues down by 15 percent from the previous year, and customers could get same-evening reservations. Some restaurants are rumored to be off by as much as 40 percent from the same time in 2008. Meanwhile, sales at McDonald's were *up* 7.2 percent worldwide in the fourth quarter of 2008.

In the United States, restaurants outside the fast-food sector are feeling the pain of this unwelcome development. In December 2008, the National Restaurant Association's comprehensive index of restaurant activity fell to its second consecutive record low, after fourteen months below its break-even level. Same-store sales were the weakest in the index's history, with nearly two-thirds of operators reporting a decline for the month. The NRA's Current Situation Index, which combines same-store sales, traffic, labor, and capital expenditures, also reached a record low.

Recession Hits Restaurants Hard

These bad times are likely to continue. The American economy is contracting and jobs are disappearing, both at high speed. GDP shrank by 3.8 percent in the fourth quarter of 2008. The Conference Board predicted further contraction of –6.7 percent and –3.8 percent in the next two quarters, with a weak recovery beginning in the second half of 2009. An estimated 3.6 million jobs have vanished since the recession began, and more are being lost at a rate of nearly 600,000 per month. On a single Monday in January, American corporations announced some 71,000 job cuts. Official unemployment was at 9.5 percent as of June 2009.

The big question in the American economy is the $787 billion recovery package and what effect it will have. Tax cuts make up more than 40 percent of the package, with the rest devoted to infrastructure projects and other employment-related steps. Unfortunately, economists almost universally rate tax cuts as the least effective form of stimulus—not completely wasted, but providing the smallest possible "bang for the buck." Worse, this less-than-$1-trillion package is meant to replace an estimated $2.9 trillion in private demand that will be missing from the economy in 2009 and 2010. While it should cushion the decline, there is valid reason to wonder how effective it will be in promoting an actual recovery. Opinion among leading economists is divided.

At Forecasting International (FI), we still believe the American economy will bottom out in the second quarter of 2009 and recover slowly thereafter. Job growth will lag considerably behind GDP, as it did in the so-called "jobless recovery" after the recession of 2001. (It took employment four years to reach pre-recession levels.) Restaurant revenues outside the fast-food sector will lag still further, as patrons will return to mid-level and high-end outlets only after they regain confidence in their economic futures. Technomics, an industry consulting firm based in Chicago, predicts that fine dining revenues in the United States will be off by 12 to 15 percent for 2009. Outlets at the extreme high end of the market could be an exception, as the wealthiest Americans, whose income depends largely on investment, are likely to feel the recovery first and most strongly.

This American experience will be mirrored at restaurants throughout the world. The details vary from country to country, but in most nations we see a common theme of economic collapse, job losses, and thickening gloom. Late in January 2009, the International Monetary Fund expected the global GDP for 2009 to come in at a positive 0.5 percent, including growth of 2.7 percent in Asia. But the situation appears worse than that when looking at individual economies.

Europe faces lean times, at least into 2010. The European Commission predicts that the aggregate GDP for sixteen original member states will fall by 1.8 percent in 2009 and then grow by just 0.4 percent in 2010. Unemployment is expected to top 10 percent, up from 7.5 percent in 2008.

For some key economies, the near future will be even worse. Germany's economy—the Continent's largest—will shrink by 2.3 percent in 2009, recovering by 0.7 percent the following year, according to the European Commission. France, Europe's second-ranked economy, will shrink 1.8 percent in 2009, then grow by 0.4 percent in 2010. Italy, in third place, has been in recession since 2008; its economy will contract another 2 percent in 2009, growing by 0.3 percent the next year. The United Kingdom faces an economic decline of 2.8 percent in 2009, with growth of only 0.2 percent in 2010 and unemployment of 8 percent or more both years.

Beijing claims its economy grew by 6.8 percent in the last quarter of 2008, but that is measured against the same quarter in 2007. Measuring the way everyone else does it—against the previous quarter—the Chinese GDP was expanding at a rate of just 1 percent. That is the closest thing to a depression for a country used to growth in or near double digits. The result is that at least twenty million migrant workers had lost their jobs by the end of January 2009.

This could be near the bottom for the world's second-largest economy. Growth is expected to come in at 5 percent in 2009—China's slowest rate in nearly twenty years, but the best we can expect from any major economy. How fast the Chinese economy expands after that depends heavily on the country's trading partners, who are unlikely to be supplying much new demand for at least two years.

If the American economy is in freefall, we need a new way to describe what is happening to Japan. In the fourth quarter of 2008, its GDP fell at an annual rate of 11.7 percent! The International Monetary Fund expects the economy to shrink by 2.5 percent in 2009 before recovering slightly in 2010. Even a 2 percent decline would make this the sharpest contraction since 1945. Unemployment in January 2009 rose to 4.4 percent, up from 3.9 percent in a single month, which was the fastest growth in unemployment Tokyo has ever recorded.

All this spells grim times for the world's restaurants.

In London, sites such as The Little Bay in Farrington are offering free meals in the hope that most customers will be too embarrassed to leave without paying. According to PricewaterhouseCoopers, one-third more restaurants in the United Kingdom went bankrupt in 2008 than the year before, and that was before the recession took hold.

In Paris, big-name chefs used to serving $400 meals are opening fast-food outlets to make ends meet. Among them: Paul Bocuse of l'Auberge du Pont de Collonges and a chain of other outlets; Yves Pinard at Le Grand Louvre; Yves Camdeborde of Le Comptoir du Relais; Guy Martin (a Michelin star) of Le Grand Véfour; and Hélène Darroze (two stars!).

In Japan, restaurant sales were off by 2.7 percent as early as September 2008, with Japanese cuisine down by 14 percent from a year earlier. Shinko Securities reports that meals at home are replacing restaurant sales, while convenience stores are selling more cheap boxed meals, such as fried chicken. At the same time, burger mongers such as Lotteria, MOS Food Services, and McDonald's have been introducing new, premium offerings to tap the market for cheap luxury. Lotteria's Zeppin includes twice as much beef as the company's regular cheeseburger, plus two kinds of cheese—Gruyère and red cheddar—and a strip of bacon. The new version costs ¥420, compared with ¥100 for a regular burger. A month after its introduction, the new burger made up nearly one-fourth of the company's sales.

In China, the recession has been mixed news even for the fast-food outlets that would be expected to flourish in a downturn. Tokyo-based Yoshinoya, Japan's largest operator of beef-bowl restaurants, had 185 outlets in China at the beginning of 2009. It planned to add sixty more over the course of the year. But McDonald's has had to cut prices in China by up to one-third just to keep business steady. Half of the company's products are now selling at or below their prices of ten years ago. Nonetheless, the company will be adding 175 new stores and hiring some 10,000 new staff in 2009, up from 1,050 outlets and more than 60,000 workers.

Other Factors Influencing the World's Restaurants

Of course, economic conditions are just one of many factors that influence the world's restaurants. At FI, we see many trends that will help to shape this industry in the years ahead. Some are limited to the United States; others are felt worldwide, or soon will be. Most are very broad waves that are sweeping societies at large; a few are specific to restaurants. In no particular order, the following sections detail ten of the most important trends for the restaurant industry.

Diners Change; Restaurants Adapt

Throughout the developed world, people on average are growing older. In the United States, those over sixty-five made up 15 percent of the population in 2000; by 2050, 27 percent of Americans will be in their traditional retirement years.

Japan's over-sixty-five population will skyrocket from 17 percent in 2000 to 22 percent in 2010 and more than 36 percent in 2050. Germany, France, Britain, Italy, and many other countries are also aging.

They are growing more diverse as well, thanks to a wave of migration that is bringing millions of people from the Eastern to the Western Hemisphere, and from south of the equator to the northern lands. In the United States, the Hispanic, Asian, and Middle Eastern populations all are expanding rapidly. In 2000, Latinos accounted for about one-eighth of the U.S. population. By 2050, they will be nearly one-fourth. And the number of Asians is almost doubling from 11.2 million in 2000 to 19.6 million in 2020. Similar changes are being seen in Europe, where hundreds of thousands of immigrants arrive each year from Eastern Europe, North Africa, the Middle East, and the Indian subcontinent.

Baby Boomers still dominate restaurant clientele. They visit full-service restaurants with per-person checks in the $10-to-$20 range more than any other age group. Once the current recession is past, they will continue to power the casual dining market for many years to come. In addition, several fast-food vendors in the United States are trying to create a middle ground known as "fast casual" in an attempt to expand beyond the saturated fast-food market. This innovation aims to take advantage of Boomers and their children who grew up on fast food but cannot yet make the leap to the higher-ticket casual dining.

A more diverse population spells growing demand for ethnic cuisines formerly outside the mainstream. In Europe, a generation of immigrants from North Africa, the Middle East, Pakistan, India, and Bangladesh have been opening restaurants that offer their native cuisines for nearly twenty years. This new fare has proved popular with indigenous Europeans. In Britain especially, demand for *halal* food acceptable to strict Muslims is growing rapidly.

New immigrants and their first-generation children prefer the foods they grew up with. This is helping to drive the American boom in Asian, Latin, and Caribbean restaurants. One of the fastest growing segments is Mexican restaurants, thanks to a growing Hispanic population with a growing income. This trend is particularly strong in California, Florida, and other areas with large Hispanic communities.

All this fits well with buying habits in the United States, where Baby Boomers and their descendants have long sought out novelty and variety. They are looking not just for food, but for new and exciting experiences as well. This extends to new cuisine, exotic surroundings, and almost anything that is just different. What these restaurant customers seek is not so much nutrition and convenience, but the experience of dining out. The trend is to dine as entertainment. Witness the rise in America of Thai food, with its emphasis on chili oil, coconut paste, fish sauce, lemon grass, and other relatively exotic flavors. Half of restaurant operators responding to a poll early in 2009 reported that they had considered adding Asian flavors to their menus. The popularity of Cajun food in Japan and pizza and ice cream in China are similar trends.

The drive toward flavor and experience is behind the recent American fad for tapas—the Spanish equivalent of dim sum—and "grazing" menus, which offer more different flavors in a single meal. These changes increasingly are finding their way into quick-service restaurants. Arby's roast turkey ranch and bacon sandwich features Asian-style tamarind sauce, while MacDonald's recently experimented with Latin-flavored items. Though these specific fads may pass, the notion of packing more intensity and experience onto one table is with us to stay.

In the years ahead, we can expect to see more American restaurants featuring foods from out-of-the-way parts of Asia, the Caribbean, Latin America, and North Africa, with a modest boom in Indian fare; more European restaurants offering cuisine from many of these same regions; and still more restaurants in Japan specializing in American regional fare.

Even more intense flavors lie ahead as well. Aging Baby Boomers will need them to maintain their feeling of novelty and excitement as their taste buds lose their sensitivity.

As the Boomers grow older, other changes are in store. Already, retirees struggling with fixed incomes are competing with young people for restaurant jobs. This should help to minimize tightness in the labor market owing to the relatively small size of the current generations and may provide a more stable, reliable pool of workers in a traditionally volatile industry. Looking farther ahead, many restaurants are likely to find that a major part of their business consists of delivering takeout meals to local retirement communities.

Tourists Eat, Too

International tourism has grown by roughly 5 percent per year for nearly as long as anyone can remember. Until recently, international tourist arrivals were expected to reach 1.6 billion annually by 2020, up from 842 million in 2006. The global recession will set that expansion back by about three years.

The opening of European borders caused a boom in Continental tourism, especially among the younger generations, who routinely speak several languages. Young people from Italy, France, England, and Germany have been nearly as likely to spend vacations, and even long weekends, in each other's countries as in their own. The recession has throttled back that flow as well, and routed many of the remaining travelers to lower-priced destinations in eastern Europe.

For restaurants in the traditional tourist destinations, this is bad news. It is particularly significant for higher-end, full-service restaurants, which report that in an average year up to 30 percent of their sales—and more than half in some major European tourist destinations—are to vacationers and business travelers.

By 2012, however, tourism should return to its accustomed growth path, and 150 million Chinese and Indian tourists will roam the world by 2023 or so. In the long run, restaurants in the traditional destinations of Europe, Asia, and the United States can look forward to good times. By 2020, we expect to see a wave of new establishments catering to the needs of these Asian travelers.

Dining for Health as Well as Pleasure

Early in 2004, the U.S. Centers for Disease Control and Prevention warned that fully two-thirds of Americans are overweight. Obesity, the agency added, is fast closing in on heart disease (itself weight-related) as the nation's leading cause of death.

This is a global problem; in fact, the epidemic of fat has been nicknamed "globesity." According to the International Obesity Task Force, 1.7 billion people around the world need to lose weight, and 312 million are obese—at least thirty pounds over their maximum recommended weight. About 36 percent of children in Italy, 30 percent in Spain, and 22 percent in Britain are now overweight or obese. Only the poorest nations of Africa are immune to this trend. As a result, the incidence of diseases such as type 2 diabetes, hypertension, coronary heart disease, osteoarthritis, and several types of cancer is skyrocketing throughout the world. So are death rates.

Figures like these—no pun intended—are bringing new power to the health movement that began in the United States more than twenty years ago. In the industrialized West, growing numbers of consumers are changing the way they eat and care for themselves, not only at home, but also when dining out. This trend is being felt in restaurants throughout the United States and is beginning to appear overseas.

U.S. restaurants are adapting to the health concerns of their guests. Even before the low-carb fad took off, 71 percent of Americans reported that they were trying to include more fruits and vegetables in their diets, rather than meats and baked goods. For a time, the low-carb Atkins and South Beach diets were the hottest things in the fat-fighting market, and chains such as TGI Friday's and Ruby Tuesday introduced many low-carb items to their menus. A few years later, the craze has passed, but many outlets still offer heart-healthy selections. Some provide calorie and content details, either on the menu or on their websites. Even more recently, trans fats are disappearing from restaurant recipes as consumers have become concerned about medical evidence linking them to heart disease. In the United States, at least, we will see similar menu changes with every diet fad that manages to remain popular for more than a few months. Europe probably is ten years behind in this trend, with the rest of the world even farther back.

Salad entrées are rapidly becoming more popular, particularly in casual-dining restaurants, while both casual-dining and fine-dining restaurants report a marked increase in sales of seafood. These trends are likely to continue for several more years.

Mediterranean cuisine also is gaining popularity in the United States (even as its appeal wanes in Europe), thanks largely to medical studies that have praised it as heart-healthy food. This is a slow-moving trend, but one that we expect to continue for some time.

Until recently, this trend was hard on quick-service chains, which have struggled to overcome a longstanding reputation for heart-*un*healthy fare. A 2001 Harris Poll showed that about one-third of Americans ate at fast-food restaurants less often than a year before, citing health reasons. As a result, many chains added salads, low-carb dishes, and other diet choices to their menus—with indifferent results. The recession that began in 2008 has largely reversed this trend. Heart-healthy or not, quick-service hamburgers are the top choice for many Americans when lean economic times call for wallet-friendly meals.

Consumerism Compounds

The Internet has brought shoppers vast new sources of information about product quality, pricing, delivery time, and store services. At the same time, advocacy groups and regulations have been promoting better content labels, nutrition data, and other consumer-oriented requirements. This continuing growth of consumerism is inevitably making itself felt in the world's restaurants.

Savvy consumers demand high quality at the best possible price, and in good economic times quality is more important. In this, consumers in the United States and Europe are following the lead of their peers in Japan, where only the freshest and highest quality foods are salable. Their concern for quality is pushing the entire restaurant industry to improve its performance in this critical area.

This gives restaurant chains one more advantage over their single-site competitors. The ability to market a brand will remain a powerful tool in attracting quality-conscious consumers. However, the sterile uniformity of the most homogenized restaurant chains is out. Consumers increasingly are shopping for quality food delivered in an ambience of warmth and comfort.

Chef-owned restaurants will find it increasingly difficult to establish a foothold, save in the largest cities, where one person's reputation can attract customers in sufficient numbers to sustain a business.

Consistent quality is important for another reason as well: Since consumers increasingly get their information from the Internet, a single dissatisfied customer in Dubuque, Iowa, can damage a chain's reputation all over the country.

This trend will become more important in Europe as the Brussels bureaucrats of the European Union spin off ever more consumerist regulations and more upscale American restaurant chains expand their Continental operations.

High Tech, High Touch

As technology permeates our daily lives and further reduces us to small, highly pressured cogs in the global economy, our need for comfort and personal attention is growing rapidly. Restaurants increasingly are providing a haven where we can sit back, relax, and feel a little bit pampered. This is one powerful force behind the growth of the new upscale restaurant chains that are quickly building a niche between casual dining operations and the luxury restaurants.

Technology is bringing even more obvious changes outside the diner's view. Automated equipment, more sophisticated order and inventory systems, and other improvements in information technology will continue to cut operating costs for both quick-service and full-service restaurants. For example, automated food service prep machines are being integrated into the process of fulfilling customer orders. French fryers can be connected to point-of-sale hardware and automatically lower fries into the oil as orders are placed. Automatic drink dispensers fill orders with no human intervention. Anything that is repetitive and requires consistency will be replaced over time with robots. The biggest change in restaurant practice may be the arrival of RFID—radio frequency identification—chips. RFID systems can track individual items—cans of ingredients, prepackaged meals, and even plates and flatware—from the supplier's warehouse to the patron's table. This will make it possible to update inventories at each location in real time, order supplies when needed, and reduce the capital tied up in consumables.

Outsourcing is another tech-enabled option. Corporate-level accounting, personnel records, and similar functions can be shipped to reliable offshore data services with a significant impact on the bottom line.

Technology is also responsible for raising some other costs. After a brief respite in the 1990s, the price of healthcare is again rising at double-digit rates, thanks in substantial part to the high cost of new medical technologies. As new diagnostic and treatment methods reach clinical use, they will continue to drive up the cost of employee medical benefits—for the increasingly rare employer that still provides them. This trend is likely to continue as long as smoking and obesity remain common. In Europe, these costs will be felt as higher taxes rather than as direct expenses.

At the same time, restaurants are finding that technology makes it pay to retain employees, even if salary costs are slightly higher. It costs less overall to keep a skilled employee than to provide training and benefits for a new hire. In the long run, retaining practiced workers lowers costs and increases guest satisfaction. This trend is growing faster in full-service restaurants than in quick-service establishments.

Gen Xers, Dots, and Millennials

Though the Baby Boomers still dominate Western culture, their children and grandchildren are a growing force in society. They are influencing the restaurant business in a number of ways.

Members of the post-Boomer generations have more in common with their peers throughout the world than with their parents. They share values, fashion sense, and a host of other factors that mark them as something new and different. They are materialistic; individualistic, yet cooperative in groups; tech-savvy; and given to extremely short attention spans.

They also are relatively rare. Generation X (roughly the forty-plus cohort), the Dot-coms (now in their thirties), and the Millennials (their twenty-something siblings) are far smaller than the Baby Boom age group. Though there are more entry-level workers today than there were five years ago, there still are fewer than employers need. In the United States, more than half of restaurant operators say they are finding it increasingly hard to hire enough workers, particularly hourly workers. The shortage is tightest among cooks, but this problem is felt in all positions.

The worker shortage affects quick-service restaurants more severely than full-service locations. One-third of American quick-service operators report that recruiting and retaining employees is a major challenge, compared with only 14 percent of full-service operators with average check sizes over $8. This problem can only grow worse in the near future.

Generation X is highly entrepreneurial. Throughout the world, Gen Xers are starting new businesses at an unprecedented rate. The Dot-coms are proving to be even more business-oriented, caring for little but the bottom line. Twice as many say they would prefer to own a business than be a top executive. Five times more would prefer to own a business rather than hold a key position in politics or government.

If this sounds like good news for business, it's not. The bottom line these generations care about is their own, not their employer's. They have grown up to expect affluence, and even wealth. Just how they will achieve it is not clear, given that many in the United States are undereducated even for most working-class jobs. But the GenXers and Dot-coms also watched their parents remain loyal to their employers, only to be downsized out of work. The lesson was not lost on them. They will quit and move across the country at even the hint of a job that offers better pay or opportunities for training. The data are not readily available, but we strongly suspect that this is true in the other developed countries as well. The generations now entering the job market are likely to be even less reliable than their older peers.

If you are beginning to think the work ethic is in trouble, you are catching on. For younger employees, work is only a means to their ends: money, fun, and leisure. In this, Americans are just catching up with a trend that swept Europe when government pensions and labor laws guaranteed workers there free time and much greater security. Tardiness is increasing, sick-leave abuse is common, and job security and high pay just are not the motivators they once were. Fifty-five percent of the top executives interviewed recently say that erosion of the work ethic will have a major negative effect on corporate performance in the future.

The global recession of 2008–09 is bringing a painful dose of reality to the younger generations. The difficulty of finding a job—any job—in this trying economy is teaching many workers that it is worth keeping the jobs they have. For a couple of years, at least, we expect employee turnover to slow dramatically.

Yet this slowdown in employee turnover is likely to be as short-lived as the decline of SUV sales when oil prices were at their 2008 peak. To meet their need for reliable workers, restaurants in the years ahead will have to adopt all the standard recruiting techniques: raise starting salaries, provide better benefits, and expand training programs.

For today's entry-level workers, training for future jobs is a key issue; they simply do not believe in traditional careers and long-term employment, even if the restaurant industry were in a position to offer enough satisfying, well-paid positions to go around. So an essential factor in retaining young workers is to position restaurant jobs and training very clearly as stepping-stones to more desirable positions in other industries later in the recruit's working life.

Better training programs will also be needed to ensure a high quality of service from generations not particularly inclined to pay attention to detail. In this context, displaced Baby Boom workers and post-retirement job seekers become even more important as a source of reliable employees.

One more effect of this change will be to drive restaurants to use robots and artificial intelligence to run and maintain a smooth flow of production in the restaurant. Many of the skills required to maintain smooth operation will be conducted remotely at a central or regional location. Intelligent machines, in-store real-time video, and network connectivity will allow one manager to control several locations.

Clock-Watching

Computers, electronic communications, the Internet, and other technologies are making national and international economies much more competitive. Labor productivity has been skyrocketing in recent years, partly because of these new technologies, but also because companies are driving their employees to do more, faster. American workers accomplished about one-third more work per hour at the end of 2008 than they did in 1992. They also spent about 10 percent more time on the job than they did a decade earlier. European executives and nonunionized workers face the same trend.

In this high-pressure environment, dining out is becoming ever more important, both as a convenience to harried workers and as an opportunity to relax and enjoy life after the stresses of work. In a study by the National Restaurant Association, 79 percent of American diners said that eating out was a better use of their leisure time than cooking and cleaning up. Those workers will continue to expand the market for casual and higher-end dining.

"The multi-unit operators will continue research to ensure that their menu price points will drive the time-conscious harried workers to their restaurants," comments Paul Wise, dean emeritus and former head of the hospitality program at the University of Delaware. "The frequency of returning customers is a growing important element of success in an increasing competitive environment."[1]

The need to save time is one driver for the spread of American-style family restaurants in Japan. As of 2006, their numbers had nearly doubled in ten years. The global recession slowed this trend, as growing unemployment sent many patrons to quick-service chains.

One growing market is the "grab-and-go" breakfast. Though more than three-fourths of breakfasts are still eaten in the home, that number is likely to decline as working lives become ever more demanding. Many potential customers will opt for a donut or energy bar and coffee in the car. Others will stop at their preferred quick-service restaurant for something more substantial.

Government Watchdogs

Since the U.S. Congress passed regulatory reform laws in 1996, nearly 20,000 new regulations have been enacted. Not one proposed regulation has been rejected during this period. The Federal Register, where proposed and enacted regulations are published, was nearly 50 percent larger in 1998 than it had been just ten years earlier—50,000 pages in all. A decade later, it had expanded to 80,700 pages.

In Brussels, officials of the European Union are churning out new regulations at an even faster pace, creating more uniform consumer and workplace regulations throughout the Continent.

Predictably, this growing burden of legal requirements is falling at least as heavily on the restaurant industry as it does on other businesses. In addition to all the general work-related rules, laws proposed in the United States and Europe would provide nutritional data to consumers in real time, even in restaurants where menus are based upon local fresh produce and meats.

To keep up with the competition, corporate computer networks will be required to access data that may be required to run a restaurant in the future. They will automatically check on changes in corporate and industry standards, government regulations for food safety, and other information critical to business planning.

Beyond that, there really is not much to be said about the spread of government regulations. Restaurant operators will have to spend a growing fraction of their time coping with them, just as their peers in other industries do. It's just one more cost of doing business.

Security That Isn't Social

The September 11 attacks on New York and Washington inspired a wave of laws and regulations intended to keep would-be terrorists out of the country or at least to render them unable to harm others. This transformation has placed a whole new level of legal and regulatory demands on all businesses.

A bioterrorist attack on the food industry could be the most important terrorist risk in the developed world. Directly and indirectly, the food industry generates 13 percent of the U.S. GDP and employs one in eight Americans; in some European countries, the numbers are slightly higher. This makes food a target to gladden the heart of any terrorist.

Restaurants are the most accessible bull's-eyes in the industry, with the highest concentrations of relaxed, vulnerable civilians. Restaurant attacks would have enormous shock value. To date, most have been straightforward bombings of establishments where Americans and other westerners congregate. Such attacks have occurred in Germany, Bali, Morocco, India, and many other lands. They will happen again. They are possible almost anywhere in the world because most borders present relatively few obstacles for the would-be terrorist. This is especially a concern for the European Union, because a person who has entered one EU country can travel freely throughout the Continent.

Food contamination may be an even greater threat. It has happened before. As early as 1984, followers of Bhagwan Shree Rajneesh contaminated eleven salad bars with salmonella in a plot to take political control of Wasco County, Oregon, by preventing nonmembers from voting in a local election. The group reportedly possessed cultures of typhoid fever as well; the salmonella was just a proof-of-concept experiment. Nonetheless, it sickened more than seven hundred people.

It could have been far worse. To take just one possible scenario, imagine what would have happened if the person who mailed anthrax bacteria to American politicians and journalists in 2001 had instead taken a lunch-time job at a restaurant near Wall Street or in London's financial district, or even had signed on at his local McDonald's. The results might not be as immediate and dramatic as a bomb tossed through the front door, but they could prove just as devastating.

Restaurant operators should consider hiring security experts to look for vulnerabilities in their locations and operations. Consistent with the comfort and pleasure of their customers, they may want to take precautions to make themselves harder targets for would-be terrorists.

Because food contamination is an obvious tactic for terrorists, restaurants will be under growing pressure to know exactly whom they are hiring and to maintain detailed records about their employees.

One new and important overhead item is insurance coverage against terrorist incidents. In the United States, case law now holds that professional hosts such as restaurants and meeting planners are liable for injuries to their guests caused by a terrorist attack on their site.

The Rich Get Richer

We have written in other chapters about bimodal distribution—the tendency of large, successful companies to keep growing and small ones to flourish in niche markets, while mid-sized competitors are bought up or driven out of business. We have seen this pattern among automakers and computer companies, banks and hotels. We see it among restaurants as well. The consolidation seen among chains in this sector will continue. Expect a continuing stream of mergers, acquisitions, and deal-making in the restaurant industry in the years ahead.

The growing popularity of restaurant chains positioned nearer the middle of the price and service range appears to be something of an exception to this trend in the United States. We expect it to spread to Europe before this decade is over. Restaurants in the fast-casual market—such as Baja Fresh and Panera Bread—offer a wider range of menu options and more inviting décor than quick-service chains, but much less service than casual-dining establishments. Similarly, places like the Bonefish Grill, The Cheesecake Factory, and its even higher-end spinoff, the Grand Lux Cafe, offer a more upscale experience than the casual-dining chains but less service and ambience than luxury restaurants. Market segmentation clearly allows more diversity among restaurant chains than is found in most other industries. When combined with a unique identity and a reputation for quality, economies of scale can make for a winning combination in almost any part of the market.

However, the growing proliferation of restaurant names—whether chains or single-location neighborhood restaurants—is likely to cut into profits in the years ahead. According to the National Restaurant Association, nearly two-thirds of fine-dining restaurant operators and half of casual-dining and family-dining chain operators say that it is becoming more difficult to maintain customer loyalty than it used to be.

This is one more place where technology will come to the rescue. By collecting information about individual customers, restaurants will be able to customize their future dining experiences. As guests become accustomed to entering a grocery store, downloading their grocery list, and receiving special coupons designed for their individual preferences, they will start to expect this same experience when they enter their favorite restaurant chain. They will want to know which items have appeared on the menu since their last visit, and which contain peanuts or other ingredients that they dislike or that might trigger their allergies. The menu will be personalized to the individual taste. In the immediate future, this will apply largely to full-service restaurants, but the trend toward individually customized menus will soon extend to quick-service locations as well.

In All...

These trends spell interesting times for the world's restaurant operators—and according to popular tradition, the wish that someone live in interesting times is an old Chinese curse, not a blessing. Yet at FI we are optimistic about the long-term future of the restaurant industry.

There are some difficult challenges ahead, particularly with regard to staffing and overhead. Nonetheless, the restaurant industry has both a decades-long record of success and all the assets it needs to build a bright future. In prosperous, growing, and increasingly stressful nations, it supplies two of the basic necessities of life: food and comfort. And if 90 percent of independent restaurants go out of business in their first year, well-run chains and the best independent operators have always looked forward to a long and productive future. So it is today.

The restaurant industry's unique market—every man, woman, and child in every country—is huge and receptive, and its challenges are manageable. For the world's restaurant operators, a bright and prosperous future appears to be all but assured.

Key Trends for Restaurants

In this section we look at the key trends for restaurants, using entries from Appendix A. We list each relevant trend and our assessment of it and then detail the specific implications of this trend for the restaurant industry.

2. POPULATION OF THE DEVELOPED WORLD IS LIVING LONGER.

Assessment: Demographic trends such as this are among the easiest to recognize and most difficult to derail. Barring a global plague or nuclear war—wildcard possibilities that cannot be predicted with any validity—there is little chance that the population forecast for 2050 will err on the low side.

Implications for Restaurants: Older diners will make up a growing portion of restaurant clientele. Older workers also will be available to make up the slack left by the small size of younger generations.

Older diners will seek out stronger flavors, to make up for the declining sensitivity of their taste buds.

9. TIME IS BECOMING THE WORLD'S MOST PRECIOUS COMMODITY.

Assessment: This trend is likely to grow as changing technologies add the need for lifelong study to the many commitments that compete for the average worker's time. As it matures in the United States, it is likely to survive in other parts of the world. It will not disappear until China and India reach modern post-industrial status, around 2050.

Implications for Restaurants: Dining out is becoming ever more desirable, both as an escape from our increasingly pressured working lives and as a better use of time than cooking and cleaning up after meals.

Harried workers with only a few minutes to spare will continue to patronize quick-service restaurants and will favor outlets with the tastiest food and most pleasant, relaxing environments.

Fast-casual restaurant chains will continue to prosper as cheap, convenient, more comfortable alternatives to quick-service meals.

12. TOURISM, VACATIONING, AND TRAVEL (ESPECIALLY INTERNATIONAL) CONTINUE TO GROW WITH EACH PASSING YEAR.

Assessment: Travel seems to be in the DNA of the middle and upper economic classes. This trend will continue as long as national economies continue to generate new prosperity for the formerly poor.

Implications for Restaurants: Tourists increasingly are taking vacations out of season, softening the seasonality of income that has long been typical of restaurants in tourist destinations.

17. Generation X, the Dot-coms, and the Millennials are gaining social and organizational influence.

Assessment: As trends go, this is an evergreen. In a few years, we will simply add the next new generation to the list.

Implications for Restaurants: Higher salaries, better benefits, and opportunities for training will be increasingly important in motivating and retaining younger workers.

Younger workers will require a more "hands-off" management style than previous generations have been willing to accept.

Post-retirement workers will be needed, both to make up for the shortfall in the younger generations and to ensure that some employees, at least, will be motivated and reliable.

19. The economy of the developed world is growing steadily, with only brief interruptions.

Assessment: These trends have been revised many times since they were first codified in the late 1980s. Some trends have fallen out of the list as they matured or as circumstances came along to change them. Others have been added as they were recognized. This trend has remained a constant, and with each revision its effective period has been extended. To invalidate this trend would take a catastrophe on the order of the permanent loss of Middle Eastern oil from the Western economies. Not even the recession of 2008–09 rises to that level of destruction.

Implications for Restaurants: Restaurant sales will grow at least as quickly as economies in general, and probably a bit faster. This should bring good times for restaurant operators throughout the industrialized world.

Upscale restaurants will benefit from the growing prosperity of their customers, as patrons who might have dined slightly down-market feel able to spend a bit more for a meal.

However, quick-service chains will also benefit as hard-pressed workers with only a few minutes to spare choose to "grab and go" rather than spend time preparing their own meals.

21. Consumerism is still growing.

Assessment: This trend seems likely to remain healthy for at least the next fifteen years.

Implications for Restaurants: Restaurants will have to cope with a growing burden of consumer-oriented regulations.

Restaurant chains with a reputation for quality will have an enormous advantage in advertising to knowledgeable consumers.

Single-location restaurants will be at a growing competitive disadvantage, except in major cities where the reputation of a top chef can carry them.

Any problems with quality are likely to be immortalized on consumer-oriented Internet sites, where they will discourage potential customers long after they have been corrected.

28. THE WORK ETHIC IS VANISHING.

Assessment: There is little prospect that this will change until the children of today's young adults grow up to rebel against their parents' values.

Implications for Restaurants: Productivity is likely to suffer as Baby Boom executives are replaced by their Generation X and Dot-com successors.

34. TECHNOLOGY INCREASINGLY DOMINATES BOTH THE ECONOMY AND SOCIETY.

Assessment: Technology-related changes in society and business seen over the last twenty years are just the beginning of a trend that will accelerate at least through this century.

Implications for Restaurants: Our growing dependence on sterile, hard-edged technology is one of the most powerful forces behind our need for such modest luxuries as restaurant meals.

Restaurants will depend more and more on automation to make up for shortages of workers and to ensure more uniform quality of meals and service.

53. INSTITUTIONS ARE UNDERGOING A BIMODAL DISTRIBUTION: THE BIG GET BIGGER, THE SMALL SURVIVE, AND THE MID-SIZED ARE SQUEEZED OUT.

Assessment: Thanks in part to technology, this trend is likely to be a permanent feature of the business scene from now on.

Implications for Restaurants: Mid-priced, family-oriented restaurants will continue to face difficult times as large, value-oriented chains out-compete them at one end of the scale and high-quality, high-luxury establishments capture their customers on the other. The fast-casual segment will continue to grow at a comfortable rate for at least several years.

As chains proliferate and target a relatively fixed population of diners, it will be increasingly difficult to maintain customer loyalty.

55. INTERNATIONAL EXPOSURE INCLUDES A GROWING RISK OF TERRORIST ATTACK.

Assessment: This trend is unlikely to change in the next decade and relatively unlikely to change in the next twenty years. A permanent end to the international terrorist threat would require a broad philosophical and cultural change in Islam that makes terrorists pariahs in their own communities. No such change is on the horizon.

Implications for Restaurants: Today, virtually every establishment has "international" exposure, because borders are relatively porous, even in the post–September 11 environment. This is particularly true in the European Union, where anyone who enters one member country has unimpeded access to all the rest.

Restaurants are a prime target for terrorist attack, because they host large numbers of relaxed, unsuspecting victims, and because people watching news reports—the real targets of the attack—can easily picture themselves happily enjoying a meal when the attack occurred.

Contamination of food with toxins or pathogens is a serious risk, and one that it is difficult to protect against.

Restaurants and chains unable to maintain their own security departments will need consultants to identify risks, design security programs, and screen possible new hires.

 Endnote

1. Personal communication, August 2008.

10

The Past Is Prologue

PICTURE YOUR NEXT VACATION as it might be in 2075. In early July, you and your family ride the space elevator to a port terminal 62,000 miles over the equator. There you join nearly two thousand other budget-conscious tourists on an interstellar cruiser the size of an ocean liner. After a stately embarkation, you sail out through interplanetary space, past the giant storms of Jupiter, close enough to Saturn to walk on its rings, and on into the inky blackness beyond. Just four luxurious days later, you arrive at Alpha Centauri, the star closest to our own sun, tour a small but spectacular system of planets, and get out at...

Er, well, probably at a theme park in Orlando, where the whole journey took place in a few hours of virtual reality. Alas, the smart money in physics is still betting that Einstein was right about not going faster than the speed of light. We will never travel to the stars unless we learn to hibernate and spend centuries en route. $E = mc^2$: It's not just a good idea, it's the law.

Nonetheless, many other changes will come to the hospitality industry over the next few decades. None will be as dramatic as star travel, but some may be nearly as important to the participants.

What follows is a timeline of probabilities. Unlike the brief science fiction scenario above, the developments below are rooted in today's realities. A majority deal with new technologies, for obvious reasons: Technology changes much faster than social factors, and it is often the driver that eventually forces societal change. Our dates are "guesstimates"; they could be a few years off in either direction. However, we at Forecasting International will be surprised if many of these predictions fail to materialize.

Top Ten in the Next Ten Years

Let us begin with our picks for the ten most important developments for the next ten years in hospitality and travel. Then we can go on to some interesting probabilities.

10. In-air Internet, cell phones, and text messaging. Airlines remain the last bastion of privacy in an increasingly connected world, thanks largely to the fear that radio transmitters such as wireless modems and cell phones could wreak havoc with aircraft navigation systems. That is changing fast. American Airlines has announced plans to offer onboard Internet access—for a modest fee, of course—while Virgin America and JetBlue have been testing free e-mail and instant messaging. By 2018, privacy in the air will be just a memory. Whether it is a good or bad memory depends on how much you miss instant access to friends, colleagues, and the world's online information.

9. The continuing decline of travel agents. For now, the cruise industry is just about the last refuge of travel agents, thanks to cruise line executives who believe their product is too complex and costly to market effectively over the Internet—and fear that online sales would hurt their image of luxurious exclusivity. Now even that safe harbor is vanishing as large-scale cruise marketers are booking berths over the Internet. Ten years from now, even high-end cruise lines will have given in and replaced travel agents with comprehensive videos of their accommodations and itineraries and online booking systems. Travel agents will arrange only the most exclusive cruises and complex custom tours, and today's much-shrunken population of agents will be smaller still.

8. Airport information kiosks. Automated ticketing kiosks are just the beginning. Soon, digital access points modeled on them will dispense information from *Arthur Frommer's Budget Travel,* the *CIA World Factbook,* and a host of other sources. Other services will be added quickly: insurance sales, information packages customized for your planned itinerary downloaded to data cards or flash drives for your laptop computer, and even electronic books for your MP3 player or Amazon Kindle.

7. Universal easy pass. Today, a wireless credit card in a key fob can get you through highway toll gates or let you pay for gas with a wave of your hand. Visa's payWave touchless credit cards already are accepted at some 32,000 retailers, while MasterCard and American Express have rolled out similar services. Ten years down the road, any of these cards, and probably others, will pay your way in or out of any major hotel, restaurant, or tourist attraction with a casual wave of the hand. That should help to cut the waiting lines at the oh-so-exotic Starbucks and McDonald's in Beijing.

6. Technology eases security delays. Tired of waiting forever in airport security lines? Relief is not far off. By making traveler identification far more secure, biometric passports should go a long way to ease checking in and out. Most today carry only descriptive data and a digital photo of the owner. Future versions will carry fingerprints (German passports already do), retinal photos, or other hard-to-fake identifiers.

Those passports will enable the second convenience: priority lists that speed travelers through customs as frequent flier lists ease movement through airport security.

Terahertz cameras will let screeners check your soles for hidden bombs without taking off your shoes—and without raising the kind of controversy that accompanied news that full-body T-ray cameras let them see through your clothes.

No doubt we have missed other ways in which new technologies will help speed us through security lines ten years hence, but even these few should go a long way toward easing the frustration of entering or leaving an airplane, cruise ship, or country.

5. RFID. Combining a digital memory chip with a tiny radio transmitter, radio frequency identification (RFID) chips make it possible to identify and track whatever they are attached to. Biometric passports are one application of RFID. Hotel key cards are another. But it is the behind-the-scenes uses of RFID that will make the greatest difference in hospitality. Restaurants, food services, hotels—just about every kind of business that deals in physical objects—are using them to keep track of inventory so that they can order the supplies they need when they need them, rather than keeping extras on hand to avoid running out. That boosts efficiency and cuts costs. RFID should raise profit margins throughout the hospitality and travel industry, even as it improves guest satisfaction. Think how much happier air travelers will be when their baggage reliably arrives at the same destination they do!

4. Real-time translation. Forget the old-fashioned talking dictionaries where you pick a phrase and the machine speaks it in another language. Much sooner than ten years from now, handheld translators will convert whatever you say among eight or ten major languages in real time. They will not replace human translators entirely, nor foreign-language guides in major museums and tourist attractions. But they will make it a lot easier to ask, "Where's the nearest loo?" in Japanese.

Future models will add other functions such as currency exchange rates, updated daily from the Internet. But the biggest advance will be camera-equipped translators that you can aim at a shop sign, bus schedule, prescription label, or menu to find out what it means. No more ordering a meal only to find out that you have inadvertently asked for the wine steward! It's coming within ten years.

3. Recovery of the airline industry. Amid today's threatened bankruptcies and economic woes, any thought of a brighter future for the airlines may seem like a sad fantasy. Yet today's pain is forcing changes on the industry that will make for a more efficient, prosperous tomorrow. Airlines are cutting their routes, eliminating planes to raise the number of passengers per plane, and cooperating more with competitors to serve more destinations with fewer aircraft. Southwest Airlines has bucked the industry trend by eliminating miscellaneous charges and setting flat, no-surprises prices for its flights. These innovations, smaller workforces, more efficient airplanes, and other developments will help airlines control both costs and fares and put them on course for a profitable future.

2. Aging of the Baby Boom generation. Wherever they have gone in life, America's vast Baby Boom generation has dominated their world. Over the next ten years, they will be going into retirement, the period when, on average, people in the developed world have the greatest wealth and freedom to travel. Their needs will dominate much of hospitality planning. Look for new facilities and services, such as larger, elder-friendly signs, levered door and faucet handles, and louder announcement volumes; spicier foods to delight less acute taste buds, but smaller portions suited to waning appetites; special tours with early-bird specials; and enhanced medical services at resorts and other destinations.

1. China and India meet the world. They're coming! An extra seventy-five million tourists every year, fanning out across the world, fifty million from the vast new Chinese middle class and twenty-five million from India. Add a few million more from oil-rich Russia—to date, most have been visiting the Middle East, rather than more traditional destinations—and from increasingly prosperous Brazil. In the next ten years, the market for international tourism will nearly double—and that does not count the opening of new tourist destinations in India and once-reclusive China for visitors from the West. If there could be any greater development in hospitality and travel over the next ten years—or any ten years in history—we at Forecasting International cannot think what it might be.

So there they are: our nominations for the ten most important developments of the next decade in the world's most vibrant industry. No doubt we will eventually look back on this selection and wonder how we missed some other novelty that has unexpectedly transformed the field. Still, we are comfortable with this list. From Moscow to Mumbai and Fairbanks to Capetown, few participants in hospitality and travel will remain unaffected by these ten innovations for the next ten years.

The items below are slightly more speculative in that most of them depend on technologies that have yet to be developed. This is especially true of the forecasts beyond, say, 2020. Yet when we are wrong, it is likely to be because even bigger changes made these possibilities obsolete. When forecasters peer out into the farther distances, our mistakes are usually failures of the imagination. The far future is always stranger than we can anticipate.

2015

Invisible idiot. That is how one early language-translation program, converting from English to Russian and back again, interpreted the phrase "Out of sight, out of mind." The software available online today does not do much better, as anyone who has tried to read foreign-language e-mail can attest. But within a few years, well-equipped tourists will be carrying pocket computers capable of translating idiomatic speech from any of half a dozen major languages into any of the others, in real time. Just talk into the box, and that Parisian waiter will know exactly what you want. Whether he likes your accent well enough to bring it is another matter.

Who are you? In the age of terrorism, governments want to know for sure. During this period, probably by 2012, passports and visas will be replaced by biometric identity cards that carry records of your fingerprints, retinal blood vessels, and other permanent, unique proof that you are really you.

Watch the birdie. Or not. If you can see it, the tiny digital camera built into your sunglasses will capture it for your friends back home. Expect basic Video Graphic Array (VGA) resolution by 2012, and higher-quality snaps a couple of years later.

Condo cruising. The first cruise ship with apartments owned by the passengers (price tags from about $900,000) is already sailing from one luxury destination to another, with stops at major tourist events planned. How quickly other ships follow its lead depends on the global economy, but FI expects that half a dozen of these ultimate recreational vehicles will take to the water by 2014.

Superclothes. For adventurous vacationers headed to deserts, mountains, and other hostile areas, industrial-strength couturiers are developing "active" attire that cools or warms the wearer as needed, and collects and stores solar energy to keep your GPS going without heavy batteries. Look for them at trendy outfitters around 2012.

Going, going, almost gone. Travel agents, that is. They already are an endangered species, their numbers down from 35,000 in the United States at the end of 2000 to only 24,000 by late 2008. Only the cruise industry still relies on travel agents for their bookings, a throwback to the days when cruises were reserved for the wealthy elite. Though some prominent executives are reluctant to accept the obvious, their patronage is not enough to support even those agents who have survived this long. Neither can their distaste for online booking and other agent-less forms of customer service long offset the economies and efficiencies of direct sales. By 2015, tourists could visit travel agencies as they would tour the back country of New Guinea, to see a vanishing way of life.

See the world—from above. The X-Prize competition is offering $10 million to the first private team that sends three people on a suborbital junket into space and manages to repeat the feat within two weeks. At least three entrants have made atmospheric test flights, and one is almost certain to make near-space flight practical within the next five years. After that, it will take less than a decade to build the first large-scale space tourism industry. Seats will sell for a lot less than the $20 million paid by Dennis Tito and Mark Shuttleworth to visit the International Space Station. The hardest part is likely to be getting insurance for the flights.

Generations of entrepreneurs. Throughout the world, people forty and under are starting businesses at a record rate. Many of the companies they start will be in the hospitality industry. Expect a huge wave of new resorts, restaurants, tour operators, and other travel services in the next two decades.

End of immigration. Travel and almost every land will open its arms to you. Threaten to stay, and you'll be as welcome as a two-cent tip. Throughout the industrialized world, native citizens complain that guest workers and other immigrants are taking jobs, soaking up public resources, and refusing to integrate into the local culture. And though many of those jobs are positions that no one else would willingly accept, there is enough truth in the other complaints to make this movement a powerful political force. Add post-September 11 security concerns, and it's all but inevitable. Under tomorrow's immigration policies, feel free to visit, but remember to leave.

2020

Faster than a speeding bullet train. The world's fastest trains today operate at a paltry 200 mph or so, though magnetic levitation trains running on closed courses have topped 300 mph. By 2020, the first 500-mph maglev trains will finally carry tourists around Japan, from Los Angeles to Las Vegas, and along other flat, high-density routes. The technology should be available by 2010 or so, but economic and political problems will stall its use for years.

Build it and they will come. A host of tourist attractions have proved this axiom in recent years. These include the sixty-story Burj Al Arab hotel in Dubai, with a seafood restaurant submerged in the Red Sea; the fabulous new Bibliotheca Alexandrina in Alexandria; the ice hotels rebuilt each winter in Greenland and Swedish Lapland; and the spectacularly popular London Eye. By 2020, we expect to see at least sixty new destinations built. Most will have some unique appeal, but six of the world's major cities will erect their own versions of the London Eye. China already is developing thirteen tourist destinations outside the few—such as Beijing and the Great Wall—that Westerners are familiar with.

How do you spell Kaopectate in Russian? Point your camera at a sign or label, and it will tell you what is written there. IBM already is working on the technology to translate text written in Cyrillic, Arabic, Hebrew, and Chinese characters into Western languages. Suddenly, we won't have to speak the local language to identify the drugstore and find what we need. By 2016, automatic translators for written material, probably built into cameras and other digital hardware, will be standard cargo for well-equipped tourists.

Vacation offer you can't refuse. It's a way of life in Europe. Cities empty in the summer as workers head off for a month of R&R that is guaranteed by law. The day will come when American workers also enjoy shorter workweeks and mandatory vacations, despite the objections of politically influential employers. The reason is that the jobs lost from manufacturing in recent years are just the beginning. Automation and global competition will continue to squeeze jobs from the American economy until, in the long run, it becomes impossible to create useful work for all who need it. The only answer will be to cut the workweek, add time off, and open new jobs to fill in for vacationing workers. The result will be a burst of growth in tourism like nothing the industry has ever seen.

Note that this is the most "iffy" forecast in this report. A combination of dramatically reduced birth rates, limited immigration, much better public education, rapid economic growth, and other changes might conceivably forestall a job crisis indefinitely. Yet what we are experiencing are high immigration, unexpectedly high birth rates, generally ineffectual public education, and the worst economic downturn in years. And it seems likely that the day will come when few noncreative tasks still require human hands. At some point in the future, much-expanded leisure seems all but inevitable. The late 2020s are our best guess at when this will occur, but no more than a guess.

Advertising in 3D. Today, holographic videos are cutting-edge technology. Twenty years from now, they will be consumer products. For tour operators, hotels, and other segments of the hospitality industry, 3D videos—delivered either by mail or over the Internet—will be the ultimate advertising medium, showing potential visitors exactly what they will experience at their destinations. Of course, in a few years they will be supplanted by virtual reality systems that re-create the vacation experience even more vividly.

UN *über alles*. America's go-it-alone foreign policy is an aberration that cannot last. A global economy calls for global institutions, and that means power will inevitably flow toward the United Nations, the International Court of Justice, and the few other bodies with worldwide jurisdiction. To provide broader representation in those bodies, India and one of the Scandinavian countries will finally be admitted to the UN Security Council. This will gradually provide much more uniform laws, regulations, and standards for the hospitality industry and other multinational businesses.

It's a gas, gas, gas. Technologically, hydrogen-powered cars are just over the horizon. Economically and societally, they will not make the grade until some environmentally-minded government mandates a change to hydrogen power. Once that happens, industry will ramp up hydrogen production and put fueling stations in every community. Then bigger things will happen. By 2025, ecotourists visiting the Arctic, Antarctic, and other pristine destinations will arrive by hydrogen-powered jets that emit only water as their exhaust and avoid contaminating sensitive environments.

Eco-backlash. On the other hand, having hundreds of tourists trampling the Arctic tundra and other fragile environments will not sit well with committed environmentalists, even if the vacationers do travel by eco-friendly aircraft. Global protests against this perceived despoiling of our common heritage will quickly give rise to stringent limits on the number of tourists who can visit what little true wilderness remains in the world.

2030

Beanstalk to the stars. The science fiction scenario that began this chapter contained one bit of future reality: the space elevator. First envisioned some forty years ago, the elevator will climb an enormous cable, like Jack up the beanstalk, to a terminal where passengers and cargo can board spacecraft for the trip farther out. Until recently, this was just a fantasy because there were no materials strong enough to build the cable. Today, so-called carbon nanotubes up to twenty times stronger than steel are approaching mass production, and engineers say a space elevator could be completed within fifteen years. Unfortunately, economic and political factors probably will double that lead time. According to current estimates, the first space elevator could be built for about $10 billion. Cost for a trip to space would be $200 per pound or less, compared with $40,000 per pound for the space shuttle. At that price, the space elevator will make space tourism routine.

2040

Room service? Today, there is only one hotel under the sea—the two-bedroom Jules Underwater Resort in Key Largo, Florida—and just two restaurants. Four decades ahead, underwater hotels and restaurants will be almost common. Most will appear in shallow water, where sunlight penetrates to illuminate abundant life; the most spectacular will be located on Australia's Great Barrier Reef. However, at least one small, spare, and incredibly expensive hotel will provide accommodations more than five miles down, where guests can see forests of giant tube worms, "volcanoes" of hot, mineral-rich water, and luminescent fish swimming past the tiny, foot-thick portholes.

　　Think it and they may not come after all. Scientists have dreamed for years of building computers that understand our thoughts and send data directly into our brains. But that means a kind of artificial telepathy. Think into your computer in San Francisco, and someone in Bangalore will "hear" the thought over the Internet. And that offers the ultimate virtual reality. If one person swims in the sea, walks on the moon, or runs a three-minute mile, the rest of us can share the experience from the comfort of our own living rooms. It brings up the obvious question—why leave home at all? One answer is snob appeal. Virtual reality will be good enough for many, but the rich will display their wealth by taking the time, and spending the money, to go in person.

　　You too can be the man in the moon. Or at least on it. The first permanent moon base is likely to appear in the 2030s. A decade later, it will be capable of accommodating up to 350 people, including 50 tourists. Thanks to a growing array of space elevators circling Earth's equator, a lunar jaunt will even be relatively affordable. As demand grows, a space elevator on the moon will bring the price within reach of solidly middle-class families.

2050

One world after all. Four decades ahead, the dollar and euro will be supplanted by a single world monetary unit, ending exchange problems forever. Biometric identity cards will be issued soon after birth, and the data will be stored in banks accessible by any government. This will make it nearly impossible for terrorists and other criminals to move around undetected, but routine tracking of our daily movements will further erode what little is left of the old-fashioned concept of privacy.

Universal English. Those automatic translators will be useful for only thirty-five years or so. English already is the *de facto* language of business, as French once was the language of diplomacy. By 2050, 90 percent of the people in the world will speak English, at least as a second language. In major tourist destinations, the number will be even higher.

2060

Jobs aplenty. Today, an estimated 14 percent of the world's people work in the hospitality industry. Tomorrow, it will be 25 percent. In part, we will owe this dramatic growth to the explosion of leisure time when shorter workweeks and forced vacations spread from Europe to the rest of the world. But this also is in the nature of the industry. Fifty years from now, personal service could be the only job category that still requires human workers.

Meet and greet. With a global Internet, lifelike virtual reality, and even computerized telepathy available to all, who needs in-person meetings? Nearly everyone, as it turns out. Full-contact telecommunications will do for routine conversations, but to meet new business associates, conduct difficult negotiations, or just build relationships over a round of golf, people will need to "press the flesh" for many decades to come. The meetings and expositions segment will continue to struggle with economic, social, and technological issues as far into the future as the eye can see. But there will be more corporate and industry-wide meetings in 2060 than in 2006.

2075

Water, water everywhere. At least in the low places of the world. At the rate things are going, global warming will raise the seas by two to three feet in the next seventy-five years. That will mean hard times for lands such as Bangladesh and the Louisiana lowlands, which are barely above sea level now and are sinking even as the water rises. It will also modify our travel habits, as temperatures and rainfall patterns change. Expect what is left of Florida to turn into baking jungle, while crops bloom in parts of Canada and Siberia that today hold little more than ice.

Atoms in space. Nuclear power is banned from space by international treaty. Nonetheless, by 2075 long-range space tugs powered by nuclear reactors will be ferrying cargo and very patient tourists out to Mars, the asteroid belt, and even beyond. Travel time? About three months each way for Mars, more than a year for Jupiter.

Oldies but goodies. Some of the hottest destinations tomorrow would probably be familiar to today's travel agents. As we have seen, fast, overwhelming technological change will bring a host of new options for tourism. However, it will also strengthen our taste for old, familiar things and our need to reconnect with the past. Crowds will still surround the Taj Mahal, the Great Wall of China, and the pyramids; visit the Grand Canyon and Old Faithful; tour the fjords, the Yangtze River dam, and the Amazon; and throng the halls of the Hermitage and the Acropolis.

Old friends as well. Whatever other changes buffet the hospitality industry, it will still need the same fundamental services that all industries need: somewhere to gather to make contacts and win contracts and people to provide job-related education, common standards, and certification. These are the province of industry associations, which can bring competitors together on common ground. In 2075, hospitality associations, many of them well known today, will be helping their members to manage one of the largest industries in the world.

Appendix A

Fifty-Five Trends Shaping the Future
of the Hospitality Industry and the World

Population Trends

1. THE WORLD'S POPULATION WILL GROW TO NINE BILLION BY 2050.

Early versions of this report predicted that the world's population would double by 2050, and population growth has proceeded almost exactly on schedule. However, even this estimate may be too low. According to the Center for Strategic & International Studies, most official projections underestimate both fertility and future gains in longevity. Unfortunately, the greatest fertility is found in those countries least able to support their existing people. Populations will triple in the Palestinian territories and Niger between 2000 and 2050 and will more than double in Yemen, Angola, Congo, and Uganda. In contrast, populations in most developed countries are stable or declining. The United States is a prominent exception.

Assessment: Demographic trends such as this are among the easiest to recognize and most difficult to derail. Barring a global plague or nuclear war—wildcard possibilities that cannot be predicted with any validity—there is little chance that the population forecast for 2050 will err on the low side.

Implications: Rapid population growth in the United States compared with its industrialized competitors will reinforce American domination of the global economy, as the European Union falls to third place behind the United States and China.

To meet human nutritional needs over the next forty years, global agriculture will have to supply as much food as has been produced during all of human history.

Unless fertility in the developed lands climbs dramatically, either would-be retirees will have to remain on the job or the industrialized nations will have to encourage even more immigration from the developing world. The third alternative is a sharp economic contraction and lower living standards.

A fourth alternative is the widespread automation of jobs to accomplish the work needed to support accustomed living standards. However, this requires development of a means other than wages to distribute wealth and to provide both a living income and a fulfilling occupation for workers and would-be workers displaced by machines and software.

Barring enforcement of strict immigration controls, rapid migration will continue from the Southern to the Northern Hemisphere and especially from former colonies to Europe. A growing percentage of job applicants in the United States and Europe will be recent immigrants from developing countries.

Implications for Hospitality and Travel: Rapid population growth, compared with other developed lands, will preserve America's place at the top of the global economy, with China taking second place from the European Union. This will help to keep the hospitality and travel industries growing rapidly.

2. POPULATION OF THE DEVELOPED WORLD IS LIVING LONGER.

Each generation lives longer and remains healthier than the last. Since the beginning of the twentieth century, every generation in the United States has lived three years longer than the previous one. An eighty-year-old in 1950 could expect 6.5 more years of life; today's eighty-year-olds are likely to survive 8.5 more years. Life expectancy in Australia, Japan, and Switzerland is now over seventy-five years for males and over eighty for females. A major reason for this improvement is the development of new pharmaceuticals and medical technologies that are making it possible to prevent or cure diseases that would have been fatal to earlier generations. Medical advances that slow the fundamental process of aging now seem to be within reach. (This is a controversial issue within the medical community, but the evidence appears quite strong.) Such treatments could well help today's younger generations live routinely beyond the century mark.

Assessment: See the *Assessment* for Trend 1.

Implications: Global demand for products and services aimed at the elderly will grow quickly in the immediate future, but this trend may pass as geriatric medicine improves the health of the elderly.

Developed countries may face social instability as a result of competition for resources between retirement-age Boomers and their working-age children and grandchildren. At the present rate of growth, public spending on retirement benefits in the United States and other developed countries could be one-fourth of GDP by 2050, even as the number of workers available to support each retiree declines sharply.

Barring dramatic advances in geriatric medicine, the cost of healthcare is destined to skyrocket throughout the developed lands. This could create the long-expected crisis in healthcare financing and delivery. However, dramatic advances in geriatric medicine are all but inevitable. Paying the high cost of new drugs, technologies, and therapies will reduce the overall cost of caring for patients who otherwise would have suffered from disorders delayed, eased, or cured by such advances. In the end, these reductions will offset many of the expected increases, leaving the average healthcare bill in the developed lands much lower than the doomsayers predict.

Any practical extension of the human lifespan will prolong health as well and will reduce the incidence of late-life disorders such as cancer, heart disease, arthritis, and probably Alzheimer's disease. This would dramatically reduce demand for products and services in the senior market, at least in the developed world. Forecasting International (FI) believes this development is nearer than even many researchers expect.

Healthier aging in the developed world may offer new hope to the world's poorer, sicker lands. Faced with declining growth in their pharmaceutical industries, Western nations—and particularly the United States—are likely to subsidize research and treatment for diseases that burden the poor countries of Africa and Asia. This will give those lands their first real prospects for economic growth and improved quality of life.

Implications for Hospitality and Travel: In the developed lands, aging represents the opportunity to accumulate wealth, and the elderly are the wealthiest segment of society. Healthier lifestyles and better geriatric medicine ensure that wealthy seniors are as interested in travel as they are able to afford it. Aging Baby Boomers—already the largest segment of cruisers—will be a ready market, both for traditional high-end cruises and for adventure travel and other niche vacation activities that would have been beyond the physical abilities of earlier generations. Well into their seventies, they will retain their youthful interest in pastimes such as skin diving, hiking, and other low-impact activities with high "experience value."

Catering to the growing population of older travelers will require adaptation from the hospitality and travel industries—doors and plumbing with handles easily operated by arthritic hands; large, easy-to-read signs and menus; foods with strong flavors to stimulate failing palates; fire and security systems that flash lights for the hard-of-hearing; and comprehensive medical facilities, especially for cruise ships.

Special tours and other activities should be ranked for the amount of walking, energy, or agility they require so that older customers can easily choose pastimes within their abilities. It may also be necessary to increase staffing slightly to provide older guests with extra help in checking in, coping with luggage, arranging for local transportation, and dealing with other chores that younger patrons could handle on their own.

Mature travelers tend to be experienced travelers. Many are unforgiving of lapses in service, inferior facilities, or excessively familiar tours and activities. They also want to feel that they are recognized (especially if they are repeat customers), respected, and catered to.

Despite their relative wealth as a group, many seniors are extremely careful with their money. This will further raise the demand for vacation packages that are comfortable, staffed by attentive personnel, and cheap. Seniors also represent a valuable workforce that hospitality and travel businesses will tap, with considerable benefit. Post-retirement workers tend to be diligent, well spoken, and habitually courteous to guests—unlike some younger workers who need to hone their grammatical skills or practice in traditional good manners.

3. THE ELDERLY POPULATION IS GROWING DRAMATICALLY THROUGHOUT THE WORLD.

Worldwide, the elderly (age sixty-five and over) numbered 440 million and represented 6 percent of the global population in 2002. Their numbers will nearly double by 2020 (to constitute nearly 9 percent of the total population) and more than triple by 2050 (becoming nearly 17 percent). In the developed world, people sixty years old and older made up one-fifth of the population in 2000 and will grow to one-third in the next half-century. Throughout the developed world, population growth is fastest among the elderly. In the United States, there are 4.2 million people aged eighty-five and up. By 2050, there will be 19.3 million. In Europe, the United States, and Japan, the aged also form the wealthiest segment of society.

Assessment: Again, this is a demographic trend, difficult to derail and unlikely to change while the massive Baby Boom generation remains on the scene.

Implications: Not counting immigration, the ratio of working-age people to retirees needing their support will drop dramatically in the United States,

Germany, Italy, Russia, Japan, and other countries. This represents a burden on national economies that will be difficult to sustain under current medical and social security systems.

In the next two to three decades, shortages of health workers will loom large in "aging vulnerable" countries. The United States in particular will need at least twice as many physicians specializing in geriatrics as its current 9,000, as well as half a million more nurses by 2020.

Suburban communities are likely to face a growing demand for social services such as senior day care, public transportation, and other programs for the elderly. This will place a growing strain on local government budgets.

In the developing countries, where the elderly have traditionally relied on their children for support, this system will begin to break down as middle-aged "children" find themselves still supporting their parents while anticipating their own retirement.

Implications for Hospitality and Travel: Seniors are not only the fastest growing segment of the population, they are also the wealthiest. Few will be up to making an assault on Mount Everest, but almost anyone can take a cruise or fly to Paris or Orlando for a long weekend with Mickey and the rest of the Disney gang. Fine dining, a tour of the links at St. Andrew's, or a visit to the tables in Vegas will appeal to some seniors and soon-to-be seniors.

As the older populations grow, the travel industry can only expand with them. In the process, it is likely to become more stable and less seasonal. Unlike the rest of us, most seniors can travel whenever the impulse strikes. Often, they do so when prices are down and crowds are thinner. In recent years, their off-season travel has begun to smooth the cyclical downturn typical of the hospitality and travel industry. Seniors will never eliminate seasonality, but the industry will find it less painful than in the past.

4. MASS MIGRATION IS REDISTRIBUTING THE WORLD'S POPULATION.

There are nearly one hundred million international migrant workers in the world, according to the United Nations. About thirty million live in Europe, twenty million in Africa, and eighteen million in North America. These figures include only the workers themselves, not their dependents. About four million people immigrated permanently to the countries of the Organisation for Economic Co-operation and Development in 2005, 10.4 percent more than the year before. Immigration to Western Europe from Eastern Europe, North Africa, the Middle East, and the Indian subcontinent continues despite controls enacted in the wake of terrorist attacks. Immigration is quickly changing the ethnic composition of the U.S. population. By 2050, the number of Latinos in the United States will double, to 24.5 percent of the population.

Assessment: As native workforces shrink in most industrialized lands, economic opportunities will draw people from the developing world to the developed in growing numbers. Thus, this trend will continue for at least the next generation.

Implications: Impoverished migrants will place a growing strain on social security systems in the industrialized countries of Europe and North America. Similar problems will continue to afflict the urban infrastructures of China and India. Remittances from migrants to their native lands are helping to relieve poverty in many developing countries. Globally, these payments exceeded US$230 billion in 2005, according to the World Bank.

Significant backlashes against foreign migrants, such as the skinhead movement in Europe, will be seen more frequently in the years ahead. They will appear even in the most peaceful lands. For example, in Scandinavia, resentment against foreign workers is strong, in part because they can return to their native lands after three years of employment and collect a pension equal to the minimum wage for the rest of their lives.

Since the terrorist attacks of September 11, 2001, and the rail bombings in London and Madrid, the large number of Muslim immigrants in Britain, France, and other European lands has inspired suspicion, and some persecution. Unfortunately, suspicion is to some extent justified. A tiny minority of Muslim immigrants has been linked to terrorist groups, and some have plotted or carried out terrorist attacks. So have native-born Muslims and converts to Islam.

Implications for Hospitality and Travel: Barring enactment of strict immigration controls, rapid migration will continue from the Southern to the Northern Hemisphere and especially from former colonies to Europe. A growing percentage of job applicants in the recipient lands will be recent immigrants from developing countries. This will compensate for a declining supply of entry-level and low-wage workers in the developed economies. Unlike post-retirement job-seekers, however, most new arrivals will be limited to relatively menial, behind-the-scenes jobs until they master the local language and adapt to the dominant culture of their new homes.

The market for relatively short-distance international travel should grow significantly in both the United States and Europe, thanks largely to their expanding foreign populations visiting their former homes. Routes between the United States and Mexico and Latin America will grow fastest, while those between Europe and the former colonies of Africa and the Middle East will not be far behind.

In the United States and Europe, foreign-born residents represent significant new markets for well-prepared foods from Latin America and the Middle East. Supplying this demand will fall to small restaurateurs at first, but the major chains can be expected to enter this field as soon as they are sure it will repay their investments.

This trend will serve an aging population well, because it promises to introduce strong new flavors suited to the failing taste buds of older diners.

5. IMPORTANT MEDICAL ADVANCES WILL CONTINUE TO APPEAR ALMOST DAILY.

Research into human genetics, stem cells, computer-aided drug design, tissue transplants, cloning, and even nanotechnology promises to ease or cure diseases and injuries that do not respond to today's medicine. Radical new treatments for diabetes, Parkinson's disease, perhaps Alzheimer's, and many other disorders are expected to arrive within the next five to ten years. Scientists even are beginning to understand the fundamental processes of aging, bringing the possibility of averting the diseases of old age and perhaps aging itself.

Assessment: The flow of new medical advances will not slow in the next forty years, and probably not in the next seventy-five.

Implications: In the next ten years, we expect to see more and better bionic limbs, hearts, and other organs; drugs that prevent disease rather than merely treating symptoms; and body monitors that warn of impending trouble. All of these will reduce hospital stays.

Outside the United States, transplants of brain cells, nerve tissue, and stem cells to aid victims of retardation, head trauma, and other neurological disorders will enter clinical use by 2012. Laboratory-grown bone, muscle, and blood cells also will be employed in transplants.

Expect also the first broadly effective treatments for viral diseases, experimental regeneration of lost or damaged human tissues, and effective ways to prevent and correct obesity.

By 2025, the first nanotechnology-based medical therapies should reach clinical use. Microscopic machines will monitor our internal processes, remove cholesterol plaque from artery walls, and destroy cancer cells before they have a chance to form a tumor.

FI believes that cloning and related methods will be accepted for the treatment of disease, though not to produce identical human beings.

Even without dramatic advances in life extension, Baby Boomers are likely to live much longer, and in better health, than anyone now expects. However, this trend could be sidetracked by the current epidemic of obesity, which threatens to raise rates of hypertension, diabetes, heart disease, and arthritis among Boomers if a cure is not found quickly enough.

However, a significant extension of healthy, vigorous life—to around 115 or 120 years as a first step—now seems more likely than no extension at all. The most significant question remaining, other than the scientific details, is whether it will arrive in time for the Baby Boom generation to benefit or will be limited to their children and descendents.

High development and production costs for designer pharmaceuticals, computerized monitors, and artificial organs will continue to push up the cost of healthcare far more rapidly than the general inflation rate. Many of these expenses will be passed on to Medicare and other third-party payers. Severe personnel shortages can be expected in high-tech medical specialties, in addition to the continuing deficit of nurses.

A growing movement to remove barriers to stem-cell research in the United States could speed progress in this critical field. This could be expected to produce new treatments for neurological disorders such as Parkinson's and Alzheimer's disease and many other illnesses now incurable or untreatable. It also would recover one aspect of America's lost lead in science.

Implications for Hospitality and Travel: This trend is responsible for the growing number of older, fitter seniors who remain able not only to travel, but to participate in relatively vigorous activities at their destination as well. Their numbers will grow rapidly as the Baby Boom generation reaches their retirement years. Accommodating the needs of healthy seniors will be a major priority for the hospitality and travel industry in the coming decades.

This trend also is a major source of medical tourism, in which travelers combine a vacation with low-cost, high-quality medical care in places such as India, Thailand, South Africa, or Eastern Europe. Medical tourism will bring India alone an estimated $2.2 billion per year by 2012.

6. The physical culture and personal-health movements are improving health in much of the world, but they are far from universal.

During the 1990s, health in the United States improved by 1.5 percent annually, based on such measures as smoking prevalence, health insurance coverage, infant mortality rates, and premature deaths. Since 2000, health improvement has slowed to just 0.2 percent a year, largely due to personal choices. The global obesity crisis is a significant countertrend to the physical-culture movement. Poor diet, physical inactivity, and associated obesity contribute to 47 percent of diseases and 60 percent of deaths worldwide. However, health consciousness is spreading to Europe. For example, a recent poll found that two-thirds of Britons now spend more to maintain a healthy lifestyle than they did a decade ago, and three out of four say they enjoy leading a healthy lifestyle. Unfortunately, much of the developing world still worries more about eating enough than about eating well.

Assessment: This trend always seems a case of two steps forward, at least one step back. We expect it to continue for at least the next generation.

Implications: As the nutrition and wellness movements spread, they will further improve the health of the elderly. Better health in later life will make us still more conscious of our appearance and physical condition. Thus, health clubs will continue to boom, and some will specialize in the needs of older fitness buffs.

Diet, fitness, stress control, and wellness programs will prosper. States will continue to mandate insurance coverage of mammography. By 2012, they will begin to require coverage of sigmoidoscopy and colonoscopy. By 2015, Congress will add coverage of many preventive-care activities to Medicare. The cost of healthcare for American Baby Boomers and their children could be much lower in later life than is now believed.

Asia, however, faces an epidemic of cancer, heart disease, emphysema, and other chronic and fatal illnesses related to health habits. Like tobacco companies, producers of snack foods, liquor, and other unhealthy products will increasingly target markets in developing countries where this trend has yet to be felt. Continuing health improvements in the industrialized world will be accompanied by a dramatic rise in heart disease, diabetes, cancer, and other such "lifestyle" disorders in the developing lands. Chronic diseases related to obesity burden national economies and could thwart economic progress in developing countries.

Implications for Hospitality and Travel: Most cruise lines, high-end hotels, and resorts already have adapted to their guests' wish for nutritious, low-calorie meals, exercise facilities, and tobacco-free areas, particularly in the United States. Their peers in other lands will find themselves forced to make similar concessions to health consciousness in the next decade.

This trend also means that hospitality and travel operators will be receiving more guests who are older, wealthier, and fitter and still able to indulge in vigorous activities that their counterparts of an earlier era would not have considered.

Societal Trends ───────────────────────────

7. SOCIETAL VALUES ARE CHANGING RAPIDLY.

Industrialization raises educational levels, changes attitudes toward authority, reduces fertility, alters gender roles, and encourages broader political participation. This process is just beginning throughout the developing world. Witness the growing literacy, declining fertility, and broad voter turnout seen in India over the last decade. Developed societies increasingly take their cue from Generation X and the Millennial generation (also called Generation Y or Generation Dot-com), rather than the Baby Boomers who dominated the industrialized world's thinking for most of four decades. Post–September 11 fear of terrorist attacks has led Americans to accept almost without comment security measures that their traditional love of privacy once would have made intolerable.

Assessment: This trend will continue for at least the next two decades in the industrialized lands and two generations in the developing world.

Implications: The growing influence of the post–Baby Boom generations will tend to homogenize basic attitudes throughout the world, because Generation Xers and especially the Millennials around the globe have more in common with each other than with their parents.

The highly polarized political environment that has plagued the United States since the 1980s will slowly moderate as results-oriented Generation Xers and Millennials begin to dominate the national dialogue.

As national security concerns have begun to lose their immediacy, family issues are regaining their significance in American society: long-term healthcare, day care, early childhood education, antidrug campaigns, and the environment.

Demand for greater accountability and transparency in business will be crucial for countries that wish to attract international investors.

Implications for Hospitality and Travel: Vacations also are becoming more active and participatory, as tourists become less interested in "go-and-see" and more eager to "go-and-*do*." This is the trend behind the growth of adventure tourism and ecology-oriented travel.

The trend is toward extreme quality and convenience. Customers want constant pampering, luxurious accommodations, and fresh meals that seem like labors of love—all at a price that will not wound the consumer's conscience.

"Authenticity" is another key value. Tourists who go to see other lands, rather than surf their beaches, want to find unique natural and cultural features that survive as close as possible to their original form. Travel experiences that remind guests of Navajo Indian blankets with "Made in China" tags will leave visitors feeling that they might as well have visited their local mall instead.

8. PRIVACY, ONCE A DEFINING RIGHT FOR AMERICANS, IS DYING QUICKLY.

Internet communications, a basic part of life for many people, are nearly impossible to protect against interception, and governments around the world are working to ensure their unfettered access to them. Corporate databases are collecting and marketing data on individual credit-worthiness, incomes, spending patterns, brand choices, medical conditions, and lifestyles. While privacy regulations bar distribution of much personal information in the European Union, restrictions in the United States are much weaker. Widespread surveillance of private individuals is technically feasible and economically viable, as tiny, powerful cameras now cost next to nothing. Increased surveillance has become socially acceptable in an age when many people fear terrorism and crime. Britons are caught on camera an estimated three hundred times per day, Americans about two hundred.

Assessment: Pessimists could say that privacy already is a thing of the past; society is merely coming to recognize its loss. We believe that enough effective privacy survives outside the most authoritarian countries to justify noting its continued erosion. However, this trend could easily reach its logical conclusion within ten years.

Implications: In the future, privacy is likely to be defined not by the ability to keep information truly secret, but by the legal power to restrict its distribution. Even this limited form of privacy will be eroded as both government and private organizations find legal justification for their interest in personal information. Once access is granted to any type of information, it is unlikely ever to be rescinded.

Most surveillance provisions of the USA PATRIOT Act will survive, even if the law itself is repealed or modified.

In the absence of a major terrorist event, most Americans will continue to consider privacy a "right," and privacy-related lawsuits are likely to proliferate as more people feel violated or inconvenienced by surveillance. However, courts will be unsympathetic to such suits as long as conservative appointees dominate the bench.

In large and medium-sized cities around the world, spaces that remain unwatched by video cameras will continue to shrink.

Growing numbers of companies, and even private citizens, will encrypt their computer data.

The number of criminal cases based on surveillance will grow rapidly in countries with the required technological sophistication and infrastructure.

Private citizens increasingly will use similar technologies to watch over government abuse, as in cases where bystanders have recorded police misconduct with their cell-phone cameras.

Implications for Hospitality and Travel: Hospitality and travel operators are likely to find themselves facing more demands to watch for suspicious activities in travel destinations, or even to provide security agencies with information about their guests.

9. Time is becoming the world's most precious commodity.

In the United States, workers spend about 10 percent more time on the job than they did a decade ago. European executives and non-unionized workers face the same trend. In the United Kingdom, an Ipsos MORI study found that 32 percent of people who had not visited a museum in the previous year reported having too little time to do so; in 1999, only 6 percent had cited that reason. China's rapid economic development means its workers also are experiencing faster-paced and time-pressured lives. In a recent survey by the Chinese news portal Sina.com, 56 percent of respondents said they felt short of time. Technical workers and executives in India are beginning to report the same job-related stresses, particularly when they work on U.S. and European schedules.

Assessment: This trend is likely to grow as changing technologies add the need for lifelong study to the many commitments that compete for the average worker's time. As the trend matures in the United States, it is likely to survive in other parts of the world. It will not disappear until China and India reach modern post-industrial status, around 2050.

Implications: Time pressures will grow even more intense as companies squeeze even more productivity from their existing workforce rather than hiring new people in the face of the current global recession.

Stress-related problems affecting employee morale and wellness will continue to grow. Companies must help employees balance their time at work with their family lives and need for leisure. This may reduce short-term profits but will aid profitability in the long run.

As time for shopping continues to evaporate, Internet and mail-order marketers will have a growing advantage over traditional stores. China, India, and other developing countries can expect consumer trends similar to those in the United States as workers seek out convenience foods, household help, and minor luxuries to compensate for their lack of leisure time.

Implications for Hospitality and Travel: Work pressure is eroding vacation time throughout the industrialized world. One-third of Americans take 50 percent or less of the vacation time their jobs theoretically allow. In Britain, 25 percent of employees take only part of their vacation time. In Japan, where employees are legally guaranteed seventeen days per year of vacation, the average worker takes only 9.5 days annually.

For those with little time, but adequate funds, multiple, shorter vacations spread throughout the year will continue to replace the traditional two-week vacation.

For the most well-off travelers, time pressure is a strong incentive to use travel agents and shop for packaged tours rather than do their own vacation planning. This is the one force that tends to preserve a market niche for the minority of travel agents who survive the transition to Internet booking. Less wealthy vacationers will continue to speed the task of making travel arrangements and broaden their selection of affordable vacation packages by doing their shopping on the Internet.

Anything destinations and tour operators can do to save time for their customers will encourage repeat visits.

10. The women's equality movement is losing its significance, thanks largely to past successes.

According to some, though not all, studies, women have nearly achieved pay parity with men in the United States when factors such as educational level, responsibilities, and seniority are taken into account. Younger generations of women are better educated and are even more likely to be successful than their male peers. Generation Xers and Millennials are virtually gender-blind in the workplace, compared with older generations.

This is true even in societies such as India and Japan, which have long been male-dominated, though not yet in conservative Muslim lands.

Assessment: This trend is valid only in the developed lands. In the developing world, the movement toward women's equality is barely beginning. In the United States, the trend could be seen as complete, with women's equality now taken for granted and only mopping-up operations required to complete the process. However, we believe that the women's equality movement will continue to retain some importance, less with each passing year, until the gender-blind Generation X and Millennials accede to leadership in business and politics.

Implications: In most of the developed world, whatever careers remain relatively closed to women will open wide in the years ahead. Japan will remain some years behind the curve, owing to the strength of its traditionally male-dominated culture.

Women's increasing entrepreneurialism will allow the formation of entrenched "old girl" networks comparable to the men's relationships that once dominated business. The fraction of women entering the American labor force has leveled off in recent years. The percentage of female workers is likely to remain approximately stable until some force appears to begin a new trend.

Demand for child care, universal health coverage, and other family-oriented services will continue to grow, particularly in the United States, where national services have yet to develop. Over the next twenty years, American companies may increasingly follow the example of their counterparts in Europe, whose taxes pay for national day care programs and other social services the United States lacks.

There is little sign of progress for women in much of the developing world. India is an exception because growing literacy has given women the chance to earn income outside the home and, with it, gain value other than as wives and mothers.

Implications for Hospitality and Travel: There are relatively few implications for these industries. Hospitality and travel operators have traditionally depended on women for much of their workforce, especially in critical guest-contact roles. As a result, they have been relatively willing to pay women well and promote them into management positions comparable to those occupied by men.

11. Despite some xenophobic reactions to immigrants, there is growing acceptance of diversity.

Migration is mixing disparate peoples and forcing them to find ways to coexist peacefully and productively. Because of this, the interaction of diverse cultures will continue to grow, both internationally and intranationally, throughout much of the world.

The Internet and other technologies promote long-distance communication and build links between distant, and disparate, people. The globalization of business is having a similar impact. In many countries, however, there are powerful reactions against these changes. The growth of the German neo-Nazi movement after unification in 1992 is one obvious example. American hostility toward undocumented immigrants may be viewed as another.

Assessment: This trend applies most clearly to the West, where it will continue for as long as we can foresee. In other regions, including Japan and large parts of the Muslim world, it remains weak, if it exists at all.

Implications: Groups with highly varied customs, languages, and histories of necessity will develop ways to coexist peacefully. Nonetheless, local conflicts will continue to erupt in societies where xenophobia is common.

Implications for Hospitality and Travel: Growing contact between countries and cultures in the United States and Europe should stimulate further demand for travel to foreign lands, where visitors can learn more about the cultures they have met, and begun to accept, at home.

Companies in all industries, including hospitality and travel, will hire ever more minority workers and will be expected to adapt to their values and needs. Much of the burden of accommodating foreign-born residents will continue to fall on employers, who must help them adapt to their new environment and make room for their languages and cultures in the workplace. Public schools and libraries must find more effective ways to educate this future workforce.

The more prosperous immigrant groups, such as those from Asia and the Middle East in the United States, also represent valuable markets for specialized travel services. Expect growing demand especially for services aimed at the needs of Muslim travelers from Europe and the United States. Hotels, restaurants, and cruise lines will have to be prepared to serve the special needs of religious, ethnic, and cultural minorities.

12. Tourism, vacationing, and travel (especially international) continue to grow with each passing year.

International tourism grew by more than 6 percent in the first half of 2007, thanks in part to global prosperity. By 2020, international tourist arrivals are expected to reach 1.6 billion annually, up from 842 million in 2006. By 2020, according to the World Trade Organization, 100 million Chinese will fan out across the globe, replacing Americans, Japanese, and Germans as the world's most numerous travelers. Some 50 million Indian tourists will join them.

Assessment: Travel seems to be in the DNA of the middle and upper economic classes. This trend will continue as long as national economies continue to generate new prosperity for the formerly poor.

Implications: Travel will grow by at least 5 percent per year for the foreseeable future.

The tourism industry will create 3.3 million new jobs worldwide. Jobs dependent on tourism will comprise nearly 14 percent of the global workforce.

Direct employment will not grow quite as quickly, but it will be up 1.7 percent annually, to nearly 87.5 million jobs, while indirect employment will account for some 260 million jobs around the world.

This will bring major opportunities for national economies in Southeast Asia and Africa, where Chinese and Indian tourists can take quick, inexpensive vacations.

Implications for Hospitality and Travel: Tourism offers growing opportunities for out-of-the-way destinations that have not yet cashed in on the boom. This will make it an important industry for still more developing countries. American domestic tourism will continue to grow by an average of 2.3 percent per year through at least 2011.

The fastest growth will be seen in pioneering regions. Intranationally, air travel in China is expanding rapidly, with the Indian air market lagging only a few years behind. Internationally, expect the most immediate growth to appear in the Middle East, where travelers will visit neighboring countries and, to a lesser extent, Europe. In the longer run, the fastest growth, and by far the greatest, will flow to Europe and the United States, thanks to vacationers from the newly prosperous middle classes of China and India.

The cruise segment is expected to grow at approximately the same rate as the travel market at large. By 2015, even India and China are likely to get into this market.

Cruise ships will continue to lure retirees. Some liners are offering full-time residency—creating new options for assisted living arrangements.

Travel is said to broaden the mind. It surely broadens palates. As generations X and Dot-com visit out-of-the-way destinations, they are bringing home tastes for foreign cuisines their more traditional elders never sampled. Over the next twenty years, this trend will itself be the result of other trends; the world's growing prosperity, the continuing heath of seniors well into old age, and other trends are building a world of habitual travelers, both for business and for pleasure. As a result, all parts of the travel and hospitality industry are growing rapidly. Built as it is on such a firm foundation, this trend suggests that all segments of the hospitality and travel industry will continue to expand well into the future.

13. EDUCATION AND TRAINING ARE EXPANDING THROUGHOUT SOCIETY.

Rapid changes in the job market and work-related technologies will require increased training for almost every worker, just as knowledge turnover in the professions requires continuous retraining and lifelong learning. Thus, a substantial portion of the labor force will be in job retraining programs at any given moment. All of the fastest growing occupations require some form of advanced training and continuous updating of job skills. In the next ten years, close to ten million jobs will open up for professionals, executives, and technicians in the highly skilled service occupations.

In order to give those who cannot attend their classes a chance to educate themselves, the Massachusetts Institute of Technology has put its entire curriculum on the Internet, including class notes, many texts, and sometimes videos of classroom lectures. Other institutions are following suit.

Assessment: This is a trend at the beginning of its life.

Implications: Over the next two decades, the growing demand for education and training is likely to transform our working lives and educational systems around the world. In order to keep up with growing demands for education, schools will train both children and adults around the clock.

The academic day will stretch to seven hours for children so as to enable students to compete with their peers in other countries, who already devote much more of their time to learning, with predictable results.

Adults will use much of their remaining free time to prepare for their next job. In knowledge-based economies, a region's growth prospects depend on its ability to generate and use innovation. This correlates roughly with the number of college-educated adults living there. Throughout the industrialized countries, this gives cities an advantage over rural and suburban areas. It is one reason upwardly mobile adults tend to move to the cities.

Skills are the most important factor in economic success today. Unfortunately, the people who need them most, the poor and unemployed, cannot afford schooling and therefore are least able to obtain them. Helping people overcome this disadvantage is a natural role for government.

As the digital divide is erased and minority and low-income households buy computers and log onto the Internet, groups now disadvantaged will be increasingly able to educate and train themselves for high-tech careers.

Even the smallest businesses must learn to see employee training as an investment, rather than an expense. Motorola estimates that it reaps $30 in profits for each dollar it spends on training. Both management and employees must get used to the idea of lifelong learning. It will become a significant part of work life at all levels.

Implications for Hospitality and Travel: Hotels and restaurants are likely to find this trend particularly difficult to cope with. Both need large numbers of relatively unskilled workers for maintenance tasks as well as customer contact. Yet they have few opportunities to provide the kind of generally applicable training that most entry-level workers have come to recognize as the key to a better future. This is likely to make it difficult to compete with other industries for young, low-wage workers. Creating learning opportunities for young job seekers or finding some other way to motivate them will be a difficult challenge for the hospitality and travel industries, but this is a problem they urgently need to solve.

14. Advanced communications technologies are changing the way we work and live.

Telecommuting is growing rapidly, thanks largely to e-mail and other high-tech forms of communication. About 80 percent of companies worldwide now have employees who work at home, up from 54 percent in 2003. The number of telecommuters in the United States reached an estimated twenty million in 2006.

Millennials, however, already have abandoned e-mail for most purposes, instead using instant messaging and social networking websites to communicate with their peers. These and other new technologies, such as podcasting, are building communities nearly as complex and involved as those existing wholly in the real world.

Assessment: Again, this trend has only just begun.

Implications: E-mail promised to speed business. Instead, it absorbs more time than busy executives can afford to lose. Expect the nascent reaction against e-mail to grow as many people eliminate mailing lists, demand precise e-communications rather than open-ended conversation, and schedule only brief periods for dealing with mail. Instant messaging is likely to be even more destructive of time for the under-thirty set.

However, e-mail is a major contributor to globalization and outsourcing, because it eliminates many of the obstacles of doing business across long distances and many time zones. Unfortunately, e-mail and other modern communications techniques also have made possible a variety of crimes, from online fraud to some forms of identity theft.

Advanced communications technologies also make it virtually impossible to retract ill-considered statements or embarrassing online activities. Once something exists on the Internet, it is all but immortal and nearly impossible to hide.

Implications for Hospitality and Travel: All the benefits and evils of e-mail, instant messaging, and other communications technologies apply as much to hospitality and travel as to other industries. They may be particularly significant for both large, multinational operators, which would find it difficult to coordinate their activities across time zones without rapid communications, and the smallest destinations, which could not compete effectively for customers in the industrialized lands without access to the Internet.

Generational and Family Trends

15. FAMILY STRUCTURES ARE BECOMING MORE DIVERSE.

In periods of economic difficulty, children and grandchildren move back in with parents and grandparents to save on living expenses. Many bring their own children with them. In the United States, one-third of Generation Xers have returned home at some point in their early lives. Among Millennials, the figure is even higher. The 2001 Census found that so-called "multigenerational households" are the fastest growing group in the United States. Yet the nuclear family also is rebounding in the United States, as Baby Boomer and Gen X parents focus on their children and grandparents retain more independence and mobility.

Same-sex households also are gaining new acceptance. At least five American states now permit same-sex marriage or have enacted domestic partnership laws that provide similar protections. In this, they join such countries as Denmark, Germany, the Czech Republic, the United Kingdom and, most recently, Switzerland.

Many grandparents are raising their grandchildren because drugs and AIDS have left the middle generation either unable or unavailable to care for their children. This trend is strongest in Sub-Saharan Africa, where there will be twenty-five million AIDS orphans by 2010.

Assessment: This trend will remain in effect for at least a generation in the United States, longer in the rest of the world.

Implications: Where many European countries have largely adjusted to this trend, the United States has not. Making that adjustment will be an important challenge for the next decades.

Tax and welfare policies need adjustment to cope with families in which heads of households are retired or unable to work. Policy modification is also needed for those who receive Social Security and work to support an extended family.

In the United States, the debates over homosexuality and the "decline of the family" will remain polarizing for the foreseeable future. The next debate is likely to focus on granting parental rights to more than two parents, as when a sperm or egg donor wants a role in the life of a child whose official parents are the recipients.

Implications for Hospitality and Travel: Gays, lesbians, singles, single parents, and multigenerational families all have become lucrative markets for specialty cruises, group tours, and other niche services. They can only grow increasingly significant in the years ahead.

16. Young people place increasing importance on economic success, which they have come to expect.

Throughout the 1990s—effectively, their entire adult lives— Generation Xers, Dot-coms, and Millennials knew only good economic times. The economic downturn at the turn of the century seemed to them a confusing aberration rather than a predictable part of the business cycle. The current global recession is a frightening wake-up call. Although most expect to see growing hardship on a national level, they both want and expect prosperity for themselves. In the United States especially, most young people have high aspirations, but many lack the means to achieve them owing to high dropout rates and ineffective schools.

Assessment: This trend appeared with the Baby Boom generation and has strengthened with the later cohorts. It will be interesting to see what develops among the children of the Millennials, something we find difficult to predict with any confidence.

Implications: Disappointed ambitions will be a major source of political unrest in the United States and many other countries in the next two decades. Most of the other countries seriously affected by this trend will be in the developing world or will be host to large numbers of disadvantaged immigrants.

Entrepreneurialism will be a global trend, as members of Generation X and the Millennials throughout the world tend to share values. Generation X and Millennial entrepreneurs are largely responsible for the current economic growth in India and China, where they are becoming a major force in the Communist party. In India, the younger generations dress and think more like their American counterparts than their parents. In China, the democratic fervor that spawned Tiananmen Square has been replaced by capitalist entrepreneurialism.

If younger-generation workers find their ambitions thwarted, they will create growing pressure for economic and social reform. If change does not come fast enough in the developing world, disappointed expectations will increase the number of young people who emigrate to the developed lands. In the United States, pressure will grow to provide more, and less burdensome, economic assistance to qualified high school graduates who cannot afford to go on to college.

Pressure also will grow to ensure that all American students have access to an education capable of preparing them for college or a rewarding career.

Implications for Hospitality and Travel: Young people concerned with economic success may be even less willing to accept entry-level jobs, yet underequipped to take on more demanding roles. This is likely to increase job turnover, even in non-menial positions. The most important asset for motivating and keeping these potential workers will be a strong training program that gives them a clear path for advancement. Unfortunately, this may be difficult to provide.

17. Generation X, the Dot-Coms, and the Millennials are gaining social and organizational influence.

Members of each group—ranging from nearly fifty to the twenty-somethings— have much more in common with their peers than with their parents. Their values and concerns are remarkably uniform throughout the world. Socially and in business, they are nearly color-blind and gender-blind. Generation X is starting new businesses at an unprecedented rate, and the Millennial generation is proving to be even more business-oriented, caring for little but the bottom line. They will work for others, but only on their own terms.

Generation X and the Millennials thrive on challenge, opportunity, and training—whatever will best prepare them for their next career move. Cash is just the beginning of what they expect. Employers will have to adjust their policies and practices to the values of these new and different generations, including finding new ways to motivate and reward them.

However, they also have a powerful commitment to society. Gen Xers are mainstays of "voluntourism," a practice in which participants spend part of their vacations on volunteer work. In a recent survey, 60 percent of respondents said they would be interested in doing scientific or environmental work while on vacation. Even more would be willing to teach English or another academic subject.

Assessment: As trends go, this is an evergreen. In ten years or so, we will simply add the next new generation to the list.

Implications: In values, cultural norms, political issues, and many other ways, this change of generations will be every bit as transforming as the transition from the World War II generation to the Baby Boomers.

Employers will have to adjust virtually all of their policies and practices to the values of these new and different generations, including finding new ways to motivate and reward them. Generation X and the Millennials thrive on challenge, opportunity, and training—whatever will best prepare them for their next career move. Cash is just the beginning of what they expect.

For these generations, lifelong learning is nothing new; it's just the way life is. Companies that can provide diverse, cutting-edge training will have a strong recruiting advantage over competitors that offer fewer opportunities to improve their skills and knowledge base.

Generations X and Millennial are well equipped for work in a high-tech world, but they have little interest in their employers' needs. They have a powerful urge to do things their own way. As both customers and employees, they will demand even more advanced telecommunications and Internet-based transactions.

Implications for Hospitality and Travel: These generations have hard noses. Young business travelers may put up with delays when a massive snowstorm arrives as they are leaving for a trip. But they won't like waiting for hours because an airport's departure schedule is overbooked. Scheduling problems, faulty service, and other down-checks that today's consumers would accept with minor grumbling will have to be fixed, or tomorrow's travelers will plaster their disgust all over the Internet.

Millennials especially can be demanding. When they have a problem at an airline, they do not just bother the people at the airport ticket desk. They grab their cell phones and call or text the frequent flier department to apply pressure for a favorable resolution. Satisfying such customers will be a constant challenge. We have seen them arrive at a hotel without a reservation only to find that no rooms are available. Rather than accept the situation, they call the chain's frequent-visitor program to complain and ask whether a room might be available after all.

These generations will have no problem spending online sums that would have stopped their parents cold. They will not accept obstacles to their habit of shopping online and clicking "Buy" the instant their decision is made.

This is especially important for the cruise market. If one cruise line is too stodgy to enable online booking—and stodgy, not exclusive, is how they will be perceived—then a more up-to-date operator will get their business.

Baby Boomers rebelled in the early 1960s, then adopted their parents' materialism and took it to whole new levels. Generation X and particularly the Dot-coms and Millennials have taken another path. They enjoy a Manhattan while surrounded by Rat Pack retro elegance. Yet they always pair indulgence with a self-deprecating humor that says it's not taken seriously. The most successful hotels will find a way to match that sense of feet-on-the-ground fun while providing impeccable service to older guests.

The new generations coming of age signal changes for restaurants as well. Although younger travelers are bringing home tastes for new cuisines, it may not be the foods of Uruguay or Nepal that next capture their imagination and limited customer loyalty. Unlike previous generations, the Xers and Dot-coms tend to mix and match. A typical meal might begin with old-fashioned Mexican nachos for an appetizer, then move on to a Thai fish dish with couscous from Algeria and a Chilean wine. Restaurants hoping to attract this crowd will need both imagination and broad experience with the world's exotic flavors.

The new generations could add a few points to the growth rate for hospitality and travel. They are enthusiastic travelers, willing to drop everything when a friend suggests an adventure. This may not make them the ideal employees by traditional standards, but it does make them great customers.

Expect major growth in eco-tourism and "voluntourism," thanks to under-forty vacationers.

18. Two-income couples are becoming the norm in most of the industrialized lands, although in the United States the trend toward greater employment among women is slowing.

The percentage of working-age women who are employed or are actively looking for work has grown steadily throughout the industrialized world. In the United States, it has grown from 46 percent in 1970 to about 66 percent in 2005, compared with 77 percent of men. In Japan, a majority of households have included two earners since at least 1980.

In the United States, both the husband and the wife worked in 50.9 percent of married-couple families in 2003, according to the U.S. Bureau of Labor Statistics' Current Population Survey. This had declined since 1997, when it was 53.4 percent. Families in which only the woman worked rose for the third straight year in 2003, to 6.8 percent.

Assessment: In the industrialized nations, this trend has just about played out, as the number of two-income households has begun to stabilize. However, it will be a growing force in India and other industrializing lands for many years to come.

Implications: This emphasis on work is one big reason the richest 25 to 50 percent of the U.S. population has reached zero population growth. They have no time for children and little interest in having large families.

Demand for on-the-job child care, extended parental leave, and other family-oriented benefits can only grow. In the long run, this could erode the profitability of some American companies unless it is matched by an equal growth in productivity. This also promotes self-employment and entrepreneurialism, as one family member's salary can tide them over while the other works to establish a new business.

Expect to see many families that usually have two incomes, but have frequent intervals in which one member takes a sabbatical or goes back to school to prepare for another career. As information technologies render former occupations obsolete, this will become the new norm.

Implications for Hospitality and Travel: Two-career couples can afford to eat out often, take frequent short vacations, and buy new cars and other such goods. And they feel they deserve whatever luxuries they can afford. This is quickly expanding the market for travel and leisure activities. It will continue to skew the travel and hospitality markets away from traditional two-week vacations and toward three-day weekend getaways, "cruises to nowhere," and other forms of short-term pampering for pressured couples in need of a break.

Economic Trends

19. THE ECONOMY OF THE DEVELOPED WORLD IS GROWING STEADILY, WITH ONLY BRIEF INTERRUPTIONS.

When the United States catches a cold, the rest of the world gets pneumonia, or so economists used to say. In mid-2009, the United States has pneumonia. Home prices remain in free-fall, and the credit market remains a problem. More than six million jobs have disappeared from the American economy since the recession began at the beginning of 2008. International trade has plummeted. Most of the world is in recession. It turns out that 2008 and some of 2009 hold one of the interruptions contemplated in the trend.

Looking abroad, we can see the effects of America's problems. The entire European Union is in recession. Australia, Japan, and Russia are in or near recession. China and India are still growing, but not nearly as fast as they are accustomed to. In all, the economies of the world seem much less healthy than they did a few months ago.

Throughout the world, governments have scrambled to shore up lending institutions, stem the tide of foreclosures, restore the flow of credit, and provide jobs for the newly unemployed. These efforts will continue through 2009.

At that point, global economic growth will resume. It will be slow at first, but eventually will reach its accustomed rate, a bit more than 5 percent per year as of 2007.

Assessment: These trends have been revised many times since they were first codified in the late 1980s. Some trends have fallen off the list as they matured or as circumstances came along to change them. Others have been added as they were recognized. This trend has remained a constant, and with each revision its effective period has been extended. To invalidate this trend would take a catastrophe on the order of the loss of Middle Eastern oil from the Western economies. No such dramatic reversal of global fortune can be foreseen.

Implications: New growth among all these trading partners should create a "benevolent cycle," in which the health of each partner helps to ensure the continued health of the rest at least through 2014. According to the World Bank, the global economy is likely to shrink by about 3 percent in 2009, rebounding weakly in 2010.

This worst interruption of economic growth in recent memory should be relatively short-lived, at least by the standard of the 1930s. By 2012 or so, India will expand faster than any other market in the world, with China falling into a close second place. They will help to lift their trading partners into solidly positive economic territory.

In the long run, the newly capitalist lands of the former Soviet Union should be among the fastest growing new markets, particularly if the oil industries of Kazakhstan and its neighbors Kyrgyzstan and Uzbekistan can be developed promptly. Labor markets will remain tight, particularly in skilled fields. This calls for new creativity in recruiting, benefits, and perks, especially profit-sharing. This hypercompetitive business environment demands new emphasis on rewarding speed, creativity, and innovation within the workforce.

Implications for Hospitality and Travel: American business has been cutting back ruthlessly in 2008 and 2009, allowing only the most necessary trips. All but the most comfortable vacationers will stay close to home until they are convinced the recession is over and their jobs are secure. We expect to see air travel drop by 15 percent or more at the bottom of the downturn and recover slowly through 2011. At the same time, consumers will continue cutting back from high-end hotels to mid-priced chains and from mid-priced to economy; eating at home or at fast-food outlets rather than pricier restaurants; and—for those who still vacation abroad—favoring cheap destinations such as Mexico, Portugal, and eastern Europe over Paris and London.

Only the high end of the cruise market will be relatively unaffected: The wealthy remain able to pay for luxuries even in the worst of economic times, and 2009 will be as mild a downturn as the United States could hope for.

The flip side is that the euro and other world currencies buy much more in the States than they do at home. Europeans can hop on a plane for New York or Miami, shop until they drop—their packages, at least—enjoy a few nights out, and return home carrying loot they could not have paid for at local prices. Many of them are doing so. These bargain hunters are bringing needed profits to the American hospitality and travel industry. At the same time, they are helping to maintain demand in the cruise market and in traditional European destinations.

By late 2011, these aberrations will pass, and Americans again will be contributing their accustomed share to the global hospitality and travel markets.

As formerly poor residents of China and India grow increasingly prosperous, they too will fan out across the world as international tourists. Accommodating them will be a continuing challenge for hospitality and travel businesses.

20. The global economy is growing more integrated.

By some counts, only half of the world's one hundred largest economies are nation-states. The rest are multinational corporations. In the European Union, relaxation of border and capital controls and the adoption of a common currency and uniform product standards continue to make it easier for companies to distribute products and support functions throughout the Continent. The Internet also brings manufacturers effectively closer to remote suppliers and customers. Companies are increasingly farming out high-cost, low-payoff secondary functions to suppliers, service firms, and consultants, many of them located in other countries. Companies in high-wage countries also are outsourcing management and service jobs to low-wage countries. An estimated 3.3 million U.S. jobs are expected to migrate to India and China by 2015. Some 40 million jobs are believed vulnerable to outsourcing.

Assessment: This trend will continue for at least the next two decades.

Implications: The growth of e-commerce enables businesses to shop globally for the cheapest raw materials and supplies. In niche markets, the Internet also makes it possible for small companies to compete with giants worldwide with relatively little investment. This has brought new opportunities for quality-control problems and fraudulent cost-cutting by suppliers, as seen in the recent spate of tainted food and other products coming from China.

The Internet has created a generation of "e-preneurs" whose businesses exist largely on the Internet, with production, fulfillment, and other functions all outsourced to specialty firms.

Demand will continue to grow for employee incentives suited to other cultures, aid to executives going overseas, and the many other aspects of doing business in foreign countries. However, rising demand for foreign-language training is likely to be a temporary phenomenon, as more countries adopt English as part of their basic school curricula.

Western companies may have to accept that proprietary information will be shared not just with their immediate partners in Asian joint ventures, but also with other members of the partners' trading conglomerates. In high technology and aerospace, that may expose companies to extra scrutiny due to national security concerns.

Establishing overseas branches mitigates this concern by keeping trade secrets within the company, even while gaining the benefits of cheaper foreign labor and other resources. Economic ties can give richer, more powerful countries considerable influence over their junior partners. Thus far, China has been the most successful at wielding this "soft" power. This has given it the ability to undermine American foreign policy even as it secures its energy and raw materials needs.

Implications for Hospitality and Travel: Online business-to-business (B2B) sales and services will play a growing role in minimizing costs for all hospitality and travel businesses. For the same reason, some out-of-sight functions such as accounting may increasingly be outsourced to services in India, China, and Eastern Europe. However, most customer service operations will remain in the firm's home country, where quality is easier to oversee.

21. Consumerism is still growing.

Consumer advocacy agencies and organizations are proliferating, promoting improved content labels, warning notices, nutrition data, and the like on packaging, TV, the Internet, and even restaurant menus. On the Internet, shoppers themselves have access to a growing universe of information about pricing, services, delivery time, and customer satisfaction. Japan, China, and other markets are beginning the same revolution that has replaced America's neighborhood stores with cost-cutting warehouse operations—discounters such as Wal-Mart, and "category killers" like Staples and Home Depot. As a result, consumer movements are springing up in countries where they have never existed. Consumer laws and regulations will follow.

Assessment: This trend seems likely to remain healthy for at least the next fifteen years.

Implications: Consumer advocacy agencies and organizations will continue to proliferate, promoting improved content labels, warning notices, nutrition data, and the like on packaging, TV, the Internet, and even restaurant menus.

Although Europe, Japan, China, and other markets are undergoing the same transformation that has replaced America's neighborhood stores with discounters, the cultural and political power of farmers and small shop owners has slowed this trend in some areas, particularly in Japan.

Thanks to recent contamination of food imported from China, the U.S. Food and Drug Administration will be required to improve screening of incoming food products. However, it will not receive adequate funding to do the job effectively.

As prices fall to commodity levels and online stores can list virtually every product and brand in their industry without significant overhead, service is the only field left in which marketers on and off the Internet can compete effectively. Branded items with good reputations are even more important for developing repeat business.

Consumer debt may be an even greater problem for Millennials than it has been for their elders.

Implications for Hospitality and Travel: Fliers increasingly will expect quality service to go with their cheap seats. Airlines therefore will have to do a better job of getting their planes into the air on time, even if that means scheduling them for odd hours. Meals can remain optional, but if customers choose to buy them, they had better be good. And so on. We believe the consumerism of the past will prove to have been no more than prologue for the greater demands to come.

A good example is the new Terminal 5 at Heathrow, where nearly everything is bigger, better, and more luxurious. Check-in kiosks scattered throughout the spacious facility mean that waiting lines are no more than two or three deep. There are six lounges, a luxurious travel spa, more bathrooms than in older terminals, and even showers for travelers.

There are twenty-two places to eat, from simple snack shops to high-end restaurants. There are designer clothing stores, a luggage shop and a luxury leather store, a computer shop, bookstore, six newsstands, and even a Harrods. When Terminal 5 is fully operational, 80 percent of passengers at Heathrow will pass through it. Chances are that they will be glad to do so. Travelers are likely to be happier still when other air terminals are as convenient and comfortable as Terinal 5.

Cruise lines increasingly face similar pressures. The prestige-oriented days of booking through a travel agent are coming to an end. Today's consumers want value and convenience when buying a cruise package just as they do in any other form of shopping. That means picking through all the tours that seem appealing, selecting the one that gives the best possible value for the price, and buying it then and there.

In a networked consumerist society, a respected brand is any chain's most important asset. This will be particularly significant for hotels and restaurants. A reputation for comfortable accommodations, pleasant surroundings, and top-notch service requires constant effort to establish and maintain. It can be lost in moments if a disappointed customer complains in the Internet's many forums and chat rooms. More than ever before, quality and service are all-important.

Consumer legislation and "bills of rights" are no more than reminders of business basics. The travel and hospitality industries exist to serve their guests. Companies that do it brilliantly will continue to prosper. Those that do not will find many new, fast-growing competitors eager to build a customer base at their expense. The essence of a consumer society turns out to be intense, endless competition to be the best in the industry.

22. RESEARCH AND DEVELOPMENT PLAY A GROWING ROLE IN THE WORLD ECONOMY.

Total U.S. outlays on R&D have grown steadily in the past three decades. In 2006, the United States spent about $330 billion on R&D. China has taken second place in the world's R&D spending, with a budget estimate at $136 billion in 2006. China says it will raise its R&D spending from about 1.23 percent of GDP in 2004 to 2.5 percent in 2020. R&D outlays in Japan have risen almost continuously, to nearly 3 percent of GDP, some $130 billion in 2006. R&D spending in the European Union (EU-15) amounted to $230 billion in 2006, about 1.9 percent of GDP. The European Commission has set a goal of raising R&D spending to 3 percent of GDP by 2010. In Russia, R&D funding is roughly 1.5 percent of GDP, up from just 0.7 percent in 1997; this amounted to about $26.25 billion in 2006. These figures do not include whatever clandestine military research escapes notice.

Assessment: This trend is stabilizing as developed nations, particularly the United States, devote more of their resources to less productive activities. We believe this is a temporary phenomenon. The trend will regain momentum in the years ahead. It will not fall off this list before the middle of this century.

Implications: This is a significant factor in the acceleration of technological change. The demand for scientists, engineers, and technicians will continue to grow, particularly in fields where research promises an immediate business payoff.

Low-wage countries such as China once took only low-wage jobs from advanced industrialized countries such as the United States. Today, higher-paid jobs in science, technology, and the professions also are at risk.

Countries such as India, China, and Russia once suffered a brain drain as those with high-tech skills emigrated to high-demand, high-wage destinations. Today, many students and professionals spend time in the West to learn cutting-edge skills and then return to their native lands to work, start companies, and teach. This promotes the growth of some developing countries, while reducing the competitive advantages of the developed world.

Implications for Hospitality and Travel: Trend 22 is responsible for much of the acceleration in technological advances seen in Trend 34 (Technology increasingly dominates both the economy and society).

23. SERVICES ARE THE FASTEST-GROWING SECTOR OF THE GLOBAL ECONOMY.

Service jobs have replaced many of the well-paid positions lost in manufacturing, transportation, and agriculture. Most of these new jobs, often part-time, pay half the wages of manufacturing jobs. On the other hand, computer-related service jobs pay much more than the minimum for workers with sound education and training. Service industries provide 79 percent of the GDP in the United States, 77 percent in France, 74 percent in the United Kingdom, 73 percent in Japan, and 70 percent in Germany. In each case, services are growing rapidly, other sectors less so, and they provide substantial majorities of private non-farm employment. Production and less-skilled jobs, in contrast, are disappearing. By 2014, the United States is expected to have more chief executives than machine tool operators, more lawyers than farm workers.

Assessment: There is no foreseeable end to this trend.

Implications: In the United States, the growth of service industries is helping to deplete the middle class, as well-paid jobs in manufacturing are replaced by relatively ill-paid service positions, leaving a country of "have-a-lots" and "have-nots," but relatively few "have-enoughs."

Services are now beginning to compete globally, just as manufacturing industries have done over the last twenty years. By creating competitive pressure on wages in the industrialized lands, this trend will help to keep inflation in check.

The growth of international business will act as a stabilizing force in world affairs, as most countries find that conflict is unacceptably hard on the bottom line.

Implications for Hospitality and Travel: This trend brings the opportunity to spin off peripheral functions to service firms that specialize in them. For example, there is no longer any reason for a major hotel to do its own laundry, wash its own cutlery, or even operate its own food service. All these functions can be farmed out to other companies and treated as an operating expense comparable to utilities. Many more such opportunities will appear in the years ahead, bringing still greater efficiency to the industry's core customer-service functions.

24. WOMEN'S SALARIES ARE APPROACHING EQUALITY WITH MEN'S—BUT VERY SLOWLY.

In the 1980s and 1990s, the overall income in the United States for women was catching up with that of their male co-workers. More recently, it has stagnated. In 1995, university-educated women earned 75.7 cents for every dollar earned by men, on average. In 2005, it had fallen to 74.7 cents.

During the same period, lower-income women continued to gain on their male peers, though very slowly. One reason may be that women are less interested than men in working seventy hours or more per week during their prime reproductive years, and growing numbers have chosen to stay home and rear their children. Women also appear to be less likely to choose and pursue a career on the basis of income. Studies that attempt to compensate for differences in factors such as education, occupation, experience, and union membership find much smaller income differences than others. One reported that women receive about 91 percent as much as men. Another held that incomes are virtually equal when measured with appropriate rigor. Some studies also suggest that the pay gap has largely disappeared for women in the newest cohort of workers. This would make sense, given the nearly total gender blindness of the Millennials.

The same trend is visible in most other industrialized countries. According to the European Commission, women on the Continent earn 15 percent less than men, on average, down from 17 percent in 1995. In Britain, the gap was 20 percent, down from 26 percent. Japan is an exception to this trend. The gender gap there remains near 35 percent.

Assessment: In the United States, this trend may be in its last generation, thanks to the gender-blind values of the Millennials. In other countries, and particularly Japan, it may have another 30 years to run.

Implications: The fact that women's salaries are lagging despite higher academic achievement than men suggests that many college-educated women may be underemployed. Whether this occurs by choice or for some other reason has yet to be determined.

More new hires will be women, and they will expect both pay and opportunities equal to those of men.

Women's average income could exceed men's within a generation. College graduates enjoy a significant advantage in earnings over peers whose education ended with high school. In the United States, some 65 percent of young men and women enroll in college after high school, but women are more likely to graduate. About 58 percent of college graduates are women.

To the extent that experience translates as prestige and corporate value, older women should find it easier to reach upper-management positions. This will blaze the trail and help raise the pay scale for women still climbing the corporate ladder.

Competition for top executive positions, once effectively limited to men, will intensify even as the corporate ladder loses many of its rungs.

The glass ceiling has been broken. One-fourth of upper executives today and nearly 20 percent of corporate board members are women—far more than in any previous generation. Look for more women to reach decision-making levels in government and business. At the same time, the remaining obstacles to women's advancement may explain why women now start businesses at roughly twice the rate of men.

Implications for Hospitality and Travel: This trend has fewer implications for hospitality and travel than for most other industries. Barriers to women's advancement have been relatively few in hospitality and travel for many years, and women's pay has been much nearer to that of men in similar positions than is common in other fields.

Work and Labor Force Trends

25. Specialization continues to spread throughout industry and the professions.

For doctors, lawyers, engineers, and other professionals, the size of the body of knowledge required to excel in any one area precludes excellence across all areas. The same principle applies to artisans. Witness the rise of post-and-beam homebuilders, old-house restorers, automobile electronics technicians, and mechanics trained to work on only one brand of car. Modern information-based organizations increasingly depend on teams of task-focused specialists. For hundreds of tasks, corporations increasingly turn to consultants and contractors who specialize more and more narrowly as markets globalize and technologies differentiate.

Assessment: This process will continue for at least another twenty years.

Implications: In an information age, each new level of specialization provides greater efficiencies, reducing the cost of doing business even as it creates new opportunities. This should continue to make global business more productive and profitable for as long as it continues.

This trend creates endless new niche markets to be served by small businesses and individual consultants. It also brings more career choices as old specialties quickly become obsolete, but new ones appear even more rapidly.

Implications for Hospitality and Travel: Again, the implications for these industries parallel the common experience: greater business efficiency and the rapid proliferation of small businesses designed to provide the best possible service to niche markets.

26. The traditional age of retirement is losing its significance.

Organisation for Economic Co-operation and Development (OECD) data show that people are retiring earlier in the developed world. In 2004, less than 60 percent of the fifty-four to sixty age group in the OECD countries had a job. This varied from 50 percent in the earliest-retiring nations to 76 percent in the latest. According to the Pew Research Center, as of 2006 the average American worker planned to retire at age 61 but actually did so at 57.8. These "retirements" may not be permanent. Americans in particular often return to work and delay complete retirement for several years. About one in five people, and 40 percent of seniors, say they plan to continue working until they die.

Assessment: In the United States, this trend will be complete in a generation. Where social safety nets are stronger, it is likely to continue through at least 2030.

Implications: Given the widespread shortage of retirement savings and investments, most Americans will delay retirement until they can no longer work, whether they wish to or not. Since the penalty on earnings of Social Security recipients has been rescinded, more American retirees will return to work, and those not yet retired will be more likely to remain on the job.

This trend will spread to other industrialized countries as the retirement-age population grows and the number of active workers to support them declines.

People increasingly will work at one career, "retire" for a while (perhaps to travel) when they can afford it, return to school, begin another career, and so on in endless variations. Retirees will act as technical aides to teachers, especially in the sciences.

True retirement, a permanent end to work, will be delayed until very late in life.

By 2015, we expect the average retirement age in the United States to be delayed well into the seventies. Benefits may also continue their decline, and they will be given based on need, rather than as an entitlement. Even though the Social Security program has been the "third rail" of American politics, within five years, the retirement age will be moved back at least to seventy for early retirement and full benefits at seventy-two.

In the long run, it may prove impossible to maintain the tradition of retirement, except through personal savings and investment.

Implications for Hospitality and Travel: Divide seniors into three groups:

- Those who can afford to do so are likely to retire early. They will spend much of their time traveling, eating out, and otherwise enjoying life. They will be a prime source of business for high-end hotels, resorts, and cruise lines.

- Those who are not quite so well-to-do but still can retire on time also will travel regularly but are likely to economize on accommodations, generally taking a trip to Orlando, rather than Paris, or a relatively brief Caribbean cruise, rather than a round-the-world trip.

- There will be many as well who really cannot afford to retire completely. These older workers will partially make up for any future shortages of entry-level employees. The chance to remain in the workplace will reduce the risk of poverty for many elderly people who otherwise would have had to depend on Social Security to get by.

27. SECOND AND THIRD CAREERS ARE BECOMING COMMON, AS MORE PEOPLE MAKE MIDLIFE CHANGES IN OCCUPATION.

Americans born at the tail end of the Baby Boom (1956 to 1964) held an average of ten jobs between the ages of eighteen and thirty-eight, according to the U.S. Bureau of Labor Statistics. These job jumpers continue with short-duration jobs even as they approach middle age: 70 percent of the jobs they took between the ages of thirty-three and thirty-nine ended within five years. In the United States, 23 percent of workers surveyed in 2004 reported being dissatisfied with their careers and considering a change of occupation. Seventy percent of Irish workers surveyed in 2004 also said they hoped to make a career change soon. Women and the twenty-six to thirty-five age group were most likely to report the desire to change careers. "Personal fulfillment" was the biggest reason cited for making the change.

Assessment: This trend will not disappear unless the pace of technological change slows dramatically—or we reach the so-called "singularity," when man's inventions grow so intelligent themselves that they entirely displace human beings from the workforce.

Implications: Boomers and their children will have not just two or three careers, but five or six, as dying industries are replaced by new opportunities.

"Earn while you learn" takes on new meaning: Most people will have to study for their next occupation, even as they pursue their current career.

In many two-earner couples, one member or the other will take a sabbatical to prepare for a new career.

Self-employment is becoming an increasingly attractive option, as being your own boss makes it easier to set aside time for career development. This is especially true for Generation Xers and Millennials. Growing numbers of retirees will start their own businesses, both to keep occupied and to supplement their meager savings with new income. This trend has already begun. Retirement plans must be revised so that workers can transfer medical and pension benefits from one career to the next—a change that has long been needed. We believe this will occur soon after the Baby Boom generation begins to retire in 2011.

Implications for Hospitality and Travel: These industries have obvious appeal for mid-life career changers. These first-time entrepreneurs start a substantial fraction of new one-off restaurants, travel destinations, bed-and-breakfasts, and business services. They will continue to be a source of creativity for hospitality and travel.

28. The work ethic is vanishing.

More than one-third of U.S. workers reported calling in sick when they were not ill at least once in the past twelve months, and 10 percent had done so at least three times, according to a 2004 survey by CareerBuilder.com. Job security and high pay are not the motivators they once were, because social mobility is high and people seek job fulfillment. Some 48 percent of those responding in a recent Harris Poll said they work because it "gives a feeling of real accomplishment." Fifty-five percent of the top executives interviewed in the poll say that erosion of the work ethic will have a major negative effect on corporate performance in the future.

Assessment: There is little prospect that this will change until the children of today's young adults grow up to rebel against their parents' values.

Implications: Both employers and voters must do their best to find candidates who can be trusted, but must expect to fail in their search. This makes safeguards against wrongdoing, both at work and in public lives, more important than ever.

The new generation of workers cannot simply be hired and ignored. They must be nurtured, paid well, and made to feel appreciated or they will quickly look for a friendlier, more rewarding workplace.

Training is crucial. Without the opportunity to learn new skills, young people will quickly find a job that can help them prepare for the rest of their many careers.

Implications for Hospitality and Travel: This trend will make it more difficult to ensure a high level of customer service in all industries. Since customer service is the core of the hospitality and travel industry, it will likely be hit harder than other industries by any decline in employee diligence.

29. Labor unions are losing their power to secure rights for workers and to shape public policy in regard to workplace issues.

Union membership has been falling for the past two decades. In the United States, some 20 percent of workers were union members in 1983. In 2006, just 12.0 percent of employed wage and salary workers were union members, down from 12.5 percent a year earlier. In the United Kingdom, where the Thatcher government broke union power in the 1980s, union membership has declined almost continuously to 28.4 percent in December 2006. In South Korea, where organized labor once was invincible, no more than 11 percent of workers are union members. One reason for this decline is that companies are freely seeking and finding nonunionized workers around the world. They also contract out a growing proportion of business activities to nonunion firms.

Assessment: In spite of determined, and occasionally successful, recruiting efforts in formerly nonunion industries, union memberships and power will continue to decline for the next fifteen years until organized labor is little more than a fringe phenomenon. The trend will be reversed only if Washington and other national governments rescind pro-business labor laws and policies enacted in the last twenty-plus years.

Implications: For large companies, this trend promises continued stability in employee wages and benefits.

Unions eager to regain their membership will target any substantial industry or firm with less-skilled employees to organize. This could raise labor costs for companies that unions once would have considered too small to organize.

In ten to fifteen years, American labor unions will compete with the American Association of Retired Persons (AARP) to lead the battle for the rights of late-life workers and for secure retirement benefits. They face an inherent conflict between the interests of workers in what once would have been the retirement years and those of younger members, who rightly see the elderly as having saddled them with the cost of whatever benefits older generations enjoy. Unions' political strength is also diminishing and is increasingly being surpassed by powerful blocs such as the AARP, Hispanics, and African Americans. The old paradigm of unions vs. corporations is obsolete. In today's economy, workers negotiate alongside management, winning shared bonuses.

Implications for Hospitality and Travel: Nonunion segments of these industries represent an appealing "market" for union organizers desperate to shore up their memberships. Any major company in hospitality and travel can expect unions to focus on workers who have yet to be organized.

Energy Trends

30. Despite efforts to develop alternative sources of energy, oil consumption is still rising rapidly.

The world used only 57 million barrels of oil per day in 1973, when the first major price shock hit. By 2004, it was using 83 million barrels daily, according to the U.S. Energy Information Administration. Consumption is expected to reach 97 million barrels daily by 2015 and 118 million by 2030. Much of this increase will be due to China, which is the second-largest user of oil in the world, and the fastest growing.

Assessment: Nothing is likely to reverse this trend in the next twenty-five years.

Implications: At the height of the price spike in 2008, oil was expensive enough to justify developing new fields, such as the Arctic National Wildlife Refuge and the deep fields under the Gulf of Mexico. Eventually, though probably not in the next few years, a more controlled price rise will stimulate the development of unused oil resources. Environmentally sensitive areas will be developed using new drilling techniques, double-walled pipelines, and other precautions that make it possible to extract oil with less damage to the surroundings. Any prolonged rise of oil prices to triple digits will erode support for environmental protections in the United States, leading to widespread development of whatever energy sources are most readily available, regardless of the long-term consequences.

Implications for Hospitality and Travel: For airlines, high oil prices are a crushing burden. This more than any other single factor has driven the wave of industry consolidation in the last few years. It will continue to do so until prices stabilize.

For other hospitality and travel operators, energy costs represent a relatively small expense—significant, but much less so than staff paychecks and benefits. High oil prices are a problem that most of them can live with, at least temporarily.

31. CONTRARY TO POPULAR BELIEF, THE WORLD'S CONFIRMED OIL SUPPLY IS GROWING, NOT DECLINING.

As a result of intensive exploration, the world's proven oil reserves have climbed steadily since the 1980s and now hover at over 1.3 trillion barrels. Natural gas reserves stood at about 6.2 trillion cubic feet in 2007, about 1 percent more than a year earlier. Recent discoveries of major oil fields in Canada, Brazil, and under the Gulf of Mexico have substantially increased the world's known oil reserves.

Assessment: Talk of "peak oil"—the suggestion that crude production has topped out or soon will—is unjustified and, in FI's view, unjustifiable. Our best estimate is that the world has used about one-fourth of its recoverable oil, and almost certainly no more than one-third. This trend will remain intact until at least 2040.

Implications: Higher oil prices should make it cost effective to develop new methods of recovering oil from old wells. Technologies already developed could add nearly 50 percent to the world's recoverable oil supply.

The Organization of the Petroleum Exporting Countries (OPEC) will continue to supply most of the oil used by the developed world. According to the U.S. Department of Energy, OPEC oil production will grow to about fifty-seven million barrels of oil per day by 2020.

Russia and Kazakhstan will be major suppliers if the necessary pipelines can be completed and political uncertainties do not block investment by Western oil companies. Russia will grow into the world's second-largest oil producer by 2010.

Alternative energy sources face problems with economic viability. Barring substantial incentives, this will inhibit efforts to stem global warming for the foreseeable future.

A generalized war in the Middle East after the United States leaves Iraq could drastically reduce the region's oil output. This is unlikely, but the probable impact of such a conflict is so great that the possibility cannot be ignored.

The spread of fundamentalist Muslim regimes with a grudge against the West also could keep OPEC oil out of the American market. If the United States loses access to Middle Eastern oil, it will buy even more from Canada and Venezuela, tap the Arctic National Wildlife Refuge, and develop the deepwater fields under the Gulf of Mexico much faster than expected.

In a prolonged energy emergency, America also would be likely to develop its vast reserves of oil shale, which have long been economically viable at crude prices over $40 per barrel. New technology reportedly makes it profitable at any price over $17 per barrel. With enough shale oil to supply its own needs for three hundred years, the United States could become one of the world's largest petroleum exporters.

Developing shale would devastate the environment, but with crude oil prices in triple digits during a Mideast war, the environment would be considered expendable.

Implications for Hospitality and Travel: This trend will help to keep the cost of energy at livable levels for at least five years to come—but see Trend 32.

32. WHEN NOT PERTURBED BY GREATER-THAN-NORMAL POLITICAL OR ECONOMIC INSTABILITY3, OIL PRICES AVERAGE AROUND $65 PER BARREL.

New energy demand from the fast-growing economies of China and India has raised the floor that until 2004 supported oil in the $25-per-barrel range. Nonetheless, the spike in prices to nearly $150 per barrel in mid-2008 was an aberration. At least four factors contributed to the bubble in energy prices. Perhaps 30 percent of the increase in oil prices to their June 2008 high stemmed from the long-term decline in the value of the U.S. dollar on foreign exchange markets. Another $10 to $15 per barrel represented a "risk premium" due to fears of instability triggered by the Iraq war and Washington's threats to attack Iran. Without those two factors, $145 oil would have been $100 oil. A worldwide shortage of refinery capacity helped to drive up the cost of gasoline, fuel oil, and other energy products. It appears that rampant futures speculation in the energy markets also helped to spur oil prices. None of these factors was permanent.

Assessment: Given the condition of the American dollar, it might be better to denominate oil prices in euros—though this could be even more devastating for the American economy in the event of future episodes of instability. Aside from that, the long-term trend toward stable energy prices can only strengthen as the West reigns in consumption and alternative energy technologies become practical.

Implications: Barring some economic or political disaster, such as a devastating terrorist attack on Saudi oil fields or an American attack on Iran, the price of oil will not reach its 2008 heights until the world really does begin to run out of crude, at least half a century into the future. Until then, we expect to see oil prices hover in the general neighborhood of $65 per barrel.

In response to high (by American standards) gas prices, the U.S. government probably will boost domestic oil production and refining to increase the reserve of gasoline and heating oil. This stockpile would be ready for immediate use in case of future price hikes. This will make it easier to negotiate with OPEC.

A key step in controlling oil prices, and an indicator of Washington's seriousness about doing so, would be governmental development of at least four new refineries around the country, probably for lease to commercial producers. To avoid problems with neighbors, the refineries could be located on former military bases, which the government already owns. We rate the odds at no more than 50:50.

In the long run, the United States almost certainly will drill for oil in the Arctic National Wildlife Refuge, though efforts will be made to minimize environmental damage. For example, drilling will take place only in the winter, when the tundra is rock hard. This small new supply of oil will have a negligible effect on oil prices.

By 2020, the new fields under the Gulf of Mexico will come online, putting even more pressure on oil prices.

Implications for Hospitality and Travel: Air carriers face difficult times when the price of their largest single expense goes up. Many have added fuel surcharges to ticket prices, but rising prices eventually make it harder to fill seats. This puts an even greater premium on efficiency and cost-cutting. It also is likely to trigger more cooperation among competing airlines, with many sharing planes when passenger demand cannot fill separate flights.

Like the airlines, cruise operators are being forced to adopt fuel surcharges to maintain their profit margins. This will not seriously affect luxury cruise lines, but it could begin to erode the family and economy cruise markets.

For the hotel sector, energy costs are an important expense, but far from the largest. So long as the price of oil does not go much higher, it should have only a modest effect on the bottom line of hotels and other lodging facilities. In the United States, rising gas prices often inhibit drive-in traffic, particularly in family-oriented markets dependent on long-distance travel. This should be only a minor problem.

Sporadic price spikes also inhibit travel in Europe for brief periods, as they did when Russia temporarily closed its pipelines, causing oil shortages. We do not expect such problems to last any longer than it takes Moscow to make its political points. By 2015 or so, Europe will have developed other petroleum sources, making the unreliability of supplies from Russia much less troublesome.

While no one likes paying more for gas and electricity, high oil prices should have a relatively modest effect in the restaurant sector, where personnel costs trump all others. Restaurants can experience problems when high gas prices combine with other economic uncertainties to discourage dining out.

Americans are cutting back temporarily while the U.S. economy is in decline, but travel will recover quickly once GDP growth returns to positive territory. Common sense suggests that elective travel would be a highly elastic market, declining rapidly when prices follow costs higher. In recent years, however, elective travel has proved to be much more inelastic and comfortable with rising costs than many observers might have imagined.

33. GROWING COMPETITION FROM OTHER ENERGY SOURCES ALSO WILL HELP TO LIMIT THE PRICE OF OIL. NUCLEAR POWER IS GROWING RAPIDLY.

In Russia, plans call for construction of twenty-six more nuclear plants by 2030, when 25 percent or more of the nation's electricity will be nuclear. China plans to build thirty reactors by 2020, quadrupling its number and bringing nuclear energy consumption from 16 billion kWh in 2000 to 142 billion kWh. Even the United States is weighing the construction of new reactors.

For transportation, ethanol is the most useful alternative to petroleum. Brazil already gets more than 40 percent of its fuel for cars from ethanol made from sugar cane.

Renewable sources such as wind, wave, and solar power also are growing rapidly, but they are unlikely ever to make up more than a small fraction of the world's energy supply, save in areas where natural resources are plentiful. Iceland's drive to develop geothermal power is one example.

Assessment: This trend will remain in effect for at least thirty years.

Implications: Though oil will remain the world's most important energy resource for years to come, two or three decades forward it should be less of a choke point in the global economy. We should feed our stomachs before we feed our cars. Producing ethanol from switchgrass would cut the cost of corn by 20 percent, according to the Worldwatch Institute. This would significantly ease the global food crisis.

Declining reliance on oil eventually could help to reduce air and water pollution, at least in the developed world. By 2060, a costly but pollution-free hydrogen economy may at last become practical.

Fusion power remains a distant hope. Cold fusion also remains a long shot for practical power, but FI believes it can no longer be discounted. If the U.S. Navy's reports of successful experiments can be corroborated, power plants based on the process could begin to come online by 2030.

Implications for Hospitality and Travel: Except in places where there is an abundance of alternative energy resources, operators will continue to depend primarily on oil for their power. This will render them vulnerable to oil price shocks until a major alternative fuel source, such as fusion, becomes available.

Technology Trends

34. TECHNOLOGY INCREASINGLY DOMINATES BOTH THE ECONOMY AND SOCIETY.

New technologies are surpassing the previous state of the art in all fields. Laptop computers and Internet-equipped cell phones provide constant access to e-mail and websites. Flexible general-service personal robots will appear in the home by 2015, expanding on the capabilities of robotic vacuum cleaners and lawn mowers. New materials are bringing stronger, lighter structures that can monitor their own wear. By 2015, artificial intelligence, data mining, and virtual reality will help most organizations to assimilate data and solve problems beyond the range of today's computers. The promise of nanotechnology is just being explored, but real possibilities range from high-powered super-batteries to cell-sized health monitors. Ultimately, speculation that we are approaching the "singularity"—the time when our artifacts become so intelligent that they can design themselves and we cannot understand how they work—may prove correct. At that point, humanity will be largely a passenger in its own evolution as a technological species.

Assessment: Technology-related changes in society and business seen over the last twenty years are just the beginning of a trend that will accelerate at least through this century.

Implications: New technologies should continue to improve the efficiency of many industries, helping to keep costs under control. This increased productivity, however, has retarded U.S. job creation since at least 2002. Other developed countries are likely to feel the same effect in the future.

Technology made international outsourcing possible. It will continue to promote outsourcing to the benefit of the recipient countries, but cause painful job losses in the donor lands.

New technologies often require a higher level of education and training to use them effectively. They also provide many new opportunities to create businesses and jobs.

Automation will continue to cut the cost of many services and products, making it possible to reduce prices while still improving profits. This will be critical to business survival as the Internet continues to push the price of many products to the commodity level.

New technology also will make it easier for industry to minimize and capture its effluent. This will be essential in the environmentally conscious future.

In 1999, a team at the technology organization Battelle Memorial Institute compiled a list of the ten most strategic technological trends for the next twenty years. The list is available at the Battelle website at http://www.battelle.org/SPOT-LIGHT/tech_forecast/technology2020.aspx. Key technologies for 2020, as forecast by Battelle:

- Gene-based medical care, from custom-tailored pharmaceuticals to cloned organs for transplantation

- High-powered energy packages such as advanced batteries, cheap fuel cells, and micro-generators

- "Green integrated technology" to eliminate manufacturing waste and make products completely recyclable

- Omnipresent computing with computers built into consumer products, clothing, and even implanted under the skin

- Nanomachines measured in atoms rather than millimeters that do everything from heating and cleaning our homes to curing cancer

- Personalized public transportation that integrates our cars into a coordinated transport network, automatically picking the fastest routes and bypassing traffic jams

- Designer foods and crops genetically engineered to resist disease and pests and be highly nutritious

- Intelligent goods and appliances such as telephones with built-in directories and food packaging that tells your stove how to cook the contents

- Worldwide inexpensive and safe water from advanced filtering, desalination, and perhaps even extraction from the air

- Super senses that use implants to give us better hearing, long-distance vision, and the ability to see in the dark

Implications for Hospitality and Travel: Air travel will benefit more, and more immediately and directly, from new technologies than any other segment of hospitality and travel. New safety systems over the next decade are likely to include improved heads-up displays, en-route collision-avoidance equipment, and automated airport routing, both in the air and on the ground.

Better sensors will tighten airport security by recognizing explosives that slip past today's detectors. However, this equipment will not be installed until another Lockerbie-style bombing or a major hijacking renews public demand for greater safety.

These innovations will not be cheap. In-airplane safety systems will be mandated at the company's cost, while external equipment such as new satellites for the GPS system will be paid for by user fees.

New materials that sense their own condition are beginning to appear, particularly from nanotechnology research. They will be incorporated into critical aircraft components such as engine mounts by 2020. Soon after, skin alloys will alert mechanics to fatigue and incipient cracks.

By 2018, the first supersonic business jets will take to the air, with twenty-passenger models likely to appear around 2025. By 2030, efficient supersonic travel will replace first-class sections on long routes over water.

Cruise lines face changes, too. Online travel agencies will account for only 9 percent of cruise sales in 2009, according to PhoCusWright. That will not long be true. Over the next decade, the most important technological development for cruise lines will be the continued growth of online booking. Early suggestions that cruise travel was too complex and expensive to book without human contact are fast proving to have been wrong. Carnival, Princess, Disney, and others have set up convenient and successful online booking systems for Internet-savvy cruisers. Operators with less efficient sites, or none at all, will find themselves at a growing competitive disadvantage. Five years from now, the tradition of booking through a travel agent will have vanished, save in the extreme high end of the market—and there is reason to wonder how long agents can survive to serve the luxury market after losing the rest.

Cruise lines hoping to do well in an increasingly Internet-savvy marketplace will have to pay scrupulous attention to their reputation. Tales of poor service and disappointed travelers go a long way in online forums, chat rooms, and blogs, and they can take forever to disappear. An impeccable brand is the only assurance the online shopper has that his or her cruise investment will be money well spent.

The Internet has changed the cruise market in another way that dismays some operators. Bright European buyers are starting to check prices online and then buy from American agents, often at considerable savings. In one example, a trip through the Western Caribbean on the *Costa Mediterranea* cost £514 for a Class 1 inside cabin, or about $1,010, when booked through an agent in the United Kingdom. Buying from an American website, the price was $569, or about £289. Thus far, some cruise lines are attempting to protect their profits by refusing to accept bookings except through agents in the customer's home country. That tactic is unlikely to work for very long.

For hotels, the biggest techno-trend is well recognized already. As database systems grow more sophisticated, operators are able to capture ever more detailed information about hotel patrons, from their choice of rooms to their dining preferences and local itinerary. This enables hotel staff to give returning patrons a highly personalized experience and all but guarantees return visits. This technology is quickly raising the level of play in the battle for customer loyalty. Cruise lines, resorts, and other destinations are quickly copying these methods.

On the negative side, long-distance calling through the hotel telephone system once was a significant profit center. Cell phones have seriously eroded this business. The last of it can be expected to vanish now that the major cell providers are offering unlimited calls for just $100 per month.

Probably the biggest development for most sectors will be the growing use of radio frequency identification (RFID) chips to track supplies, automate ordering, and make delivery more efficient, and therefore cheaper.

One nascent restaurant chain in California features order entry computers at each table. Customers use the terminal to read the menu, view each menu item, and place their order. They see human staff only when handing over their credit cards—before ordering—and when the food is delivered. Computerized ordering will not soon penetrate high-end restaurants or fast-food chains, but it will be welcome at mid-range family restaurants, where savings are sorely needed. Also expect to see innovation at self-bussing restaurants, where patrons will deliver their plates and tableware directly to the maw of the automated washers.

Some of the most interesting new technologies for restaurants and food services will operate far behind the scenes. In laboratories around the world, scientists are building artificial "tongues" and "noses" more sensitive than human organs. Models now in development can distinguish among closely related wines, various cheeses and breads, and coffees. In the near future, food producers will use them to guarantee product quality. This innovation will provide restaurants with better, more consistent materials and give diners more predictable, and probably more satisfying, meals.

35. THE UNITED STATES IS CEDING ITS SCIENTIFIC AND TECHNICAL LEADERSHIP TO OTHER COUNTRIES.

"The scientific and technical building blocks of our economic leadership are eroding at a time when many other nations are gathering strength." This warning comes from the National Academy of Sciences in a 2005 report, and continues: "Although many people assume that the United States will always be a world leader in science and technology, this may not continue to be the case inasmuch as great minds and ideas exist throughout the world. We fear the abruptness with which a lead in science and technology can be lost—and the difficulty of recovering a lead once lost, if indeed it can be regained at all."

Although research and development (R&D) spending is growing in raw-dollar terms, when measured as a percentage of the total federal budget or as a fraction of the U.S. GDP, research funding has been shrinking for some fifteen years. In 2005, the United States spent about 2.68 percent of its GDP on R&D, down from 2.76 percent in 2001. Washington has often reduced the post-inflation buying power of its R&D funding request. In the FY 2007 budget, for the first time, it cut R&D funds in absolute dollars as well. Washington's neglect of basic science is being felt in many ways. For example, only half of American patents are granted to Americans, a number that has been declining for decades. Another example: only

29 percent of the research papers published in the prestigious *Physical Review* in 2003 were written by American authors, down from 61 percent in 1983.

More than half of American scientists and engineers are nearing retirement. At the rate American students are entering these fields, the retirees cannot be replaced except by recruiting foreign scientists. Between 25 and 30 percent of high school graduates who enter college plan to major in science or engineering. Fewer than half of them receive a degree in those fields. The number of U.S. bachelor's degrees awarded in engineering in 2005 was nearly 15 percent below the peak twenty years earlier

Assessment: This trend emerged from a wide variety of ill-conceived political decisions made over the last thirty years. It will take at least a generation to reverse.

Implications: If this trend is not reversed, it will begin to undermine the U.S. economy and shift both economic and political power to other lands. According to some estimates, about half of the improvement in the American standard of living is directly attributable to research and development carried out by scientists and engineers.

The Bureau of Labor Statistics predicts that the number of job openings in science and engineering will grow by 47 percent in the five years ending in 2010—three times as fast as nontechnical fields. The United States will not produce nearly enough home-grown technical specialists to fill them. Demand to import foreign scientists and engineers on H-1B visas also will continue to grow. Publicity about the H-1B program, and about the offshoring of R&D to company divisions and consulting labs in Asia, in turn, will discourage American students from entering technical fields. This has already been blamed for shrinking student rolls in computer science.

In 2005, China for the first time exported more IT and communications goods ($180 million) than the United States ($145 million). Its lead has grown each year since then.

Implications for Hospitality and Travel: In the short run, this suggests that a growing fraction of the new technologies adopted by hospitality and travel businesses will originate with companies outside the United States. In the longer term, this trend could begin to reduce the relative wealth of Americans compared to the rest of the world. This may eventually cause a decline in per capita spending by Americans on hospitality and travel, particularly outside the United States. Loss of science-based prestige also could reduce America's appeal for some foreign travelers, discouraging tourism to the United States.

36. Transportation technology and practice are improving rapidly.

The newest generation of aircraft, such as the Boeing 787 and future Airbus A350 XWB, are using lightweight materials and more efficient engines to cut fuel costs, stretch ranges, and increase cargo capacity. In the United States, two companies have even announced plans to build supersonic business jets and have them in the air by 2013 or so. One has already taken deposits for several dozen aircraft. At the same time, rail travel is getting faster. The new TGV Est line, which runs 300 kilometers (180 miles) from Paris to Frankfurt, operates at 320 kph (198.8 mph) inside France, compared with 300 kph on other parts of the TGV system. China has begun to install a network of high-speed trains to compensate for its shortage of regional air transportation.

Assessment: These advances will continue at least through mid-century.

Implications: One of the fastest-growing transport industries is trucking, thanks to the expanded use of just-in-time inventory management and Internet-based companies that rely on trucks to deliver their products. This field will grow more efficient as GPS-based truck tracking, RFID-based cargo management, more efficient engines, and other new technologies spread through the industry.

To reduce the number and severity of traffic accidents, trucks on the most heavily used highways will be exiled to car-free lanes, and the separation will be enforced.

New hybrid car models will begin to gain significant market share from traditional gas guzzlers between 2010 and 2015. By 2010, smart-car technologies will begin to reduce deaths due to auto accidents in Europe and, a few years later, in the United States.

Cities increasingly will struggle to reduce auto congestion by limiting the use of private automobiles, as in Munich, Vienna, and Mexico City; by taxing auto use in congested areas, as in London; or by encouraging the development and use of mass transit, as in Copenhagen and Curitiba, Brazil.

Technology may offer other alternatives. One proposal is "dual-mode transportation" in which private cars would be used normally on short hauls, but would run on automated guideways for long-distance travel.

Implications for Hospitality and Travel: The arrival of lightweight aircraft with high-efficiency engines should help to reduce the impact of fuel costs on airlines, making it possible to profit in this industry without charging excessively high ticket prices or leaving travelers feeling that they are being "nickel-and-dimed" to death by fees that once were included in the basic ticket cost.

Following European practice, even "legacy" air carriers in the United States will begin to replace the spokes of their existing hub-and-spokes system with high-speed trains for journeys of 100 to 150 miles.

By 2015, improved technologies and concerns about the long-term cost of energy will lead even the rail-resistant United States to begin modernizing its train system.

New aircraft navigation and safety technologies will reduce the number and severity of crashes.

37. THE PACE OF TECHNOLOGICAL CHANGE ACCELERATES WITH EACH NEW GENERATION OF DISCOVERIES AND APPLICATIONS.

In fast-moving engineering disciplines, half of the cutting-edge knowledge learned by college students in their freshman year is obsolete by the time they graduate. The design and marketing cycle—idea, invention, innovation, imitation—is shrinking steadily. As late as the 1940s, the product cycle stretched to thirty or forty years. Today, it seldom lasts thirty or forty weeks. Almost any new consumer product can be exactly duplicated by Chinese factories and sold on e-Bay within a week after it is introduced. The reason is simple: Some 80 percent of the scientists, engineers, technicians, and physicians who ever lived are alive today and exchanging ideas real time on the Internet.

Assessment: This trend will continue for many years. However, we may grow less able to perceive it.

Implications: Subjectively, change soon will move so rapidly that we can no longer recognize its acceleration, save as an abstract concept.

All the technical knowledge we work with today will represent only 1 percent of the knowledge that will be available in 2050. Industries will face much tighter competition based on new technologies. Those who adopt state-of-the-art methods first will prosper. Those who ignore them will eventually fail.

Products must capture their market quickly, before the competition can copy them. Brand names associated with quality are becoming even more important in this highly competitive environment.

Lifelong learning is a necessity for anyone who works in a technical field—and for growing numbers who do not. In what passes for the long run—a generation or two—the development of true artificial intelligence is likely to reduce human beings to managers. Rather than making new discoveries and creating new products, we will struggle to understand and guide the flow of novelties delivered by creations we cannot really keep up with.

Implications for Hospitality and Travel: As new technologies arrive, hospitality and travel operators will be forced to hire more technology specialists and train other employees to cope with new demands.

The next major development will be the spread of RFID chips throughout the hospitality and travel industry. Airlines, hotels, and restaurant chains will need to hire technicians with experience in RFID to set up and monitor new automated inventory and ordering systems, while everyone from chefs to warehouse personnel will need training in their use.

38. The Internet continues to grow, but at a slower pace.

In mid-2007, Internet users numbered about 1.173 billion, up just less than one-fourth in three years. Most growth of the Internet population is now taking place outside the United States, which is home to only 19 percent of Internet users. In mid-2007, the most recent available data showed 162 million Internet users in China (12.3 percent of the population), 42 million in India (3.7 percent), and 86.3 million in Japan (67.1 percent.)

The growth of e-commerce also is slowing, with 2007 sales coming in at $116 billion. Sales growth, as much as 25 percent per year in 2004, is expected to slow to 9 percent annually by 2010. The current recession may trim up to 2 percent off that pre-2009 forecast, but growth will continue at its expected pace thereafter.

Assessment: Internet growth will continue until essentially no one in the world lacks easy access to e-mail and the web, about thirty years by our best estimate.

Implications: Americans will continue to dominate the Internet as long as they produce a substantial majority of web pages, but that is not likely to be very long.

Analysts believe that Internet growth will not accelerate again until broadband service becomes less expensive and more widely available. This is a matter of government policy as much as of technology or basic costs.

Demands that the United States relinquish control of the Internet to an international body can only gain broader support and grow more emphatic as Americans make up a smaller part of the Internet population.

B2B sales on the Internet are dramatically reducing business expenses throughout the Internet-connected world, while giving suppliers access to customers they could never have reached by traditional means.

The Internet has made it much easier and cheaper to set up a profitable business. An online marketing site can be set up with just a few minutes' work at a cost of much less than $100. This is fostering a new generation of entrepreneurs.

Internet-based outsourcing to other countries has only just begun. Growth in this field will accelerate again as overseas service firms polish their English, French, and German and find even more business functions they can take on.

Cultural, political, and social isolation has become almost impossible for countries interested in economic development. Even China's attempts to filter the Internet and shield its population from outside influences have been undermined by hackers elsewhere, who provide ways to penetrate the barriers.

Implications for Hospitality and Travel: Continuing growth of the Internet will bring these industries the same benefits others enjoy—lower business expenses, greater efficiency, and easier access to customers even for the smallest operators. Online marketing will grow even more significant for destinations as China and India grow more prosperous and travel-prone.

Social networking sites such as Facebook, MySpace, and Twitter are some of the hottest online phenomena of recent years. Now hospitality and travel firms are getting into the act. KLM Royal Dutch Airlines, one of the earliest adopters and still among the most impressive, offers its customers three invitation-only communities where they can meet like-minded colleagues: one for people doing business in China, one for Africa hands, and one for golfers. Fliers can make contacts, meet offline at club events sponsored by the airline, and set up their own real-world meetings. Forty percent of users have been logging in an average of once a month, which KLM rates as a success. Similar offerings are available from a growing host of specialty sites. Virgin America even put a social networking system into seatback computers to help people connect with fellow passengers.

Internet savants also are starting to talk about the "semantic web," a natural-language interface to the Internet's vast stores of information. Picture a website where you can ask for "a week for two in South America next February. We want to explore a rain forest, but spend at least three days on the beach at a luxury resort. We can spend $2,500 each, including air fare from Miami." By 2012, travel sites will be able to understand the question, search their databases, offer a choice of vacation plans, and make reservations as soon as the customers make their decision.

39. Technology is creating a knowledge-dependent global society.

More and more businesses and entire industries are based on the production and exchange of information and ideas rather than exclusively on manufactured goods or other tangible products. At the same time, manufacturers and sellers of physical products are able to capture and analyze much more information about buyers' needs and preferences, making the selling process more efficient and effective. The number of Internet users in the United States more than doubled between 2000 and 2007, to nearly 231 million, or 69 percent of the population. Yet the percentage of the population online has remained almost unchanged since 2004. And while the percentage of Internet users in China is smaller than in the United States, the *number* of users there passed the United States early in 2008.

Assessment: This trend will not reach even its halfway mark until the rural populations of China and India gain modern educations and easy access to the Internet.

Implications: This trend is raising the level of education required for a productive role in today's workforce. For many workers, therefore, the opportunity for training is becoming one of the most desirable benefits any job can offer.

Even entry-level workers and those in formerly unskilled positions require a growing level of education. For a good career in almost any field, computer competence is mandatory.

Knowledge workers are generally better paid than less skilled workers, and their proliferation may raise overall prosperity. However, data and communications technologies also are exposing workers in the developed world to competition from low-wage countries. It is not yet clear at what pay level these competing forces will balance.

This trend also is enlarging the income gap between well-educated workers and those with a high school degree or less. That gap will continue to grow.

In ten years, most digital devices will combine multimedia communication functions and real-time voice translation, so that conversations originating in one of seven or eight common languages can be heard in any of the others. These technologies will enable even more people to become knowledge workers or, at least, knowledge-enhanced workers.

Telecommuting will make many companies more efficient, cutting their expenses in the process. New technologies create new industries, jobs, and career paths, which can bring new income to developing countries. An example is the transfer of functions such as technical support, and more recently R&D, to Asian divisions and service firms.

For some developing countries, computer skills are making it faster and easier to create wealth than a manufacturing economy ever could. India, for example, is rapidly growing a middle class, largely on the strength of its computer and telecom industries. Other lands will follow its example.

Implications for Hospitality and Travel: For both marketing and management, this trend is changing all segments of hospitality and travel. Online sales have grown into a major outlet for airlines and hotels, severely eroding the market for travel agencies. This trend will accelerate in the years ahead, as Generation X and especially the Millennials bring their computer skills to travel shopping. Within five years, even the cruise industry, which has been committed to sales through travel agencies, will be substantially dependent on Internet sales.

This also levels the field for smaller and less-well-known destinations, which now can get their message to potential guests on the same basis as larger operators. As a result, we will see a steady proliferation of small travel businesses throughout the world for at least the next twenty years.

In hospitality management, the greatest technological change in the next five years will be the arrival of RFID chips. Combining a small piece of computer memory with a tiny radio transmitter, RFID chips can remotely identify and track whatever object they are attached to. This dramatically reduces the manpower required for inventory and order functions and cuts inventory requirements. Just-in-time ordering will streamline procedures for hotels, restaurants, cruise lines, and most other hospitality and travel operations.

Information technologies also are raising the level of technical skill required for many hospitality-industry functions.

Cruise ships today require complete network management staffs for their Internet systems as well as for vessel controls, and crews tech-savvy enough to help guests with onboard computers, HDTV, and other increasingly complicated hardware.

Environmental Trends

40. People around the world are becoming increasingly sensitive to environmental issues as the consequences of neglect, indifference, and ignorance become ever more apparent.

The World Health Organization (WHO) estimates that three million people die each year from the effects of air pollution, about 5 percent of the total deaths. In the United States, an estimated 64,000 people a year die of cardiopulmonary disease caused by breathing particulates. In Sub-Saharan Africa, the toll is between 300,000 and 500,000 deaths per year. Pollution-related respiratory diseases kill about 1.4 million people yearly in China and Southeast Asia. And contaminated water is implicated in 80 percent of the world's health problems, according to WHO. An estimated 40,000 people around the world die each day of diseases directly caused by contaminated water, more than 14 million per year.

Though some debate remains about the cause, the fact of global warming has become undeniable. At Palmer Station on Anvers Island, Antarctica, the average annual temperature has risen by three to four degrees since the 1940s, and by an amazing seven to nine degrees in June—early winter in that hemisphere.

Anticipating a three-foot rise in sea levels, the Netherlands is spending $1 billion to build new dikes.

Assessment: A solid majority of voters throughout the developed world and even some in the developing lands now recognize the need to clean up the environment and especially to control greenhouse warming. They will keep this trend intact for at least the next thirty years.

Implications: Throughout most of the world, polluters and private beneficiaries of public assets will increasingly confront restrictive regulations designed to serve the interests of the community at large.

Carbon dioxide will remain a problem for many years to come. If air pollution were halted instantly, it would take an estimated two hundred years for carbon dioxide and other greenhouse gases to return to pre-industrial levels.

Impurities in water will become an even greater problem as the populations of the developed countries age and become more susceptible to infectious diseases.

Recent analyses posit a 90 percent chance that the planet's average annual temperature will rise between three and nine degrees Celsius over the next century. This will cause severe dislocations both for plant and animal populations and for many human activities.

Environmental policies will provoke a political backlash wherever they conflict with entrenched interests, as they have long done in the American West.

Implications for Hospitality and Travel: Hospitality operators throughout most of the world can expect many more legal mandates for cleaner facilities and practices.

Once the airline industry's current economic problems have been endured, aviation will face more demands to reduce emissions linked to global warming.

Cruise lines found to be avoidably polluting the seas, whether deliberately or by accident, will be penalized especially harshly.

In the long run, incentives for "green" practices will take some of the financial pain out of making the necessary changes. So will long-term savings on energy, waste disposal, and expendables.

Eco-friendly travel will continue to be one of the fastest growing segments of the industry for the next fifteen years. After that, it will simply be the way things are done.

41. Water shortages will be a growing problem for much of the world. In many regions, they are severe already.

The northern half of China, home to perhaps half a billion people, already is short of water. The water table under Beijing has fallen nearly two hundred feet since 1965. Australia's Murray-Darling river system, which supplies water for 40 percent of the country's crops and 80 percent of its irrigation, no longer carries enough water to reach the sea without constant dredging. Salinity in the Murray is rising so quickly that the water is expected to be undrinkable in twenty years. There is worse to come. According to UN studies, at least 3.5 billion people will run short of water by 2040, almost ten times as many as in 1995. Ten years later, fully two-thirds of the world's population could be living in regions with chronic, widespread shortages of water.

Assessment: This trend will remain with us for the very long term.

Implications: Providing adequate supplies of potable water will be a growing challenge for developing and developed countries alike.

Such problems as periodic famine and desertification can be expected to grow more frequent and severe in coming decades.

In many lands, including parts of the United States, growing water shortages may inhibit economic growth and force large-scale migration out of afflicted areas.

Climate change is expected to reduce the flow of Australia's parched Murray River by a further 5 percent in twenty years and 15 percent in fifty years.

Water wars, predicted for more than a decade, are a threat in places such as Kashmir: much of Pakistan's water comes from areas of Kashmir now controlled by India.

Other present and future water conflicts involve Turkey, Syria, and Iraq over the Tigris and Euphrates; Israel, Jordan, Syria, and Palestine over water from the Jordan River and the aquifers under the Golan Heights; India and Bangladesh over the Ganges and Brahmaputra; China, Indochina, and Thailand over the Mekong; Kyrghyzstan, Tajikistan, and Uzbekistan over the Amu Darya and

Jaxartes rivers; and Ethiopia, Sudan, and at least six East African countries, including Egypt, over the Nile.

In the United States, repair of decayed water systems is likely to be a major priority for older cities such as New York, Boston, and Atlanta. Cost estimates for necessary replacement and repair of water mains range up to $1 trillion.

Implications for Hospitality and Travel: In the American Southwest, northern China, Australia, and other parched regions, water supplies will be a growing concern for hotels, restaurants, and other destinations. This is not likely to ease in the foreseeable future.

As water becomes ever more scarce throughout much of the developing world, regional instability could put otherwise attractive destinations off limits for Western travelers. Parts of the Middle East are the obvious candidates for future avoidance.

42. Recycling has delayed the "garbage glut" that threatened to overflow the world's landfills, but the problem continues to grow.

Americans now produce about 4.5 pounds of trash per person per day, twice as much as they threw away a generation ago. Seventy percent of U.S. landfills will be full by 2025, according to the Environmental Protection Agency. Japan expects to run out of space for industrial waste as soon as 2012 and for municipal solid waste by 2015. In London and the surrounding region, landfills will run out of room by 2012.

Recycling has proved to be an effective alternative to dumping. As of 2005, Germany recycled 60 percent of its municipal solid waste, 65 percent of manufacturing waste, 80 percent of packaging, and 87 percent of construction waste, according to the Federal Ministry for the Environment, Nature Conservation and Nuclear Safety. Largely as a result, the number of landfills for domestic waste has been reduced from about 50,000 in the 1970s to just 160.

Assessment: The challenge of dealing with garbage will grow as long as the world's middle classes continue to expand or until technology finds ways to recycle virtually all of the materials used in manufacturing and packaging. This trend will remain intact through at least 2050.

Implications: Recycling and waste-to-energy plants are a viable alternative to simply dumping garbage. This trend will push the development of so-called lifecycle design, which builds convenient recyclability into new products from their inception.

Expect a wave of new regulations, recycling, waste-to-energy projects, and waste management programs in the United States and other countries in an effort to stem the tide of trash. In the United States, this wave will of course begin in California, a jurisdiction often cited by policy forecasters as a bellwether of change.

State and local governments will tighten existing regulations and raise disposal prices in Pennsylvania, South Carolina, Louisiana, and other places that accept much of the trash from major garbage producers such as New York. Trash producers in the developed world will ship much more of their debris to repositories in developing countries. This will inspire protests in the receiving lands.

Beyond 2025 or so, the developing countries will close their repositories to foreign waste, forcing producers to develop more waste-to-energy and recycling technologies. Ultimately, it may even be necessary to exhume buried trash for recycling to make more room in closed dump sites for material that cannot be reused.

Waste-to-energy programs will make only a small contribution to the world's growing need for power.

Implications for Hospitality and Travel: Hotels, resorts, restaurants, and other large-scale waste generators can expect to face the same kind of recycling requirements that many private homeowners have been complying with for years. This will increase handling expenses for recyclable bottles, cans, plastics, and paper, but it should ultimately reduce the cost of disposal.

This may bring even more scrutiny to cruise lines. Any ship caught dumping waste at sea can expect to bring its company catastrophic publicity with a risk of boycotts. The rest may profit from advertising their "green" credentials, especially if they donate to ocean-oriented environmental groups.

43. PREFERENCE FOR INDUSTRIAL DEVELOPMENT OVER ENVIRONMENTAL CONCERNS IS FADING SLOWLY IN MUCH OF THE DEVELOPING WORLD.

The Pew Research Center reports that less than one-fourth of respondents in any African country rated environmental problems as the world's most important threat. In Ethiopia, where desertification is at its worst and drought is a constant threat, only 7 percent did so. Although Beijing has made repairing the environment a national priority, 70 percent of the energy used in China comes from coal-burning power plants, few of them equipped with pollution controls. The country intends to build more than five hundred new coal-fired plants in the next ten years. Even Germany has committed to building more power plants fired by high-sulfur brown coal.

Assessment: View this as a counter-trend to Trend 40 (People around the world are becoming increasingly sensitive to environmental issues as the consequences of neglect, indifference, and ignorance become ever more apparent). It will remain largely intact until the poor of India and China complete their transition into the middle class, around 2040.

Implications: Broad regions of the planet will be subject to pollution, deforestation, and other environmental ills in the coming decades. Acid rain like that afflicting the United States and Canada will appear wherever designers of new power plants and factories neglect emission controls. In India, an area the size of the United States is covered by a haze of sulfates and other chemicals associated with acid rain. Look for this problem to appear in most other industrializing countries.

Diseases related to air and water pollution will spread dramatically in the years ahead. Already, chronic obstructive pulmonary disease is five times more common in China than in the United States. As citizens of the developing countries grow to expect modern healthcare, this will create a growing burden on their economies.

This is just a taste of future problems, and perhaps not the most troublesome. Even the U.S. government now admits that global warming is a result of human activities that produce greenhouse gases. It now seems that China and India soon will produce even more of them than the major industrialized nations. Helping the developing lands to raise their standards of living without creating wholesale pollution will require much more aid and diplomacy than the developed world has ever been willing to give this cause.

Implications for Hospitality and Travel: All these problems will make the worst afflicted areas much less attractive to travelers in the coming years. They also will subject hotels, resorts, cruise lines, and other segments to new regulations designed to minimize their use of energy and to promote recycling and other environmentally friendly practices.

44. CONCERN OVER SPECIES EXTINCTION AND LOSS OF BIODIVERSITY IS GROWING QUICKLY.

An estimated fifty thousand species disappear each year, up to one thousand times the natural rate of extinction, according to the UN Environment Program. By 2100, as many as half of all species could disappear. Eleven percent of birds, 25 percent of mammals, and 20 to 30 percent of all plants are estimated to be nearing extinction. Some 16,118 species are now listed as threatened (7,925 animal species and 8,393 plant and lichen species), according to the 2006 Red List of the International Union for Conservation of Nature and Natural Resources. This is an increase of nearly 2,700 in four years. The real list is likely much larger, as the group has evaluated only forty thousand of the 1.5 million species on its list. The chief cause for species loss is the destruction of natural habitats by logging, agriculture, and urbanization.

Assessment: This trend has at least three decades to run.

Implications: Saving any significant fraction of the world's endangered species will require much more effort and expense than many governments find acceptable. For species such as corals, if the loss is attributable largely to climate change, it may not be possible.

Species loss has a powerful negative impact on human well-being. Half of all drugs used in medicine are derived from natural sources, including fifty-five of the top one hundred drugs prescribed in the United States. About 40 percent of all pharmaceuticals are derived from the sap of vascular plants. So far, only 2 percent of the three hundred thousand known sap-containing plants have been assayed for useful drugs. Most of the species lost in the years ahead will disappear before they can be tested.

The Indonesian economy loses an estimated $500,000 to $800,000 annually per square mile of dead or damaged reef. Australia may lose even more as degradation of the Great Barrier Reef continues. The UN Intergovernmental Panel on Climate Change predicts that the Reef will be "functionally extinct" by 2030.

Diverse ecosystems absorb more carbon dioxide than those with fewer species. Loss of biodiversity thus is a potential cause of global warming.

Implications for Hospitality and Travel: For the near term, environmentally conscious travelers will flock to endangered regions such as the Galápagos, the Great Barrier Reef, and the Amazon rain forests to witness their biological diversity while it is still available. In the long run, however, the loss of coral and other extinction events will destroy the tourist appeal of some of the world's favorite destinations for environmental and adventure tourism.

45. Urbanization, arguably the world's oldest trend, continues rapidly.

Forty-eight percent of the world's population currently lives in cities, according to the Population Reference Bureau's 2006 World Population Data Sheet. By 2030, that figure will grow to 60 percent, as some 2.1 billion people are added to the world's cities.

Cities are growing fastest in the developing world. In 1950, there were just eight megacities, with populations exceeding five million, in the world. By 2015, there will be fifty-nine megacities, forty-eight of them in less developed countries. Of these, twenty-three will have populations over ten million, all but four in the developing lands.

Natural increase now accounts for more than half of population increase in the cities; at most, little more than one-third of urban growth results from migration.

Assessment: After surviving for some 3,500 years, this trend is unlikely to disappear in the next fifty.

Implications: Cities' contribution to global warming can only increase in the years ahead. As the world's supply of potable water declines, people are concentrating in those areas where it is hardest to obtain and is used least efficiently. This trend will aggravate water problems for as long as it continues. Many more people will die due to shortages of shelter, water, and sanitation. Epidemics will become still more common as overcrowding spreads HIV and other communicable diseases more rapidly.

Since urban growth is now attributable more to natural increase than to migration, programs designed to encourage rural populations to remain in the countryside may be misplaced. Education and family planning seem more likely to rein in the growth of cities.

Implications for Hospitality and Travel: Many cities in the developing world will become even more congested and polluted, reducing their appeal even when historical arts and artifacts might otherwise draw tourism.

Management Trends

46. More entrepreneurs start new businesses every year.

In the United States, about 9 percent of men and 6 percent of women are self-employed. These fractions have been growing in about two-thirds of the OECD countries. Many women are leaving traditional jobs to go home and open businesses, even as they begin a family. At least half of the estimated 10.6 million privately held firms in the United States are owned by women, employing 19.1 million people and generating $2.46 trillion in sales annually.

For the fourteen years ending in 2003, the most recent period for which data are available, small businesses (those with fewer than five hundred employees) created 92 percent of the net new jobs in the United States, according to the U.S. Census Bureau. The smallest companies, those with fewer than twenty employees, created 85 percent. However, jobs from small companies also disappear faster because those companies are much more likely to fail than larger concerns. Although big-company layoffs have gotten the most publicity in the current recession, losses from smaller firms are likely to be even more severe.

Assessment: This is a self-perpetuating trend, as all those new service firms need other companies to handle chores outside their core business. It will remain with us for many years, not only because it suits new-generation values, but also because it is a rational response to an age in which jobs can never be counted on to provide a stable long-term income.

Implications: It is driven as well by the attitudes and values of Generation X and the Millennials and by the rapid developments in technology, which create endless opportunities for new business development. Specialty boutiques will continue to spring up on the Internet for at least the next fifteen years.

This trend will help to ease the poverty of many developing countries, as it is already doing in India and China.

Implications for Hospitality and Travel: We can expect a wave of new hospitality and travel businesses to appear in the years ahead. Many will be new destinations in areas where the travel industry is just beginning to grow. Others will be specialty tour operators focused on either niche sports and other activities or on consumer groups with special needs, such as non-English-speakers, religious or cultural minorities, seniors, or all-female tour groups.

47. INFORMATION-BASED ORGANIZATIONS ARE QUICKLY DISPLACING THE OLD COMMAND-AND-CONTROL MODEL OF MANAGEMENT.

The typical large business has reshaped itself or is struggling to do so. Soon, it will be composed of specialists who rely on information from colleagues, customers, and headquarters to guide their actions.

Upper management is giving fewer detailed orders to subordinates. Instead, it sets performance expectations for the organization, its parts, and its specialists and supplies the feedback necessary to determine whether results have met expectations.

Assessment: This is a well-established trend. At this point, many large corporations have restructured their operations for greater flexibility, but many others still have a long way to go.

This trend will continue in the United States for at least the next fifteen years. The developing world may largely bypass this step in its new organizations and go straight to networked management structures.

Implications: This management style suits Generation Xers and Millennials well, as it tends to let them work in whatever fashion suits them as long as the job gets done.

Downsizing has spread from manufacturing industries to the service economy. Again, this process encourages the entrepreneurial trend, both to provide services for companies outsourcing their secondary functions and to provide jobs for displaced employees.

Many older workers have been eliminated in this process, depriving companies of their corporate memory. Companies have replaced them with younger workers whose experience of hard times is limited. Many firms may discover that they need to recruit older workers to help them adapt to adversity.

This also drives the entrepreneurial trend. Many older workers find themselves self-employed by default, as they need income and cannot find work in their accustomed fields.

Implications for Hospitality and Travel: The growing demand for specialists to join in task-oriented teams will reduce the number of broadly experienced industry generalists needed by large hospitality and travel operators. Unfortunately, relying on specialists for their expertise in relatively narrow aspects of company operations will make it difficult to train promising staff members in the broad range of skills needed for promotion to higher management positions.

48. ORGANIZATIONS ARE SIMPLIFYING THEIR STRUCTURES AND SQUEEZING OUT PERSONNEL.

Computers and information management systems have stretched the manager's effective span of control from six to twenty-one subordinates. Information now flows from frontline workers to higher management for analysis. Thus, fewer mid-level managers are needed, flattening the corporate pyramid.

The span of control could stretch again if computer science finally delivers on its long-delayed promise of artificial intelligence. Opportunities for advancement are shrinking because they increasingly must come within the worker's narrow specialty, rather than at the broader corporate level. In 2001, only one person in fifty was promoted, compared with one in twenty in 1987.

Assessment: In the United States, downsizing, restructuring, reorganization, and cutbacks of white-collar workers will continue at least through 2025. The pace will not slow unless technology ceases to deliver new ways to replace human workers with faster, cheaper, more reliable hardware and software.

Implications: The current recession will be filled by another "jobless recovery" as companies squeeze still more productivity out of their existing workforce, rather than hiring new employees.

A typical large business in 2015 will have fewer than half the management levels of its counterpart in 1995, and about one-third the number of managers.

Information-based organizations have to make a special effort to prepare professional specialists to become business leaders. Broad experience of the kind needed by a CEO no longer comes naturally during an executive's career.

Top managers must be computer-literate to retain their jobs and must make sure to oversee the increased spans of control that computers make possible.

Finding top managers with the broad experience needed to run a major business already has become difficult. It can only grow more so as the demand for specialization grows. This will reduce promotion from within and encourage companies to seek upper-level execs from other firms, and even industries.

Executives increasingly will start their own companies rather than trust the old-fashioned corporate career path to provide advancement.

Ultimately, this trend will require a wholesale rethinking of the social contract, as it becomes difficult or impossible to create enough fulfilling, well-paid jobs for human workers to support the population. The end of salaried work is not yet near, but it could arrive within the lifetimes of today's younger generations.

Implications for Hospitality and Travel: This trend could endanger the tradition of promoting from within that has been prevalent in the hospitality and travel industry. Because there will be fewer opportunities for promotion, it will be difficult to provide employees with the breadth of experience required of top executives. Thus, high-level managers are likely to come increasingly from competitors and from other industries. This is likely to increase the turnover of management personnel, who can no longer look forward to the rewarding careers that these industries once offered.

This also will force corporate managers to develop new ways to motivate their employees and provide them with the kind of experience needed to fill the few positions remaining at the upper levels of the company.

49. GOVERNMENT REGULATIONS WILL CONTINUE TO TAKE UP A GROWING PORTION OF THE MANAGER'S TIME AND EFFORT.

In 1996, the U.S. Congress passed regulatory reform laws intended to slow the spread of government regulations. Nonetheless, by 2001 more than fourteen thousand new regulations were enacted. Not one proposed regulation was rejected during this period. The Brussels bureaucrats of the European Union are churning out rules at an even faster rate, overlaying a standard regulatory structure on the national systems of member countries.

This is not all bad. A study by the Office of Management and Budget estimated that major federal regulations enacted in the decade ending September 2002 cost between $38 billion and $44 billion per year. However, the estimated benefits added up to between $135 billion and $218 billion annually.

Assessment: If the future holds an end to this trend, it is not yet in sight.

Implications: Regulations are necessary, unavoidable, and often beneficial. Yet it is difficult not to see them as a kind of friction that slows both current business and future economic growth.

The proliferation of regulations in the developed world could give a competitive advantage to countries such as India and China, where regulations that impede investment and capital flow are being stripped away, and health, occupational safety, and environmental codes are still rudimentary or absent.

However, there is a significant penalty for the kind of risk that comes from inadequate regulation. China pays an estimated risk penalty of 6.49 percent for international borrowing. Per capita GDP, access to capital, foreign direct investment, and other measures of a country's economic health all decline directly with a rising Opacity Index, which is heavily influenced by the lack of effective regulations to guarantee a level playing field for those doing business there. As a result, lands such as Russia will remain at a competitive disadvantage until they can pass and enforce the regulations needed to ensure a stable, fair business environment.

Implications for Hospitality and Travel: Airline regulations will focus on safety and customer convenience. The most costly would be installation of an effective bomb detection system for checked luggage. It will be required only if an American flight is bombed. (It is far from impossible. Officials at the U.S. Transportation Security Administration worry that a bomb could still be smuggled aboard as tiny parts, then assembled for use.) Other rules are likely to demand installation of more crash-worthy seating, new user fees, and switching schedules to relieve peak-hour congestion.

A regulation proposed recently would require foreign-flagged cruise ships leaving from the United States to spend at least two days in a foreign port before returning, and at least one day in a foreign port for every two in an American port. The rule, proposed to limit competition for two American-flagged ships operated out of Hawaii by Norwegian Cruise Line, would change itineraries for thousands of cruises. It might also devastate profits at American home ports. Juneau, Alaska, alone would lose an estimated $68 million in one summer. Forecast: This regulation is unlikely to pass scrutiny. If enacted, it will be rescinded quickly.

Hotels already are so well regulated that this sector should be *relatively* immune to new government-mandated complications. Of course, any new rules that apply to restaurants will apply to hotel-based eating establishments just as they do to freestanding outlets.

Restaurant operators trying to avoid cluttering their menus with nutrition information are fighting a losing battle. Calorie counts, fat content, and other unpleasant details soon will be there for patrons to see when choosing their meals. And that sausage and pepperoni pizza will have a warning label that could scare the customer into a heart attack. This could easily sink the market for some traditionally popular but unhealthy dishes and raise demand for fish (omega-3 fatty acids), cruciferous vegetables (cancer fighters), and other "healthy" alternatives. We can expect significant menu revisions in the next few years.

The biggest regulatory changes ahead for travel are the global move to biometric passports, prompted largely by Washington's fear of another major terrorist attack, and—within the United States—the REAL ID program. According to the plan, anyone seeking to enter the United States—including American citizens who have been out of the country—will need a biometric passport to get in. Countries from Switzerland to Singapore have adopted them in recent years. However, delays in pulling the American program together have forced Washington to waive the scheme for some travelers.

Under REAL ID, before granting a driver's license, states must carry out extensive checks to confirm the applicant's identity. By 2014, anyone under fifty living in a state that does not provide compliant licenses will be unable to board an airliner or enter a federal building. Those over fifty can fly until 2017. Several states have said they will not comply with the program, and their citizens now face the prospect of being unable to travel by air.

Thus far, the Department of Homeland Security has backed down from a possible confrontation with these states, but we believe the REAL ID program eventually will be enforced.

Institutional Trends

50. MULTINATIONAL CORPORATIONS ARE UNITING THE WORLD AND GROWING MORE EXPOSED TO ITS RISKS.

The continuing fragmentation of the post–Cold War world has reduced the stability of some lands where government formerly could guarantee a favorable—or at least predictable—business environment. The current unrest in Iraq is one example. One risk now on the decline is the threat of sudden, extreme currency fluctuations. In Europe, at least, the adoption of the euro is making for a more stable financial environment.

Assessment: This trend will continue for at least the next thirty years as companies in the developing world diversify into less developed markets.

Implications: It is becoming ever more difficult for business to be confident that decisions about plant location, marketing, and other critical issues will continue to appear wise even five years into the future. All long-term plans must include an even greater margin for risk management. This will encourage outsourcing rather than investment in offshore facilities that could be endangered by sudden changes in business conditions.

Countries that can demonstrate a significant likelihood of stability and predictable business outcomes will enjoy a strong competitive advantage over neighbors that cannot. Witness the rapid growth of investment in India now that deregulation and privatization have general political support, compared with other Asian lands where conditions are less predictable.

Although Russia has continued to attract Western investment, particularly in its energy industry, increasingly autocratic governance by the Putin regime and any successors could eventually discourage foreign companies from doing business there or require much more favorable terms to justify accepting the associated risks.

Major corporations also can help to moderate some risks in unstable countries by threatening to take their business elsewhere.

Implications for Hospitality and Travel: Unfortunately, multinational operations bring risks beyond those of national stability or its absence. Some Western firms have cut back or abandoned their operations in Russia, concluding that Moscow's capricious treatment of foreign concerns could be too costly to ignore. Others have found it difficult to deal with autocratic government and petty corruption in China. Primitive banking and legal systems, poor communications and infrastructures, and other such problems in developing lands can make it difficult for Western firms to operate in the developing world. No industry is more exposed to these problems than hospitality and travel.

51. CONSUMERS INCREASINGLY DEMAND SOCIAL RESPONSIBILITY FROM COMPANIES AND EACH OTHER.

Companies increasingly are being judged on how they treat the environment, their workers, and their customers. Many are changing their business practices as a result. For example, home-improvement retailers Home Depot and Lowe's have stopped buying wood from countries with endangered forests, while Nike now publishes its discoveries of worker abuse by offshore suppliers. Costco offers much better benefits than its competitors and has half the employee turnover rate as a result. In a 2005 survey of nearly 1,200 companies, 81 percent—and 98 percent of large firms—said corporate citizenship is a priority; 84 percent said that being socially responsible has improved profits. With the departure of the business-friendly Bush administration, government intervention will rebound in sectors from finance to industrial chemicals. To avoid political backlash from the Right, regulation is likely to be carefully targeted and limited, at least for a time.

Assessment: This trend is well established in the industrialized world, but only beginning in the developing world. It can be expected to grow more powerful as the no-nonsense, bottom-line-oriented Generation Xers and Millennials gain influence.

Implications: A new administration in Washington means that government intervention will supplant deregulation in the airline industry (in the interest of safety and services), financial services (to control instability and costs), electric utilities (nuclear problems), and the chemical industry (toxic wastes).

In the United States, frequent incidents of political corruption may spread the demand for greater responsibility into the field of government and public service, although that is not yet clear. As the Internet spreads Western attitudes throughout the world, consumers and environmental activists in other regions will find more ways to use local court systems to promote their goals. Litigation is likely to become a global risk for companies that do not make the environment a priority.

Implications for Hospitality and Travel: This will bring still more pressure to minimize fuel consumption and cut air and noise pollution. The impact of jet exhaust on the ozone layer will continue to draw unwelcome publicity to air travel, but with little impact on seat-miles or the bottom line. Cruise lines whose itineraries permit may wish to add day trips to rain forests and other environmentally sensitive locations. Carefully managed excursions to poor areas are another possible option, if they can be structured to benefit the community. "Green" furnishings and supplies are the trend at hotels and resorts. Look for bamboo flooring in the rooms, eggs from free-range chickens in the kitchen, and a growing demand from guests for better worker benefits and pay. In all but extreme-luxury locations, hotels will save energy and water by providing fresh towels and linens only every other day, or when guests request them.

Even simple measures, such as saving water by providing it only at the customer's request, can help to burnish a restaurant's eco-reputation. However, many necessary—or at least unavoidable—measures will be harder to accept. Demands for nutritional information on the menu eventually will become impossible to resist. They will be accompanied by calls for eco-conscious sourcing of foods and other supplies, better pay and at least minimal benefits for restaurant workers, and American-style work rules in offshore subsidiaries. Look at the pressure that has been put on Nike to improve working conditions at the plants of overseas suppliers, and you see the future of the restaurant industry.

Trends such as eco-tourism and "pro-poor" tourism are just getting started. While tourists from China and India will still be eager to see Paris and Orlando, their more experienced peers from Europe and America will be looking for the last few elephants, coral reefs, and communities still living by the ways of their ancestors. However, they will want the people and sites they visit to benefit from their spending, not just the companies arranging their vacations.

52. ON AVERAGE, INSTITUTIONS ARE GROWING MORE TRANSPARENT IN THEIR OPERATIONS AND MORE ACCOUNTABLE FOR THEIR MISDEEDS.

Many different forces are promoting this change in various parts of the world. In the United States, the wave of business scandals in 2004, the exposure of child abuse within the Catholic Church, and other perceived offenses by large organizations have inspired demands for greater transparency and accountability. China, rated by Kurtzman Group as the most opaque of the major nations, was forced to open many of its records as a precondition for joining the World Trade Organization. In India, a country often regarded as one of the world's most corrupt, the Central Vigilance Commission has opened the country's banking system to more effective oversight. Lesser "vigilance commissions" now oversee many parts of the Indian economy and government. More generally, wars against terrorism, drug trafficking, and money laundering are opening the world's money conduits to greater scrutiny. They also are opening the operations of nongovernmental organizations that function primarily as charitable and social service agencies but are linked to terrorism as well.

Assessment: There are roughly as many reactions against this trend as there are governments, agencies, and individuals with something to hide. At the same time, the benefits of transparency are so clear that the general decline of barriers to oversight is likely to continue until societies develop a consensus about how much—or little—secrecy is really necessary. We give this trend at least twenty years of continued vigor.

Implications: Countries with high levels of transparency tend to be much more stable than more opaque lands. They also tend to be much more prosperous, in part because they find it easier to attract foreign investment. Greater transparency reduces the operational effectiveness of the world's miscreants. It impedes drug traffickers and terrorist organizations, as well as dishonest governments and corrupt bureaucrats.

Implications for Hospitality and Travel: Like other companies, large hospitality firms are likely to face demands for more rigorous accounting practices and other transparency-oriented changes in their operations.

Companies based in lands such as China and India may find it more costly to borrow capital for expansion than those in the West. Western firms expanding into some of the developing countries also may find themselves paying higher rates for capital, particularly if they are forced to take on local partners.

53. Institutions are undergoing a bimodal distribution: the big get bigger, the small survive, and the mid-sized are squeezed out.

Economies of scale enable the largest companies to win out over mid-sized competitors, while "boutique" operations can take advantage of niches too small to be efficiently tapped by larger firms. We see the result in a wide range of industries throughout the developed world. In agriculture, banking, auto manufacturing, telecommunications, and many other sectors, the largest firms have been buying up their mid-sized competitors or driving them out of business. At the same time, hundreds or thousands of tiny operators have arisen in each industry to get rich by serving markets beneath the notice of the giants.

Assessment: Thanks in part to technology, this trend is likely to be a permanent feature of the business scene from now on.

Implications: No company is too large to be a takeover target if it dominates a profitable market or has other features attractive to profit-hungry investors. No niche is too small to attract and support at least one or two boutique operations. Thus far, industries dominated by small, regional, often family-owned companies have been relatively exempt from the consolidation now transforming many other businesses. Takeovers are likely even in these industries in the next decade.

This consolidation will extend increasingly to Internet-based businesses, where well-financed companies are trying to absorb or out-compete tiny online startups, much as they have done in the brick-and-mortar world.

However, niche markets will continue to encourage the creation of new businesses. In Europe, as of 2006, no fewer than forty-eight small, no-frills airlines in twenty-two countries had sprung up to capture about 28 percent of the Continental market share. Only fifteen offered more than fifty flights per day.

Implications for Hospitality and Travel: FI expects airlines to continue merging for as long as there are airlines available to do so. At the same time, small startup airlines are appearing almost constantly, taking advantage of routes or other niche opportunities that their predecessors either have not recognized or did not consider sufficiently attractive. These startups will provide the next big wave of airline mergers.

We have long seen the same trend in the cruise industry. Royal Caribbean and P&O Princess joined forces in 2001. Four years later, diminutive Clipper Cruise Line announced its pending merger with Australia's Peregrine Adventures. And recently, Royal Caribbean/Celebrity spun off the new, upscale Azamara Cruises to compete with Oceania Cruises. There will be more such examples in the future.

Hotel chains have been merging constantly at least since Bowman-Biltmore bought United Hotels back in 1929. There is no sign the deal-making will stop in the near future. Given the weakness of the dollar and of the American real estate market, we expect to see a wave of offers by European hospitality firms for their peers in the United States.

In this aspect, the restaurant industry parallels hotels almost exactly. Mergers and acquisitions and startups and failures change the industry almost too quickly to follow.

This is truly a universal trend. The implication for travel is the same as for all these sectors: Large companies will continue to snap up mid-sized competitors or, by outcompeting them, drive them out of business. At the same time, new companies will prosper in niche markets. Some will remain small and highly profitable for their owners. Others will grow until they attract the attention of the giants. A very few may become giants themselves. Look for the fastest turnover in the online travel search and marketing operations, where niche startups abound.

All segments of hospitality and travel have been in ferment for as long as we can remember. They will remain in ferment long into the future.

Terrorism Trends

54. MILITANT ISLAM CONTINUES TO SPREAD AND GAIN POWER.

It has been clear for years that the Muslim lands face severe problems with religious extremists dedicated to advancing their political, social, and doctrinal views by any means necessary. Most of the Muslim lands are overcrowded and short of resources. Many are poor, save for the oil-rich states of the Middle East. Virtually all have large populations of young men, often unemployed, who are frequently attracted to violent extremist movements. During its proxy war with the Soviet Union in Afghanistan, the United States massively fortified the Muslim extremist infrastructure by supplying it with money, arms and, above all, training. It is making a similar mistake today. The overthrow of Saddam Hussein and the American occupation of Iraq has inspired a new generation of *mujahideen* who have been trained and battle-hardened in the growing insurgency. In a now-declassified National Intelligence Estimate, the American intelligence community concluded that al-Qaeda was more powerful in 2007 than it had been before the so-called "war on terror" began—more dangerous even than it had been when it planned the attacks of September 11, 2001.

Assessment: This trend may wax and wane, but it seems unlikely to disappear this side of a Muslim reformation comparable to those that transformed Christianity and Judaism.

Implications: Virtually all of the Muslim lands face an uncertain and possibly bleak future of political instability and growing violence. The exceptions are the oil states, where money can still buy relative peace, at least for now. These problems often have spilled over into the rest of the world. They will do so again.

In a 1994 terrorism study for the Department of Defense and other government clients, FI predicted that by 2020 a strong majority of the world's twenty-five or so most important Muslim lands could be in the hands of extremist religious governments. At the time, only Iran was ruled by such a regime. That forecast still appears sound.

Iraq is likely to become the next fundamentalist Muslim regime. Once American forces leave, Iran will support the establishment of a Shiite regime much like its own in Baghdad. There is a one-in-ten chance that this will set off a general war in the Middle East, as Sunni-dominated states intercede to protect Iraqi Sunnis against Shi'a domination. However, Iraq and Saudi Arabia already are negotiating to keep this situation under control.

Any attempt to reduce the commitment of Western forces to the task of stabilizing Afghanistan will result in the restoration of the Taliban to power.

Implications for Hospitality and Travel: In Bangkok and Pattani, Thailand, hotel bombs kill four people. Another bomb shakes the Al Deira hotel, west of Gaza City. In Kabul, Afghanistan, one journalist dies in a hotel bombing. In Islamabad, Pakistan, a restaurant bombing kills twenty people. In Baqouba, Iraq, a car bomb outside a restaurant kills at least seventy. In Mumbai, three hotels and a restaurant are among ten targets struck by terrorists. All these incidents happened in 2008—and outside Iraq, it was a relatively slow year for terrorism.

In 1994, FI predicted that as government installations were "hardened" against attack, terrorists would turn to softer targets and particularly those of the hospitality and travel industries. That forecast has been amply proved correct. Hotels, restaurants, and transportation facilities have become the preferred targets of both local and international terrorists.

The next generation of terrorists is now being trained in Iraq and Pakistan. As the American wars in those regions prove unsustainable, the most zealous among them will continue their war against their chosen enemies. Most will return to their home countries to attack local rulers. Others will focus on the United States and its allies in the Iraq war. All of them will continue to find hotels and restaurants easy targets with high publicity value. Some may attempt to attack passenger aircraft, while others will aim their bombs at public transportation. A few may even choose cruise ships, conference centers, or casinos as their victims of choice.

Terrorism will become more common in the future, not less so, and the hospitality and travel industries will remain appealingly vulnerable to attack.

55. INTERNATIONAL EXPOSURE INCLUDES A GROWING RISK OF TERRORIST ATTACK.

Terrorism has continued to grow around the world as the Iraq war proceeds, even as the rate of violence in Iraq itself has, at least temporarily, declined. State-sponsored terrorism has nearly vanished, as tougher sanctions have made it more trouble than it was worth. However, nothing will prevent small, local political organizations and special-interest groups from using terror to promote their causes. These organizations have found inspiration in the successes of al-Qaeda, and many have found common cause. The most dangerous terrorist groups are no longer motivated primarily by specific political goals, but by generalized virulent hatred based on religion and culture.

On balance, the amount of terrorist activity in the world will continue to rise, not decline, in the next ten years. This was seen in corrections to the State Department's April 2004 report on terrorism, which originally seemed to show a sharp drop in terrorist incidents. In fact, at that time, terrorist attacks had risen sharply since the invasion of Iraq, both in number and in severity.

Assessment: This trend is unlikely to change in the next decade and relatively unlikely to change in the next twenty years. A permanent end to the international terrorist threat would require a broad philosophical and cultural change in Islam that makes terrorists pariahs in their own communities. No such change is on the horizon.

Implications: Terrorism against the West is likely to grow, not decline, when fighters trained and bloodied in the Iraq war are able to turn their attention elsewhere.

Western corporations may have to devote more of their resources to self-defense, while accepting smaller profits from operations in the developing countries.

Like the attacks on the World Trade Center and Pentagon, the American embassies in Kenya and Tanzania before them, and the bombings of the Madrid rail system and London subways since then, any attacks on major corporate facilities will be designed for maximum destruction and casualties. Bloodshed for its own sake has become a characteristic of modern terrorism.

Where terrorism is most common, countries will find it difficult to attract foreign investment, no matter how attractive their resources.

Though Islamic terrorists form only a tiny part of the Muslim community, they have a large potential for disruption throughout the region from Turkey to the Philippines.

The economies of the industrialized nations could be thrown into recession at any time by another terrorist event on the scale of September 11. This is particularly true of the United States. The impact would be greatest if the incident discouraged travel, as did the September 11 attacks.

The U.S. economy is being affected already by American anti-terrorism measures. Since Washington began to photograph incoming travelers and to require more extensive identification from them, tourism to the United States is off by some 30 percent. The number of foreign students coming to American universities has declined by a similar amount.

Implications for Hospitality and Travel: Until the terrorist problem is brought under control—probably not for at least a generation—tourism to the more volatile parts of the Middle East will be a relatively hard sell for Western vacationers, despite the appeal of historic places.

This stigma is likely to spread almost instantaneously to any destination that suffers a major terrorist incident. That threat is likely to be one of the great unpredictable risks of the international tourist industry for at least the next twenty years.

Terrorist hazards are not limited to Muslim lands. The communist insurgency in Nepal, which now seems to be winding down, has significantly inhibited vacation travel from China and India.

American-owned facilities and those where Americans congregate will be favorite targets for many terrorists now being trained in Iraq and Pakistan. These facilities will have to devote a larger portion of their budgets to security.

Disgruntled employees and former employees are the single greatest threat, because they are familiar with security procedures and weaknesses. Therefore, some of the most important security measures will be invisible to customers, but highly intrusive for staff. These may include comprehensive background checks for new hires, much as airports need to screen such behind-the-scenes personnel as baggage handlers and fuel-truck drivers. Those recently fired are a frequent source of problems.

Appendix B
Vital Signs of National Stability

Socio-Political Indicators

- *Population of men between age fifteen and thirty:* Young men are the most prone to violence.

- *Unemployment rate among young males*

    - Young men are most volatile, and most likely to adopt violent causes, if they are unemployed and without hope.

    - A sudden, permanent loss of job opportunities, as when a war is lost, heightens the possibility of terrorism.

- *Educational status of young males:* Young men are most susceptible to terrorist causes if they have been educated for a middle-class life that is no longer available to them.

- *Percentage of ethnic minorities:* Ethnic divisions reduce national stability, particularly in regions with traditional tribal animosity. However, division among many ethnic groups can produce relative peace, as long as power and prosperity are shared.

- *Political power of ethnic minorities*

    - An effective political voice promotes stability among minority populations and reduces the likelihood of terrorist activity.

    - States dominated by an ethnic minority may be even less stable and more prone to terrorism than those in which the minority is persecuted.

- *Percentage of religious minorities:* The effects of religious divisions mirror those of ethnic divisions, but may be even more vicious and intractable.

- *Prevalence of political corruption:* Widespread political corruption undermines the legitimacy of governments and tends to promote the growth of dissident and terrorist movements.

- *Prevalence of police corruption:* Police corruption is equivalent to political corruption at the local level. It can be even more damaging to social stability, and more conducive to terrorism, because the police have both weapons and a coherent management structure to use them.

- *Length of visa lines outside embassies:* Eagerness to leave the country reveals instability; any sudden change in this indicator is particularly important.

- *Hoarding of food, medical supplies, and gasoline:* These all suggest a general expectation of hard times to come and a decline in national stability.

- *Number of foreign students in the United States in technical, business, and liberal arts courses:* American colleges are a traditional haven for the younger members of wealthy families in unstable lands.

- *Percentage of homes with indoor plumbing:* A low number indicates widespread poverty and a population with little investment in the existing regime.

- *Degree of religious freedom:* Great religious freedom indicates a nation with little to fear from social differences.

- *Degree of press freedom:* The press can be free, monitored, or controlled; the greater the freedom, the more confident the government is likely to be in the acceptance of its power.

- *Consolidation of wealth in the hands of political leaders and their families, of military leaders, and of political cronies of the head of government:* The more wealth is consolidated within any elite, the less stable any nation will be.

- *Subsidies for food, housing, and medicine or medical care:* These indicate that the nation's underlying economy is not adequately providing for all its citizens and—when they become a major source of income for a large fraction of its citizens—suggest that social and political stability are low.

- *Changes in subsidies to the poor:* Sudden increases in subsidies often are an attempt to buy the loyalty of a population that is no longer willing to grant it.

- *Percentage of the population below the poverty line:* Social and political stability is inversely related to poverty rates.

- *Number of AIDS patients:* In extreme cases, such as in Central Africa and Thailand, high rates of AIDS can undermine entire economies and cause instability.

- *Rates of morbidity and mortality:* High rates indicate that the society has not been able to deliver basic social services to its population, which will have little loyalty to the existing government.

- *Life expectancy:* This extends the previous indicator.

- *Sharing data and information on technology, politics, economics, social conditions, criminal activity, military intelligence, and terrorism:* Governments unwilling to share basic information often are uncertain of their hold on power.

Economic Indicators

- *Percentage of home ownership:* A high rate of home ownership suggests that wealth is being distributed relatively fairly and indicates that much of the population has a stake in the country's continued stability and prosperity.

- *Percentage of imports:* In the absence of some balancing factor, the need to import an unusually high fraction of a nation's goods suggests the absence of a native manufacturing base, and perhaps the existence of widespread poverty.

- *Percentage of exports*
  - Strong exports of manufactured goods suggest a prosperous economy, and therefore a stable nation; an export economy based on raw materials suggests the reverse.
  - Oil-based economies will be vulnerable to unrest for as long as petroleum remains relatively cheap.
- *Difference in income and wealth between the richest and poorest deciles of the population*
  - A wide gap between the rich and poor is one of the most reliable warnings of social and political instability.
  - Developed by Forecasting International many years ago, this indicator has recently been adopted by the Central Intelligence Agency for the country reports presented in the *CIA World Factbook,* which is available on the Internet.
- *Transfer of wealth to other countries:* In the absence of other investment incentives, this may suggest strong doubts about political stability among those well positioned to make such a judgment.
- *Movement of cash to the United States:* This is one measure of the previous indicator.
- *Investment in U.S. stocks or bonds:* And yet another.
- *Increased sales of diamonds:* This may reveal conversion of wealth to easily portable form, a traditional sign of instability.
- *Increased numbers of expensive homes on the market:* Another harbinger of impending flight by the wealthy.
- *Growing investment in homes or real estate in the United States or Canada by the wealthy elite, by high-ranking military officers, and by politicians:* This strongly confirms the previous indicator.
- *Form in which workers are paid*
  - Payment in goods or credit—in any form other than a regular salary—indicates a severely unhealthy economy in which unrest is likely.
  - For a time, Russian teachers were paid in vodka, which is easily sold and resisted inflation better than rubles. They had refused to accept payment in toilet paper or credit toward funeral costs.
- *Access to drug funds:* Drug money represents a convenient and lucrative way both to support terrorist activity and to make it pay.

Technology Indicators

- *Number of automobiles:* A high rate of automobile ownership suggests at least moderate general prosperity and the existence of a well-developed infrastructure to maintain and supply the cars and roads; both these implications suggest political and economic stability.

- *Availability of modern communications facilities:* General access to information-related technologies suggests the existence of a high-tech infrastructure to manufacture, operate, and maintain the equipment; a population both sufficiently well educated to have use for telephones, computers, and the like and wealthy enough to buy them; and a government that trusts its citizens with information and with access to the world at large. Specific indicators include:

  - Number of cell phones per capita
  - Number of regular telephones per capita
  - Number of computers per capita
  - Number of printers per capita
  - Number of copiers per capita
  - Number of fax machines per capita
  - Number of shortwave radio receivers per capita
  - Number of satellite receivers per capita
  - Number of Internet users per capita

Military Indicators

- *Percentage of military:* In a stable country, the military usually employs a small fraction of the population and forms a minor segment of the economy.
- *Military salaries:* Military pay scales substantially above those of the population at large may indicate a nation with little social cohesion.
- *Numbers of palace guard or "elite" guard:* The existence of a strong elite guard indicates that leaders cannot trust even their own military.
- *Changes in salary of palace guard per year*
  - A sudden, substantial pay raise for an elite guard is often an attempt to buy loyalty where none is otherwise available and is a clear sign of impending unrest.
  - This was one of the most important symptoms of social and political instability in Iran in the years before the fundamentalist revolution in 1980. More than any other single factor, it allowed Forecasting International to warn its clients of impending trouble fully two years before the event.
- *Role of military in politics:* Relatively few governments remain stable for long unless the military is subservient to civilian rule.
- *Nuclear, biological, and chemical weapons capabilities:* There is little impetus for nations to develop weapons of mass destruction in the face of international sanctions unless they perceive some imminent threat to their sovereignty or are planning future aggression.
- *Use of underground tunnels or laboratories:* The felt need to hide weapons development and other such military preparations is a clear warning that war is contemplated.

Appendix C
Hospitality Associations and Publications

Listing of Associations

Association of Correctional Food Service Affiliates
304 West Liberty Street, Suite 301
Louisville, KY 40202
Tel: 502-583-3783
Fax: 502-589-3502
Website: www.acfsa.com

American Culinary Federation
P.O. Box 3466
St. Augustine, FL 32085
Tel: 904-824-4468
Fax: 904-825-4758
Website: www.acfchefs.org

American Dietetic Association
216 West Jackson Boulevard, Suite 800
Chicago, IL 60606-6995
Tel: 312-899-0040
Fax: 312-899-1758
Website: www.eatright.org

American Hotel & Lodging Association
1201 New York Avenue NW, #600
Washington, DC 20005-3931
Tel: 202-289-3100
Fax: 202-289-3199
Website: www.ahla.com

American Hotel & Lodging Educational Institute
800 North Magnolia Avenue, Suite 300
Orlando, FL 32803
Tel: 407-999-8100; 800-752-4567
Fax: 407-236-7848
Website: www.ei-ahla.org

American Society for Healthcare Food Service Administrators
840 North Lake Shore Drive
Chicago, IL 60611
Tel: 312-280-6416
Fax: 312-280-4152
Website: www.ashfsa.org

Cruise Lines International Association
910 SE 17th Street, Suite 400
Fort Lauderdale, FL 33316
Tel: 754-224-2200
Fax: 754-224-2250
Website: www.cruising.org

Club Managers Association of America
1733 King Street
Alexandria, VA 22314
Tel: 703-739-9500
Fax: 703-739-0124
Website: www.cmaa.org

Council of Hotel and Restaurant Trainers
741 Carleton Road
Westfield, NJ 07090
Tel: 908.389.9277
Fax: 908.389.0767
Website: www.chart.org

Dietary Managers Association
406 Surrey Woods Drive
St. Charles, IL 60174
Tel: 800-323-1908
Fax: 630-587-6308
Website: www.dmaonline.org

Foodservice Consultants Society International
Many addresses and telephone numbers; see website
Website: www.fcsi.org

International Flight Services Association
1100 Johnson Ferry Road, Suite 300
Atlanta, GA 30342
Tel: 404-252-3663
Fax: 404-252-0774
Website: www.ifsanet.com

International Association of Amusement Parks and Attractions
1448 Duke Street
Alexandria, VA 22314
Tel: 703-836-4800
Fax: 703-836-4801
Website: www.iaapa.org

International Association of Culinary Professionals
1100 Johnson Ferry Road, Suite 300
Atlanta, GA 30342
Tel: 404-252-3663
Fax: 404-252-0774
Website: www.iacp.com

International Council on Hotel, Restaurant & Institutional Education
2613 North Parham Road, Suite 230
Richmond, VA 23294
Tel: 804-346-4800
Fax: 804-346-5009
Website: www.chrie.org

International Foodservice Distributors Association
1410 Spring Hill Road, Suite 210
McLean, VA 22102
Tel: 703-532-9400
Website: www.ifdaonline.org

International Food Service Executives Association
500 Ryland Street, Suite 200
Reno, NV 89502
Tel: 775-825-2665
Fax: 775-825-6411
Website: www.ifsea.com

International Foodservice Manufacturers Association
Two Prudential Plaza
180 North Stetson Avenue, Suite 4400
Chicago, IL 60601
Tel: 312-540-4400
Fax: 312-540-4401
Website: www.ifmaworld.com

MICROS Systems, Inc.
7031 Columbia Gateway Drive
Columbia, MD 21046-2289
Tel: 443-285-6000
Website: www.micros.com

National Association of Black Hospitality Professionals, Inc.
P.O. Box 5443
Plainfield, NJ 07060
Tel: 908-354-5117

National Association of College University Foodservice
2525 Jolly Road, Suite 280
Okemos, MI 48864
Tel: 517-332-2494
Fax: 517-332-8144
Website: www.nacufs.org

National Association of Concessionaires
35 East Wacker Drive, Suite 1816
Chicago, IL 60601
Tel: 312-236-3858
Fax: 312-236-7809
Website: www.naconline.org

National Automatic Merchandising Association
20 North Wacker Drive, Suite 3500
Chicago, IL 60606
Tel: 312-346-0370
Fax: 312-704-4140
Website: www.vending.org

National Club Association
1201 15th Street, N.W., Suite 450
Washington, DC 20005
Tel: 202-822-9822
Fax: 202-822-9808
Website: www.nationalclub.org

National Restaurant Association
1200 17th Street N.W.
Washington, DC 20036-3097
Tel: 202-331-5900
Website: www.restaurant.org

National Restaurant Association Educational Foundation
175 West Jackson Boulevard, Suite 1500
Chicago, IL 60604
Tel: 800-715-1010
Fax: 312-715-1010 in Chicagoland
Website: www.nraef.org

National Society for Healthcare Foodservice Management
355 Lexington Avenue, 15th Floor
New York, NY 10017
Tel: 212-297-2166
Fax: 212-370-9047
Website: www.hfm.org

North American Association of Food Equipment Manufacturers
161 North Clark Street, Suite 2020
Chicago, IL 60601
Tel: 312-821-0201
Fax: 312-821-0202
Website: www.nafem.org

Research & Development Associates for Military Food & Packaging Systems, Inc.
16607 Blanco Road, Suite 501
San Antonio, TX 78232
Tel: 210-493-8024
Fax: 210-493-8036
Website: www.militaryfood.org

School Nutrition Association
700 South Washington Street, Suite 300
Alexandria, VA 22314-3436
Tel: 800-877-8822
Fax: 703-739-3915
Website: www.asfsa.org

Society for Foodservice Management
15000 Commerce Parkway, Suite C
Mount Laurel, NJ 08054
Tel: 856-380-6829
Fax: 856-439-0525
Website: www.sfm-online.org

Technomic, Inc.
300 South Riverside Plaza, Suite 1200
Chicago, IL 60606
Tel: 312-876-0004
Fax: 312-876-1158
Website: www.technomic.com

U.S. Travel Association
1100 New York Avenue N.W., Suite 450
Washington, DC 20005-3934
Tel: 202-408-8422
Fax: 202-408-1255
Website: www.tia.org

Publications and Journal Publishers ————————————

Activities Report and Minutes of Work Groups and Sub-Work Groups of the R&D Associates
R&D Associates
16607 Blanco Road, Suite 1506
San Antonio, TX 78232
Tel: 210-493-8024
Fax: 210-493-8036

Club Director
1201 15th Street, N.W., Suite 450
Washington, DC 20005
Tel: 202-822-9822
Fax: 202-822-9808
Website: www.nationalclub.org

Club Management
Club Managers Association of America
1733 King Street
Alexandria, VA 22314
Tel: 703-739-9500
Fax: 703-739-0124
Website: www.cmaa.org

Cornell Hospitality Quarterly
Sage Publications
2455 Teller Road
Thousand Oaks, CA 91320
Tel: 805-499-9774
Fax: 805-499-0871
Website: http://online.sagepub.com/

Food Executive
500 Ryland Street, Suite 200
Reno, NV 89502
Tel: 775-825-2665
Fax: 775-825-6411
Website: www.ifsea.org

Food Industry Review
The Food Institute
One Broadway
Elmwood Park, NJ 07407
Tel: (201) 791-5570
Fax: (201) 791-5222
Website: www.foodinstitute.com

Food Management; Restaurant Hospitality
Penton Media Inc.
1300 E. 9ᵗʰ Street
Cleveland, OH 44114
Tel: 216-931-9373
Fax: 215-245-4060

Food Technology; Journal of Food Science
Institute of Food Technologists
525 West Van Buren, Suite 1000
Chicago, IL 60607
Tel: 312-782-8424
Fax: 312-782-8348
Website: www.ift.org

FoodService Director
Bill Communications, Inc.
355 Park Avenue South
New York, NY 10010
Tel: 212-592-6200

Health Care Management Review
Aspen Publishers, Inc.
7201 McKinney Circle
Frederick, MD 21704
Tel: 800-234-1660
Fax: 800-901-9075

HOTELS
Reed Business Information
8878 Barrons Boulevard
Highlands Ranch, CO 80129-2345
Tel: 800-446-6551
Website: www.hotelsmag.com

Journal of the American Dietetic Association
The American Dietetic Association
120 South Riverside Plaza, Suite 2000
Chicago, IL 60606-6995
Tel: 800-877-1600
Website: www.eatright.org

Journal of Child Nutrition and Management
School Nutrition Association
700 South Washington Street, Suite 300
Alexandria, VA 22314
Tel: 703-739-3900
Fax: 701-739-3915

Journal of Food Protection
6200 Aurora Avenue, Suite 200W
Des Moines, IA 50322-2864
Tel: 515.276.3344
Fax: 515.276.8655
Website: www. www.foodprotection.org

Journal of Foodservice Management and Education
National Association of College & University Food Services (NACUFS)
2525 Jolly Road, Suite 280
Okemos, MI 48864-3680
Phone: 517-332-2494
Fax: 517-332-8144

Journal of Hospitality & Tourism Research
Sage Publications
2455 Teller Road
Thousand Oaks, CA 91320
Tel: 805-499-9774
Fax: 805-499-0871
Website: http://online.sagepub.com/

Journal of Nutrition Education
Society for Nutrition Education
9100 Purdue Road, Suite 200
Indianapolis, IN 46268
Tel: 317-328-4627 or 800-235-6690
Fax: 317-280-8527
Website: www.jneb.org

Lodging Magazine
385 Oxford Valley Road, Suite 420
Yardley, PA 19067
215-321-9662
Fax: 215-321-5124
Website: www.lodgingmagazine.com

Nation's Restaurant News
425 Park Avenue, 6th Floor
New York, NY 10022
Tel: 800-453-2427
Website: www.nrn.com

Smith Travel Research
735 East Main Street
Hendersonville, TN 37075
Tel: 615-824-8664
Fax: 615-824-3848
Website: www.strglobal.com

Training and Development
American Society for Training and Development
1640 King Street, P.O. Box 1443
Alexandria VA 22313
Tel: 703-683-8100
Website: www.astd.org

Appendix D
College Programs in Hospitality

Académie Internationale de Management (AIM): Hotel Management. Paris, France
http://www.academy.fr

Alexandria Technical College: Hotel—Restaurant Management.
Alexandria, MN
http://www.alextech.org/hotelrestaurant

Arkansas Tech University: Hospitality Administration. Russellville, AR
http://www.atu.edu

Art Institutes International Minnesota: Culinary Arts. Minneapolis, MN
http://www.aim.artinstitutes.edu

Asheville-Buncombe Tech. Comm. College: Hospitality Department.
Asheville, NC
http://www.asheville.cc.nc.us/bh/hospitality/default.asp

Blue Mountains International Hotel Management School: Tourism & Hospitality
Management. Leura, Australia
http://www.hotelschool.com.au

Borough of Manhattan Community College. New York, NY
http://www.bmcc.cuny.edu

Boston University: School of Hospitality Administration. Boston, MA
http://www.bu.edu/hospitality/

Canadian Tourism College: Hospitality & Tourism Management.
Vancouver, BC
http://www.tourismcollege.com

Champlain College: Hospitality Industry Management. Burlington, VT
http://www.champlain.edu/majors/hospitality

College of Charleston: Department of Hospitality and Tourism Management.
Charleston, SC
http://www.cofc.edu/~baecon/tourism.htm

Columbus State Community College: Hospitality Management Department.
Columbus, OH
http://www.cscc.edu/hospitality

Cornell University: School of Hotel Administration. Ithaca, NY
http://www.hotelschool.cornell.edu

Culinary Institute of America (CIA). Hyde Park, NY
http://www.ciachef.edu

Culinary School of the Rockies: Professional Culinary Arts.
Boulder, CO
http://www.culinaryschoolrockies.com

Delaware State Univ.: Hospitality & Tourism Management. Dover, DE
http://www.deu.edu

Douglas College: Hotel and Restaurant Management. Coquitlam, BC
http://www.douglas.bc.ca

East Carolina University: Dept. of Hospitality Management. Greenville, NC
http://www.ecu.edu/che/hmgt/

Eastern Michigan University: Hotel and Restaurant Management.
Ypsilanti, MI
http://www.emich.edu/sts/hrm/

Emirates Academy of Hospitality Management. Dubai, UAE
http://www.emiratesacademy.edu

ESHOTEL: Ecole Supérieure de Gestion Hôtelière et de Tourisme.
Paris/Lille, France
http://www.eshotel.fr

Fairleigh Dickinson Univ.: Hotel and Restaurant Management. Teaneck, NJ
http://view.fdu.edu/default.aspx?id=1563

Florida Gulf Coast University: Resort & Hospitality Management (RHM).
Fort Myers, FL
http://cps.fgcu.edu/resort

Florida International University: Hospitality and Tourism Management.
North Miami, FL
http://hospitality.fiu.edu

Florida State University: Dedman School of Hospitality.
Tallahassee, FL
http://cob.fsu.edu/dsh/

Foothill College: Travel Careers Department. Los Altos Hills, CA
https://www.foothill.fhda.edu/bss/tc/index.php

Fort Lewis College: Tourism and Resort Management. Durango, CO
http://soba.fortlewis.edu/soba/students/academic_programs/tourism/index.asp

Frederick Community College: Culinary Arts & Hospitality Institute. Frederick, MD
http://www.frederick.edu/courses_and_programs/hospitality.aspx

George Washington Univ.: Tourism & Hospitality Management. Washington, DC
http://business.gwu.edu/tourism

Georgia State University: Cecil B. Day School of Hospitality. Atlanta, GA
http://robinson.gsu.edu/hospitality

Griffith University: Business and Commerce, Tourism. Queensland, Australia
http://www.griffith.edu.au/business/tourism

Harper College: Hospitality Management. Palatine, IL
http://goforward.harpercollege.edu/page.cfm?p=4626

Hesser College: Assoc. of Business Science Degree, Travel & Tourism.
Manchester, NH
http://www.hesser.edu

Highline Community College: Hotel and Hospitality Management. Seattle, WA
http://www.flightline.highline.edu/hotelhospitality/

Hong Kong Polytechnic University: School of Hotel & Tourism Management
http:hotelschool.shtm.polyu.edu.hk/eng/index.jsp

Humber College: School of Hospitality, Recreation & Tourism. Toronto, Canada
http://hospitality.humber.ca/

Imperial Hotel Management College: Vancouver, BC
http://www.ihmc.ca

Indiana Univ.-Purdue Univ. (IPFW): Hospitality Management. Fort Wayne, IN
http://bulletin.ipfw.edu/preview_program.php?catoid=8&poid=1595&bc=1

International College of Management. Manly (Sydney) Australia
http://www.manlyaustralia.com.au/business/default.asp?ID=2969

International Hotel, Tourism and Culinary Management Institute and International Tourism Institute. Switzerland
http://www.imi-luzern.com

Iowa Lakes Community College: Hotel & Restaurant Management.
Emmetsburg, IA
www.iowalakes.edu

IUPUI: School of Physical Education & Tourism Management. Indianapolis, IN
http://petm.iupui.edu

J. Sargeant Reynolds Comm. College: The Center for Culinary Arts, Tourism & Hospitality. Richmond, VA
www.reynolds.edu/hospitality

Johnson State College: Hospitality & Tourism Management. Johnson, VT
www.jsc.edu

Johnson & Wales University—College of Culinary Arts. North Miami, FL
http://www.jwu.edu/college.aspx?id=30742

Kemmons Wilson School of Hospitality & Resort Management: Univ. of Memphis. Memphis, TN
http://memphis.edu/hospitality

Kendall College: The Les Roches School of Hospitality Management.
Evanston, IL
http://hospitality.kendall.edu/

Lexington College: The Women's Hospitality Management College. Chicago, IL
http://www.lexingtoncollege.edu

Lincoln University: Bachelor of Tourism Management. Lincoln (Canterbury),
New Zealand
http://www.lincoln.ac.nz

Mercyhurst College: Hospitality Management. Erie, PA
http://hm.mercyhurst.edu/

Miami Dade College: Hospitality and Tourism Management.
Miami, FL
http://www.mdc.edu/business/program.htm

Michigan Licensed Beverage Association. East Lansing, MI
http://www.mlba.org

Michigan State University: *The* School of Hospitality Business. East Lansing, MI
http://www.bus.msu.edu/shb

Montclair State University: Recreation and Leisure Studies. Upper Montclair, NJ
http://sbus.montclair.edu/departments/mis/programs/hopitality-management/

National Schools: National Culinary & Bakery School. La Mesa, CA
http://www.nationalschools.com

New England Culinary Institute (NECI): Hospitality & Restaurant Management
Montpelier, VT
http://www.neci.edu/

New York Univ. The Preston Robert Tisch Center for Hospitality, Tourism, and
Sports Management. New York, NY
http://www.scps.nyu.edu/areas-of-study/tisch/

Niagara University: College: of Hospitality and Tourism Management.
Niagara Falls, NY
http://www.niagara.edu/hospitality

Normandale Community College: Hospitality Management. Bloomington, MN
http://www.normandale.edu

North Carolina Central University: Hospitality and Tourism.
Durham, NC
http://www.nccu.edu/curriculum/index.cfm

Northeastern State Univ.: Hospitality & Tourism Management. Tahlequah, OK
http://arapaho.nsuok.edu/~mdm

Northern Alberta Institute of Technology (NAIT): Hospitality Management.
Alberta, Canada
http://www.nait.ca/program_home_27432.htm

Northern Arizona University: School of Hotel & Restaurant Management.
Flagstaff, AZ
http://www.nau.edu/hrm

Oklahoma State Univ.: School of Hotel and Restaurant Administration.
Stillwater, OK
http://ches.okstate.edu/hrad/

Pennsylvania State University: School of Hotel, Restaurant and Recreation
Management. University Park, PA
http://www.hrrm.psu.edu

Professional Development Institute of Tourism (PDIT). Parksville, BC
http://www.pdit.ca

Purdue University: Hospitality and Tourism Management. West Lafayette, IN
http://www.cfs.purdue.edu/htm

Red Deer College: Hospitality & Tourism Program. Red Deer, Alberta
http://www.rdc.ab.ca/future_students/departments/hospitality_and_tourism

Richland College: Travel, Exposition & Meeting Management.
Dallas, TX
http://www.richlandcollege.edu/travel/

Robert Morris University: Hospitality/Tourism Management.
Pittsburgh, PA
http://www.rmu.edu

Rochester Institute of Technology: School of Hospitality and Service
Management. Rochester, NY
http://www.rit.edu/cast/hsm

Roosevelt University: The Manfred Steinfeld School of Hospitality & Tourism
Management. Chicago, IL
http://www.roosevelt.edu/etsuc/hosm.htm

San Diego State University: School of Hospitality and Tourism Management.
San Diego, CA
http://htm.sdsu.edu/

Schiller International University: School of Tourism and Hospitality Mangement.
Engelberg, Switzerland
www.schiller.edu/BAIHTMNGMT.cfm

Seneca College: School of Tourism. King City, Ontario
http://www.senecac.on.ca/tourism

Seton Hill University: Hospitality & Tourism Program. Greensburg, PA
http://www.setonhill.edu/academics/hospitality/index.cfm

Sinclair Community College: Hospitality Management & Tourism. Dayton, OH
http://www.sinclair.edu/academics/bps/departments/hmt

Southern Cross University: School of Tourism and Hospitality Mangament.
Sydney, Australia
http://www.scu.edu.au/schools/tourism/index.php/38

Southern Illinois University Carbondale: Hospitality & Tourism.
Carbondale, IL
http://coas.siu.edu/default2.asp?active_page_id=331

St. Cloud State University: Travel and Tourism. St. Cloud, MN
http://bulletin.stcloudstate.edu/ugb/programs/geog.asp

Sullivan University: National Center for Hospitality Studies. Louisville, KY
http://www.sullivan.edu/nchs

SUNY College of Agriculture and Tech.: Culinary Arts, Hospitality & Tourism Department. Cobleskill, NY
http://www.cobleskill.edu/academics/busschool/caht

SUNY Delhi: Business and Hospitality. Delhi, NY
http://www.delhi.edu/academics/academic_divisions/business_and_hospitality/index.php

Temple University: School of Tourism & Hospitality Management (STHM). Philadelphia, PA
http://www.temple.edu/sthm

Texas Tech University: Nutrition, Hospitality and Retailing. Lubbock, TX
http://www.depts.ttu.edu/hs/nhr/rhim/

Travelcampus: Education Systems. Salt Lake City, UT
http://www.travelcampus.com

University of Arkansas, Food, Human Nutrition and Hospitality. Fayetteville, AR
http://hesc.uark.edu/2622.htm

University of Calgary: World Tourism Education and Research Centre (WTERC). Calgary, Alberta
http://haskayne.ucalgary.ca/faculty/research/centres/wterc

University of Delaware: Hotel, Restaurant and Institutional Management. Newark, DE
http://www.udel.edu/HRIM/home.html

University of Denver: School of Hotel, Restaurant and Tourism Management. Denver, CO
http://www.daniels.du.edu/hrtm

University of Guelph: School of Hospitality & Tourism Management. Guelph, Ontario
http://www.htm.uoguelph.ca

University of Hawaii-Manoa: School of Travel Industry Management. Honolulu, HI
http://www.tim.hawaii.edu

University of Houston: Conrad N. Hilton College of Hotel and Restaurant Management. Houston, TX
http://www.hrm.uh.edu/

University of Massachusetts Amherst: Department of Hospitality and Tourism Management. Amherst, MA
http://www.isenberg.umass.edu/htm/

University of Missouri-Columbia: Hotel and Restaurant Management.
Columbia, MO
http://majors.missouri.edu/viewmajor.php?mid=8

University of Nebraska Kearney: Travel & Tourism.
Kearney, NE
http://www.unk.edu/UploadedFiles/offices/careerserv/students/
Travel%20and2%0Tourism.pdf

University of Nevada, Las Vegas: Harrah Hotel College.
Las Vegas, NV
http://hotel.unlv.edu

University of New Brunswick: Bachelor of Applied Management,
Hospitality and Tourism. New Brunswick
http://www.unbsj.ca/business/bam/bamht.html

University of Central Florida: Rosen College of Hospitality Management.
Orlando, FL
http://www.hospitality.ucf.edu

University of New Hampshire: Department of Hospitality Management.
Durham, NH
http://orbit.unh.edu/dhm/links/links2.htm

University of New Orleans: Lester E. Kabacoff School of Hotel, Restaurant &
Tourism Administration. New Orleans, LA
http://business.uno.edu/hrt/

University of North Texas: School of Merchandising and Hospitality
Management. Denton, TX
http://www.smhm.unt.edu

University of San Francisco: Hospitality Industry Management. San Francisco, CA
http://www.usfca.edu/sobam/undergrad/ug-hopsitality.html

University of South Florida/Sarasota-Manatee: Bachelor of Science in Applied
Science in Hospitality Management. Sarasota, FL
http://www.ugs.usf.edu/academic/bsascon.htm

University of Tennessee: Knoxville Hotel, Restaurant, and Tourism
Knoxville, TN
http://catalog.utk.edu/preview-program.php?catoid=1&poid=168

University of Wisconsin-Stout: Hospitality and Tourism Department
Menomonie, WI
http://www3.uwstout.edu/hosptour

Virginia State University: Hospitality Management. Petersburg, VA
http://www.vsu.edu/pages/751.asp

Virginia Tech: Department of Hospitality & Tourism Management.
Blacksburg, VA
http://www.cob.vt.edu/htm

Washburne Culinary Institute. Chicago, IL
http://kennedyking.ccc.edu/washburne/home.asp

Washington State University: School of Hospitality Business Management.
Pullman, WA
http://www.business.wsu.edu/academics/Hospitality/Pages/index.aspx

Widener University: School of Hospitality Management. Chester, PA
http://www.widener.edu/soh

Bibliography

Hotels

Barsky, Jonathan. "Hotels Keep Customers Happy Despite Cuts in Staff and Service." *HSMAI eConnect/Market Metrix*. 10 June 2009. Accessed June 13, 2009, at http://www.hsmaieconnect.org/news/154000320/4041834.html.

Darson, Lauren. "Hotel CEOs: 'The Worst Is Behind Us.'" *Management Travel*. 3 June 2009. Accessed June 13, 2009, at http://www.management.travel/news.php?cid=hotel-executives.Jun-09.03.

Freitag, Jan. "Extended-Stay Segment Extends Performance into Downturn." *HotelNews Now.com*. 9 June 2009. Accessed June 13, 2009, at http://www.hotelnewsnow.com/Articles.aspx?ArticleId=1335.

Gale Reference Team, "Hotel Industry to Continue Struggling in 2009 (Commercial)(Report)." *Mortgage Banking*. 1 April 2009. Accessed June 13, 2009, at http://www.amazon.com/industry-continue-struggling-Commercial-Report/dp/B00287GKKC/ref=sr_1_4?ie=UTF8&s=books&qid=1244877465&sr=8-4.

Hogan, John. "What Is Your Definition of Leadership?" *HSMAI eConnect*. 9 June 2009. Accessed June 13, 2009, at http://www.hsmaieconnect.org/news/154000320/4041819.html.

Lomanno, Mark. V. "Thoughts from NYU." *HotelNewsNow.com*. 5 June 2009. Accessed June 13, 2009, at http://www.hotelnewsnow.com/blog.aspx?PageType=Blogs&b=1311.

Rackoff, Katie. "Hyatt Hotels & Resorts Goes Mobile to Support Its Guests and Their On-the-Go Lifestyles." *HSMAI eConnect/Global Hyatt*. 8 June 2009. Accessed June 13, 2009, at http://www.hsmaieconnect.org/news/154000320/4041800.html.

Roth, Bill. "Hotel Industry Embraces Green Revolution." *Entrepreneur.com*. 5 June 2009. Accessed June 13, 2009, at http://www.msnbc.msn.com/id/31124522/.

"U.S. Hotel Industry Enters 19th Month of Recession." *HNN Newswire*. 8 June 2009. Accessed June 13, 2009, at http://www.hotelnewsnow.com/Articles.aspx?ArticleId=1321.

Walterscheidt, Katy. "New Council Focuses on Future of Hospitality Technology." *HSMAI eConnect*. 11 June 2009. Accessed June 12, 2009, at http://www.hsmaieconnect.org/news/154000320/4041883.html.

Woodworth, Mark. "U.S. Lodging Turning Point Arrives But Growth Remains on Distant Horizon." *HSMAI eConnect*. 11 June 2009. Accessed June 12, 2009, at http://www.hsmaieconnect.org/news/154000320/4041866.html.

Restaurants

Andrew Freeman & Co, "2009 Hotel & Restaurant Trends." *Food Fete*. 16 December 2009. Accessed June 13, 2009, at http://foodfete.wordpress.com/2008/12/16/2009-restaurant-and-bar-trends-from-andrew-freeman-co/.

Baum, Joseph, and Michael Whiteman Co. Inc. "Consultants Predict 13 Top Restaurant and Hotel Food Trends for 2009." 15 November 2008. Accessed June 13, 2009, at http://www.baumwhiteman.com/trends2009.pdf.

Dumanovsky, Tamara, and Christina Huang. "Read 'em Before You Eat 'em: New York City's Policy to Post Calories in Chain Restaurants." *Obesity Management* (April 2009). Accessed June 13, 2009, at http://www.liebertonline.com/doi/abs/10.1089/obe.2009.0205.

Gellman, Keith. "Restaurant Trends—Growing and Emerging Concepts—Data Reflects Change and Activity from February 1, 2009 to June 1, 2009." *Hospitality Trends.* 9 June 2009. Accessed June 13, 2009, at http://www.htrends.com/trends-detail-sid-39264.html.

Hasek, Glenn. "Food Service Operators Are Discovering the Gold in Grease." *Hospitality Trends.* 11 June 2009. Accessed June 13, 2009, at http://www.htrends.com/trends-detail-sid-39336.html.

Komaiko, Leslee. "2009 Restaurant Trend Forecast." *dineLA.com.* Accessed June 13, 2009, at http://discoverlosangeles.com/play/dining/la-chefs/2009-restaurant-trend-forecast.html.

Leahy, Kate. "Restaurant Trends: 10 Things Learned From the 2009 NRA Show." *Restaurants and Institutions.* 21 May 2009. Accessed June 13, 2009, at http://www.rimag.com/article/CA6659901.html.

Mintel, "Restaurant Trends Forecasted." *4Hoteliers.* 11 June 2009. Accessed June 13, 2009, at http://www.4hoteliers.com/4hots_fshw.php?mwi=4123.

Moll, Kevin. "Top Trends for 2009 from National Restaurant Consultants." *National Restaurant Consultants, Inc.* Accessed June 13, 2009, at http://www.nationalrestaurantconsultants.com/top_trends.

Palmer, Daniel. "Restaurant Trends 2009." *Australian Food News.* 11 December 2008. Accessed June 13, 2009, at http://www.ausfoodnews.com.au/2008/12/11/restaurant-trends-2009.html.

"Restaurant Industry Outlook Continues to Improve as Restaurant Performance Index Hits Highest Level in 11 Months." *Hospitality Trends.* 1 June 2009. Accessed June 13, 2009, at http://www.htrends.com/trends-detail-sid-39088.html.

Rowe, Megan. "What's Hot for '09." *Restaurant Hospitality.* 1 January 2009. Accessed June 13, 2009, at http://restaurant-hospitality.com/features/whats_hot_restaurants_0109/.

Urban, Chris. "5 Top Restaurant Trends for 2009." *Restaurant News Resource.* 18 December 2008. Accessed June 13, 2009, at http://www.restaurantnewsresource.com/article36304.html.

Williams, Dick. "2009 Restaurant Trends." *NorthWest STIR.* 11 February 2009. Accessed June 13, 2009, at http://www.hotelnewsresource.com/pdf8/2009_Restaurant_Trends.pdf.

Airlines

"Airline Seat Capacity Drops 3% Worldwide in April." *Travel Weekly.* 27 April 2009. Accessed June 13, 2009, at http://www.travelweekly.com/article3_ektid193478.aspx.

"Delta Installs Wi-Fi on Nearly 50% of Domestic Fleet." *Travel Weekly.* 11 May 2009. Accessed June 13, 2009, at http://www.travelweekly.com/article3_ektid194318.aspx.

Fabey, Michael. "American Loses $375M on 15% Drop in Revenue." *Travel Weekly.* 15 April 2009. Accessed June 13, 2009, at http://www.travelweekly.com/article3_ektid192926.aspx.

———. "Delta Chief Also Sees Day When Travel Agents Will Pay Airlines." *Travel Weekly.* 21 April 2009. Accessed June 13, 2009, at http://www.travelweekly.com/article3_ektid193196.aspx.

———. "Delta Loses $794 Million in Q1; United Loses $382 Million." *Travel Weekly.* 21 April 2009. Accessed 13 Jun 2009, at http://www.travelweekly.com/article3_ektid193192.aspx

———. "Delta 2.0: A Progress Report." *Travel Weekly.* 20 May 2009. Accessed June 13, 2009, at http://www.travelweekly.com/article3_ektid194788.aspx.

———. "DOT: International Carriers Breaking Baggage-Liability Rules." *Travel Weekly.* 20 April 2009. Accessed June 13, 2009, at http://www.travelweekly.com/article3_ektid193182.aspx.

———. "FlyersRights: Biggest Airlines Guiltiest of Stranding Passengers." *Travel Weekly.* 12 May 2009. Accessed June 13, 2009, at http://www.travelweekly.com/article3_ektid194390.aspx.

———. "Southwest's $91 Million Loss Surprises Analysts." *Travel Weekly.* 16 April 2009. Accessed June 13, 2009, at http://www.travelweekly.com/article3_ektid192986.aspx.

———. "Swine Flu Could Be Another Blow to Struggling Airlines." *Travel Weekly.* 27 April 2009. Accessed June 13, 2009, at http://www.travelweekly.com/article3_ektid193524.aspx.

———. "Wary Eyes Watch Oil Prices Rise." *Travel Weekly.* 3 June 2009. Accessed June 13, 2009, at http://www.travelweekly.com/article3_ektid195496.aspx?terms=*wary+eyes+oil+prices*.

Limone, Jerry. "Airline Goes to the Dogs ... and Cats." *Travel Weekly.* 20 April 2009. Accessed June 13, 2009, at http://www.travelweekly.com/article3_ektid193174.aspx.

———. "IATA Predicts Airlines Will Lose $9 Billion This Year." *Travel Weekly* 8 June 2009. Accessed June 13, 2009, at http://www.travelweekly.com/article3_ektid195766.aspx.

———. "U.S. Airlines Expect 7% Drop in Passengers This Summer." *Travel Weekly.* 15 May 2009. Accessed June 13, 2009, at http://www.travelweekly.com/article3_ektid194576.aspx.

Tourism (Medical)

"Aeromexico Inks Deal to Promote Medical Tourism." *Travel Weekly.* 27 March 2009. Accessed June 13, 2009, at http://www.travelweekly.com/article3_ektid191858.aspx?terms=*medical+tourism*.

Alessie, Lorenza. "Medical Tourism: Vaccinated Against the Recession?" *Hospitality Trends.* 4 March 2009. Accessed June 13, 2009, at http://www.htrends.com/trends-detail-sid-37418.html.

"Bangkok Hospital Upgrades Its Health and Beauty Services to Capture Medical Tourists." *MediThai.* 6 February 2009. Accessed June 13, 2009, at http://www.medithai.net/news/bangkok-hospital-upgrades-its-health-and-beauty-services-to-capture-medical-tourists.

"Emerging Trends of Medical Tourism in India." *Health Tourism News.* 25 May 2009. Accessed June 13, 2009, at http://www.healthtourismnews.com/2009/03/25/emerging-trends-of-medical-tourism-in-india/.

"Global Medical Tourism." *BioPortfolio.* 1 December 2008. Accessed June 13, 2009, at http://www.bioportfolio.com/cgi-bin/acatalog/Global_Medical_Tourism.html.

Iftikhar, Mubbashir. "Medical Tourism Evolving Trends." *Knol.* 9 November 2008. Accessed June 13, 2009, at http://knol.google.com/k/dr-mubbashir-iftikhar/medical-tourism-evolving-trends/3so95bu0lqa34/4#.

Keller, Amy. "Medical Tourism Is Thriving." *Florida Trend.* 1 March 2009. Accessed June 13, 2009, at http://www.floridatrend.com/article.asp?aID=50631.

Madden, Christina. "Medical Tourism Causes Complications." *MediThai.* 8 November 2008. Accessed June 13, 2009, at http://www.medithai.net/news/medical-tourism-causes-complications.

Sauer, Katherine. "Medical Tourism: An Overview." *2009 ABE Medical Tourism.* 19 March 2009. Accessed June 13, 2009, at http://www.scribd.com/doc/13863004/2009-ABE-Medical-Tourism.

"SpaFinder Issues 6th Annual Full Trends Report: 'Top 10 Spa Trends to Watch in 2009.'" *SpaFinder* (2008). Accessed June 13, 2009, at http://www.spafinder.com/about/press_release.jsp?relId=152.

"SpaFinder's Medical Tourism Trends to Watch in 2009." *SpaFinder.* 29 December 2008. Accessed June 13, 2009, at http://www.treatmentabroad.net/medical-tourism/news/?entryid82=91747.

Vequist, David. "The Center for Medical Tourism Research: The First Center in the World Devoted to the Medical Tourism Industry." *Medical Tourism Magazine.* 6 February 2009. Accessed June 13, 2009, at http://www.medicaltourismmag.com/issue-detail.php?item=187&issue=8.

Wood, Andrew. "Thailand's Tourism—Waning Confidence Needs Steady Nerves." *Hospitality Trends.* 12 June 2008. Accessed June 13, 2009, at http://www.htrends.com/trends-detail-sid-33056.html.

Cruises

Baran, Michelle. "Despite Parent Company's Woes, Windstar Says It's Going Strong." *Travel Weekly* 21 May 2009. Accessed June 12, 2009, at http://www.travelweekly.com/article3_ektid194904.aspx.

"Consumer Interest in Cruise Grew 8% in December." *Travel Weekly*. 11 January 2009. Accessed June 12, 2009, at http://www.travelweekly.com/article3_ektid183804.aspx.

Jainchill, Johanna. "Antarctic Group Calls for Stricter Tourism Regulations." *Travel Weekly*. 19 February 2009. Accessed June 12, 2009, at http://www.travelweekly.com/article3_ektid189748.aspx.

———. "Big Cruise Discounts Might Be Undermining Brand-Building." *Travel Weekly*. 11 May 2009. Accessed June 12, 2009, at http://www.travelweekly.com/article3_ektid194304.aspx.

———. "Costa Unveils Two Ships Along With Its Plans for Growth." *Travel Weekly*. 09 June 2009. Accessed June 12, 2009, at http://www.travelweekly.com/article3_ektid195962.aspx.

———. "Cruise Lines Ramp Up Shore Excursions in '09." *Travel Weekly*. 02 March 2009. Accessed June 12, 2009, at http://www.travelweekly.com/article3_ektid190336.aspx.

———. "Cruise Lines See a Robust Market in Europe." *Travel Weekly*. 21 May 2009. Accessed June 12, 2009, at http://www.travelweekly.com/article3_ektid194924.aspx.

———. "Cruise Safety Legislation Reintroduced in Congress." *Travel Weekly*. 13 March 2009. Accessed June 12, 2009, at http://www.travelweekly.com/article3_ektid191080.aspx.

———. "Dispatch, Costa Pacifica 1: Costa, the Quiet Giant." *Travel Weekly*. 4 June 2009. Accessed June 12, 2009, at http://www.travelweekly.com/article3_ektid195528.aspx.

———. "INSIGHT: No Tears of Joy in Cruise Industry's Bon Voyage to 2008." *Travel Weekly*. 30 December 2008. Accessed June 12, 2009, at http://www.travelweekly.com/article3_ektid186308.aspx.

———. "With Recent Surge in Pirate Attacks, Cruise Lines Try New Security Tactics." *Travel Weekly*. 22 April 2009. Accessed June 12, 2009, at http://www.travelweekly.com/article3_ektid193334.aspx.

Kiesnoski, Kenneth. "Cruise Charters Feeling Recession's Effects." *Travel Weekly*. 15 May 2009. Accessed June 12, 2009, at http://www.travelweekly.com/article3_ektid194606.aspx.

Travel (General)

Amadeus. "Economist Intelligence Unit Predicts New Age of Austerity for Business Travelers." *Hospitality Trends.* 9 February 2009. Accessed June 13, 2009, at http://www.htrends.com/trends-detail-sid-36991.html.

American Express. "American Express Travel Survey Reveals Top 2009 Summer Travel Trends." *Hospitality Trends.* 19 May 2009. Accessed June 13, 2009, at http://www.htrends.com/trends-detail-sid-38890.html.

Frost & Sullivan. "Airlines in Turbulence—Virus Outbreaks and Their Impact on the Aviation Market." *Hospitality Trends.* 21 May 2009. Accessed June 13, 2009, at http://www.htrends.com/trends-detail-sid-38966.html.

National Business Travel Association. "Europe: Business Travel Holds Firm Despite Economic Conditions." *Hospitality Trends.* 22 May 2009. Accessed June 13, 2009, at http://www.htrends.com/trends-detail-sid-38981.html.

PhoCusWright Inc. "Top 10 Travel Technology Trends for 2009." *Hospitality Trends.* 13 April 2009. Accessed June 13, 2009, at http://www.htrends.com/trends-detail-sid-38135.html.

Plunkett, Jack W. *Plunkett's Airline, Hotel & Travel Industry Almanac 2009* (Houston, Tex.: Plunkett Research, Ltd., 2008). Accessed June 13, 2009, at http://www.amazon.com/Plunketts-Airline-Travel-Industry-Almanac/dp/1593921195/ref=sr_1_1?ie=UTF8&s=books&qid=1244877465&sr=8-1.

Travel Industry Wire. "No Vacation from the Economy: Two Thirds of Americans Plan Summer Vacation, but Nearly Half Will Spend Less Than Last Year." *Hospitality Trends.* 19 May 2009. Accessed June 13, 2009, at http://www.htrends.com/trends-detail-sid-38899.html.

———. "Travelers Say Economy, More Than Environment, Is Making Them Waste-Conscious." *Hospitality Trends.* 27 May 2009. Accessed June 13, 2009, at http://www.htrends.com/trends-detail-sid-39016.html.

———. "U.S. Travelers—Nearly 90% Taking Summer Vacation, 27% Taking More Time Than Last Year." *Hospitality Trends.* 20 May 2009. Accessed June 13, 2009, at http://www.htrends.com/trends-detail-sid-38922.html.

———. "Visa Report Shows Increase in Inbound and Outbound U.S. Tourism Spending in 2008, Decline in Early 2009." *Hospitality Trends* 6 June 2009. Accessed June 13, 2009, at http://www.htrends.com/trends-detail-sid-39291.html.

Travelocity. "Travelocity Issues First-Ever 'Traveler Confidence' Report." *Hospitality Trends* 2 (June 2009. Accessed June 13, 2009, at http://www.htrends.com/trends-detail-sid-39126.html.